W9-CIL-689

Building the Mobile Internet

Mark Grayson, Kevin Shatzkamer, Klaas Wierenga

Cisco Press

800 East 96th Street

Indianapolis, IN 46240

Building the Mobile Internet

Mark Grayson, Kevin Shatzkamer, Klaas Wierenga

Copyright© 2011 Cisco Systems, Inc.

Published by:
Cisco Press
800 East 96th Street
Indianapolis, IN 46240 USA

Printed in the United States of America

First Printing February 2011

The Library of Congress Cataloging-in-Publication data is on file.

ISBN-13: 978-1-58714-243-7

ISBN-10: 1-58714-243-0

Warning and Disclaimer

This book is designed to provide information on how to enable the mobile Internet. Every effort has been made to make this book as complete and as accurate as possible, but no warranty or fitness is implied.

The information is provided on an "as is" basis. The authors, Cisco Press, and Cisco Systems, Inc. shall have neither liability nor responsibility to any person or entity with respect to any loss or damages arising from the information contained in this book or from the use of the discs or programs that may accompany it.

The opinions expressed in this book belong to the authors and are not necessarily those of Cisco Systems, Inc.

Trademark Acknowledgments

All terms mentioned in this book that are known to be trademarks or service marks have been appropriately capitalized. Cisco Press or Cisco Systems, Inc., cannot attest to the accuracy of this information. Use of a term in this book should not be regarded as affecting the validity of any trademark or service mark.

Corporate and Government Sales

The publisher offers excellent discounts on this book when ordered in quantity for bulk purchases or special sales, which may include electronic versions and/or custom covers and content particular to your business, training goals, marketing focus, and branding interests. For more information, please contact: **U.S. Corporate and Government Sales**   1-800-382-3419   corpsales@pearsontechgroup.com

For sales outside the United States, please contact: **International Sales**   international@pearsoned.com

Feedback Information

At Cisco Press, our goal is to create in-depth technical books of the highest quality and value. Each book is crafted with care and precision, undergoing rigorous development that involves the unique expertise of members from the professional technical community.

Readers' feedback is a natural continuation of this process. If you have any comments regarding how we could improve the quality of this book, or otherwise alter it to better suit your needs, you can contact us through email at feedback@ciscopress.com. Please make sure to include the book title and ISBN in your message.

We greatly appreciate your assistance.

Trademark Acknowledgments

All terms mentioned in this book that are known to be trademarks or service marks have been appropriately capitalized. Cisco Press or Cisco Systems, Inc. cannot attest to the accuracy of this information. Use of a term in this book should not be regarded as affecting the validity of any trademark or service mark.

Publisher: Paul Boger

Associate Publisher: Dave Dusthimer

Cisco Representative: Erik Ullanderson

Cisco Press Program Manager: Anand Sundaram

Executive Editor: Mary Beth Ray

Managing Editor: Sandra Schroeder

Senior Development Editor: Christopher Cleveland

Project Editor: Mandie Frank

Copy Editor: John Edwards

Technical Editor: Scott Brim

Editorial Assistant: Vanessa Evans

Designer: Sandra Schroeder

Composition: Tricia Bronkella

Indexer: Cheryl Lenser

Proofreader: Sarah Kearns

Americas Headquarters
Cisco Systems, Inc.
San Jose, CA

Asia Pacific Headquarters
Cisco Systems (USA) Pte. Ltd.
Singapore

Europe Headquarters
Cisco Systems International BV
Amsterdam, The Netherlands

Cisco has more than 200 offices worldwide. Addresses, phone numbers, and fax numbers are listed on the Cisco Website at **www.cisco.com/go/offices.**

About the Authors

Mark Grayson is a distinguished consulting engineer at Cisco Systems with responsibility for leading Cisco's mobile architecture strategy. He has over 20 years of experience in the wireless industry, ranging from the development of military systems, the definition of satellite communication architectures, and the evolution of traditional cellular systems to the creation of the latest small-cell solutions. He holds a first class honors degree in electronics and communications engineering from the University of Birmingham (England) together with a Ph.D. in radio communications. Mark has been granted over 50 patents in the area of mobile communications and is the coauthor of *IP Design for Mobile Networks* (Cisco Press).

You can contact Mark Grayson at mgrayson@cisco.com.

Kevin Shatzkamer is a distinguished systems architect at Cisco Systems with responsibility for long-term strategy and architectural evolution of mobile wireless networks. He has worked at Cisco and in the mobile wireless industry for over 10 years, focusing on various technologies that include 3G and LTE networks, packet gateways, network-based services and security, video distribution, quality of service, and end-to-end design theory. Kevin holds four issued patents and has 16 pending patents related to all areas of work. Kevin holds a Bachelor of Engineering degree from the University of Florida and a Master of Business Administration from Indiana University.

Kevin Shatzkamer is a regular speaker at various trade shows and industry forums and has previously published *IP Design for Mobile Networks*, a Cisco Press book that discusses the technologies and requirements shaping the future of the mobile Internet, from RAN to services. Kevin's current area of focus is the end-to-end digital media value chain for mobility, working with both content providers and service providers to create unique mobile media service offerings.

You can contact Kevin Shatzkamer at kshatzka@cisco.com.

Klaas Wierenga is a senior consulting engineer in the office of the CTO at Cisco. His 15-plus years of experience include the planning, analysis, and design of numerous solutions for enterprises, municipalities, hospitals, and universities in the fields of mobility, security, and identity worldwide. Klaas is the original creator of the worldwide eduroam service for federated network access in academia and cocreator of the federated identity solution that forms the basis of the Dutch government's e-Identity portfolio. He is the author of numerous publications and has presented many times on wireless networking, security, and identity topics. Klaas is active within 3GPP, in the group responsible for the security architecture of future mobile networks. He serves as chairman of the Abfab Working Group in the IETF, which deals with federated access for non-web applications, as well as of the Task Force on Mobility and Network Middleware of TERENA, the European Association for Research and Education Networks. Klaas holds a master's degree in computer science from the University of Groningen (The Netherlands).

You can contact Klaas Wierenga at klaas@cisco.com.

About the Technical Reviewer

Scott Brim is a Senior Consulting Engineer in the office of the CTO at Cisco. He received a BA magna cum laude from Harvard University and has been active in developing communications technology since 1978. He has been at Cisco since 2000. Previous to that, he was research staff at Cornell University for 18 years and Director of Technology Strategy at Newbridge Networks for 3 years. Technically, he has spent 12 years on Internet routing, 5 years on Internet QoS, and 4 years on mobile services. His particular interest has always been making different technologies or technology layers interwork better. He is currently focused on the future mobile Internet infrastructure and how proposed fundamental changes to Internet architecture in routing, addressing, mobility and identity can create a robust, flexible, beneficial synergy.

He has also been active in a number of standards bodies, most recently the IETF, ITU-T, and GSMA.

Dedications

I dedicate this book to my parents, Anne and Bryan, for their ever-present encouragement and support. I would like to thank my wife Sharon and two sons, Charlie and Harry, not the least for their inspiration for Chapter 7; I'm sure it won't be long before your networked lives of iPods, iPads, and PCs become fully mobilized Internet experiences. Finally, I would also like to thank the many friends, coworkers, and mentors who, over the last 20-odd years, have helped me achieve so much.

—Mark Grayson

I dedicate this second book to my wife and family, who, having experienced the time and commitment to authoring a book during the first round, allowed me to write a second one. As I explained the context of this second book, my young children assured me that our content reviewers would catch that I did not reference SpongeBob SquarePants, who, much to my surprise, is the founder of the mobile Internet. Alas, you will find no reference to SpongeBob in this book, partially because we did not have adequate time to receive all relevant copyright information, and partially because we have sought to provide an alternative theory into the development of the mobile Internet. To my children— may your reality always consist of Santa Claus, the Easter Bunny, and SpongeBob SquarePants.

—Kevin Shatzkamer

I dedicate this book to my wife Licia, who has been very supportive and patient whenever I deviated from my regular pleasant and optimistic self—ahem ;-)—in trying to meet the deadlines of this book while doing my day job. To my parents for making me explain the things I was working on in a nongeek way. And to my former colleagues at SURFnet, current colleagues at Cisco, and all the others I have worked with in the past years for shaping my understanding of the topics at hand and providing the often-so-necessary critique. In particular, I would like to thank the participants in the Task Force on Mobility and Network Middleware of TERENA and the members of the Mobile Internet project team at Cisco, without what I learned in the many discussions, fights, meals, and beers I have had with you, I could not have written this book.

—Klaas Wierenga

Acknowledgments

We'd like to thank the Pearson production team for their time and effort in creating this book, for patience during the delays resulting from our jobs, and for providing valuable and insightful feedback during the entire process. Specifically:

- Thanks to Mary Beth Ray for getting this book contracted and managing the process from beginning to end. We understand that we are not always the easiest to work with, and your involvement has made the authoring process a bit less painful.

- Thanks to Christopher Cleveland, Mandie Frank, and John Edwards for their fantastic editing of the book.

- Thanks to the many others at Pearson who were part of developing and producing this book. Sometimes it is those who remain faceless and nameless that tend to do the majority of the work, and we recognize that.

- Thanks to Moray Rumney at Agilent for giving his permission to use the chart in Figure 1-9 and for his comprehensive analysis of the radio frequency challenges in today's cellular systems.

- Thanks to Morgan Stanley Research for its permission to use the chart in Figure 1-1.

- Thanks to SURFnet for making the diagrams in Figures 3-3 and 3-9 available under a Creative Commons license.

- Thanks to TERENA for its permission to use the chart in Figure 3-7.

We'd like to thank Tom Carpenter for providing technical feedback on the many topics that this book covers. Also, thanks to all the technical reviewers, especially Scott Brim, who took the time to read our gibberish and turn it into gold.

Contents at a Glance

Contents

Icons Used in This Book

Wireless
Residential
Gateway

DSLAM

WiFi Access
Point

WLAN
Controller

Wireless
Transport

Lightweight
Single Radio
Access Point

Cisco
ASA

Route Switch
Processor

Switch

ATM Switch

Bridge

Router

Policy
Server

SIP Proxy
Server

Web Server

PC

Laptop

WiFi Enabled
Tablet

Cellular
Smartphone

Cell
Phone

IP Phone

Wireless
Connection

Introduction

This book examines the different techniques for building mobility into the Internet. The breadth of approaches currently in operation should cause us all to pose the question as to whether, in the future, a single utopian mobility solution can be defined that accommodates all scenarios, or whether solving "mobility" requires a decomposition of the "mobility problem space" into a number of distinct use cases.

The tremendous success of mobile broadband–based services based on cellular architectures where mobility has been effectively performed at the data link layer has shown how that approach is perfectly acceptable for providing wide-area mobility to use cases involving a single device with a single interface.

Should such data link layer techniques be enhanced to address alternative use cases? This is an important question to answer, because we confidently predict that the mobility use cases will broaden from today's homogeneous, cellular-only view of the world:

- Devices will become more heterogeneous from an access perspective. Wi-Fi dual-mode capabilities will become widely integrated into the next generation of cellular devices.

- Users will increasingly have access to more than a single cellphone for accessing the mobile Internet.

- As the majority of users who access the Internet become mobile, applications will increasingly look to become "mobile-aware," tailoring their operation to address specific limitations of mobile access, including being able to accommodate switches in access technologies and rapid fluctuations in available bandwidth.

This book takes a look at mobility from a broad perspective of use cases and examines how mobility solutions are in fact pervasive across all layers of the protocol stack. The book provides details of how mobility functionality has been added to these layers and describes use cases that demonstrate the different approaches to building the mobile Internet.

Who Should Read This Book

This book is intended to increase the reader's understanding of how mobility can be supported in IP networking.

The book assumes at least a basic understanding of standard networking technologies, including the Internet Protocol itself. Many concepts are introduced to give the reader exposure to the key mobility functionality that can coexist across different protocol layers. The book does not give recommendations on which of these technologies should be deployed for supporting mobility use cases, nor does it provide a transition plan for existing network operators for adding mobile functionality. Each network operator is expected to evaluate his or her mobility user case(s) that must be supported and make decisions based on his or her own criteria on which technique(s) to adopt for mobilizing the Internet.

This book is written for many levels of technical expertise, including network design engineers and network planning engineers looking to design and implement mobile network migrations toward an all-IP future, networking consultants interested in understanding the technology trends that affect mobile operators, students preparing for a career in IP networking that is increasingly being impacted by mobile technologies, and chief technology officers (CTO) seeking a further understanding of the convergence of IP and mobile technologies.

How This Book Is Organized

Although this book can be read from cover to cover, it is designed to be flexible and allows you to easily move between chapters and sections of chapters to learn just the information that you need.

This book covers the following topics:

- **Chapter 1, "Introduction to 'Mobility'":** This chapter defines the mobility market in terms of device proliferation, consumption trends, and radio-specific challenges in scaling for massive adoption of the mobile Internet.

- **Chapter 2, "Internet 'Sessions'":** This chapter explains the protocols and layers that make up the Internet architecture, as well as the fundamental problem with that architecture in supporting mobility.

- **Chapter 3, "Nomadicity":** This chapter describes how users and devices are authenticated for using the network and its applications, in particular those that are not operated by the operator that the user has a subscription with.

- **Chapter 4, "Data Link Layer Mobility":** This chapter explains the benefits of solving mobility at the data link layer. Contrasting approaches for delivering local- and wide-area wireless mobility are introduced and used with Wi-Fi and cellular technologies.

- **Chapter 5, "Network Layer Mobility":** This chapter provides an overview of a number of network layer solutions for delivering seamless mobility and session continuity.

- **Chapter 6, "Transport/Session Layer Mobility":** This chapter describes the advantages of integrating mobility functionality into the transport/session layer. The required mobile modifications to existing transport/session layer protocols are introduced.

- **Chapter 7, "Application Mobility":** This chapter describes how the application layer can be enhanced with additional mobility functionality, allowing advanced mobility use cases to be supported, including the ability to move media sessions between different devices.

- **Chapter 8, "Locator-Identifier Separation":** This chapter provides an overview of the approaches for redesigning the Internet architecture to allow better mobility, as well as a discussion of the pros and cons of some typical examples of those approaches.

Chapter 1

Introduction to "Mobility"

This book provides insight into techniques for building mobility into the Internet, so perhaps a good place to start would be with a definition of mobility. As is often the case, you could look to Google to provide some inspiration about the definition of mobility. Having entered **Oxford English Dictionary** and **mobility** into the search engine, you might be interested to find that one of PageRank's highest-priority results is associated, not with the Oxford English Dictionary's (OED's) definition of mobility, but with a news report describing the new iPhone application for the OED[1].

As you are surely aware, mobility is becoming a truly pervasive quality associated with nearly all advances in Information and Communications Technology (ICT), including iPhone applications enabling ubiquitous access to online dictionaries. The ability to access any content, on any device over any network in any location, is becoming a reality. Critically, however, mobility has not been integrated into the fabric of the Internet, and instead, a range of different techniques are available for delivering such a mobile experience. This has resulted in the concepts of *mobility* being widely referenced but seldom understood.

The concept of mobility might imply a user with a laptop who wants Internet access everywhere he goes, a user with a mobile device who wants a seamless Internet experience while he is moving, a user wanting to use unlicensed Wi-Fi technology to offload traffic from a conventional cellular network, or a user who has multiple devices and wants a seamless Internet experience across those devices.

As today's networks migrate toward "all-IP," numerous protocols and solutions have been designed to handle these different types of mobility, with varying degrees of market adoption and formal standardization. This book looks at the protocols that are relevant to the mobility landscape, contrasts different approaches at delivering the mobile experience, and accurately defines and discusses the mobile Internet evolution.

Mobility Market

Clearly one of the great successes of the 1990s and early 2000s has been the phenomenal growth in the adoption of cellular service. While the first decade of cellular adoption has been driven by simple circuit-switched service voice, using the Global System for Mobile (GSM) communications or Code Division Multiple Access (CDMA) standard, and rapid adoption of services based on Short Message Service (SMS), the second decade can be characterized by the initial adoption of IP-based packet services, using low-rate General Packet Radio Service (GPRS) or cdma2000 1xRTT-based radio access networks. The next decade of cellular evolution will see increasing uptake of mobile broadband services, using High Speed Packet Access (HSPA), EVolution-Data Only (EV-DO), Worldwide Interoperability for Microwave Access (WiMAX), or Long-Term Evolution (LTE) radio access networks.

Indeed, mobile broadband subscriber growth is exceeding that of the fixed broadband. In its analysis of Internet Trends[2], Morgan Stanley estimates that by 2014, the number of mobile Internet users will surpass the number of fixed Internet users, as illustrated in Figure 1-1. With the mobile broadband subscription rate of growth being greater than twice that of fixed network subscriptions, it is clear that the end of the next decade will see the Internet being dominated by mobile hosts.

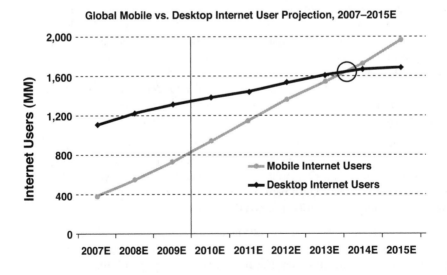

Figure 1-1   *Growth in Mobile Versus Fixed Broadband Subscribers*

Another key aspect from a mobility market perspective is the rise of multiradio devices. These devices are distinct from cellular-centric multimode devices that have been specified by the likes of the Third Generation Partnership Project (http://www.3gpp.org), a collaboration among various Standards Development Organizations (SDO) that is responsible for developing the set of technical specifications for 3G systems based on the evolved GSM core network. In particular, 3GPP has defined a triple-mode cellular architecture that allows a single radio to be shared among second-generation GPRS, third-generation HSPA, and next-generation LTE radio access modes. While this single-radio definition leads to lower bills of material for devices, the restrictions are such that these dual mode devices can only be connected to one network at any instant.

However, with the increasing adoption of IEEE 802.11–based wireless local-area network (WLAN) technology in smartphone devices, the 2010 decade will see the era of true multiple-radio devices. ABI Research recently predicted that between 2006 and 2015, the Compound Annual Growth Rate (CAGR) of Wi-Fi–enabled smartphones will be 85 percent[3]. Figure 1-2 illustrates this growth in millions of units shipped, so that by 2015, ABI Research estimates that one in three handsets shipped globally will include Wi-Fi–enabled dual-mode capability.

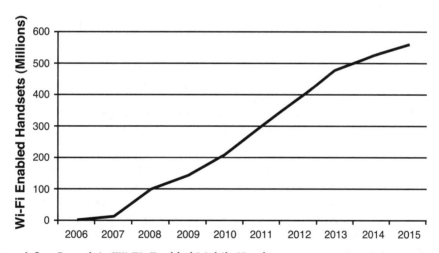

Figure 1-2   *Growth in Wi-Fi–Enabled Mobile Handsets*

Another key development in the cellular industry is the rise of multiple handsets per subscriber. In 2007, the Organization for Economic Co-operation and Development (OECD) reported that over 25 countries had cellular penetration rates in excess of 100 percent, with Italy taking the lead in reaching 150 cellular subscriptions per 100 inhabitants[4]. Many analysts are predicting this trend will continue. In 2009, the Cisco Internet Business Solutions Group (IBSG) estimated that in 2010, 35 billion devices will be connected to the Internet, equivalent to nearly six devices per person on the planet. Many of these new devices will be used to provide machine-to-machine (M2M) services, and while many M2M devices are not strictly mobile (an M2M-enabled residential utility meter is unlikely to move), it is likely that a significant proportion of these new devices will use wireless connectivity to provide access to M2M services.

Reinforcing this shift from architectures that assume a single device per user to one where each subscriber has a multitude of devices is the current revolution in tablet-style computers. Tablets, smartbooks, and netbooks will see a blurring of functionality between the legacy laptop and smartphone markets. However, Forrester Research has recently highlighted a shift in the heterogeneous PC market[5] where future growth is driven by consumers adopting a "multiple PC" approach to fit their lifestyles:

■   **Desktop PCs:** Growth will be driven in gaming as well as watching and editing high-definition and three-dimensional video and graphics.

■   **Tablets:** Growth will be driven by their ease of media consumption as well as access to email and web browser–based services.

■   **Netbooks:** Growth will be driven by web-centric operating systems and the associated cloud-based applications and storage.

So, if the future mobile market will be characterized by device divergence, with users having a plethora of specialized Internet-enabled devices for watching 3D media, interactive gaming, collaboration, and communications, through to basic Internet-enabled sensors, the networks used to support such devices are set to increasingly converge. This convergence is being driven by the increasing adoption of IP as the convergent technology across "fixed" and "mobile" networks, with IP now recognized as the fundamental building block for all next-generation communication networks.

Cellular networks are now evolving to enable the Internet to be available anytime and anywhere. IP is already impacting all aspects of the mobile operator's network, from radio bearer support through transmission and service delivery capability. Indeed, the various definitions for the next generation of mobile networks all align around an "all-IP" vision, providing purely packet-switched capabilities and solely supporting IP services.

As cellular networks transition to "all-IP" networks, the architectures of fixed and cellular networks converge. Figure 1-3 illustrates this, showing a classical fixed broadband network comprised of Customer Premises Equipment (CPE), which provides residential gateway functions, connected to a Digital Subscriber Line Access Multiplexer (DSLAM), which then connects to a Broadband Network Gateway (BNG), which provides the user's IP Point of Attachment (PoA) to the Internet. An IP/Ethernet transport network is typically used to provide connectivity between the DSLAM and the BNG. The figure then shows a tablet user wirelessly attaching to the residential gateway using, for example, IEEE 802.11–defined Wi-Fi technology, with the solid arrow showing the communications between the tablet user and a correspondent node on the Internet.

The lower portion of the figure shows a conventional "all-IP" cellular network comprising a smartphone User Equipment (UE), connected using licensed cellular technology to an Enhanced Node B (ENB) base station. The ENB is connected through an IP/Ethernet transport network to the Packet Data Network Gateway (PGW) and Serving Gateway (SGW) functionality, with the former being the IP PoA for the mobile subscriber. The dual-line arrow shows the communications between the smartphone user and a correspondent node on the Internet.

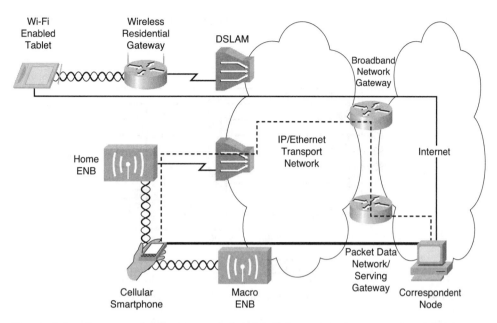

Figure 1-3 *Convergence Between Fixed and Cellular Networks*

Note 3GPP has defined an all-IP architecture with two logical gateway functionalities, SGW and PGW. From a user plane perspective, the SGW simply provides a tunnel switch capability, conceptually similar to a Layer 2 Tunneling Protocol Access Concentrator (LAC). Just as the fixed-line LAC allows multiple retail providers to provide independent IP PoA services over a common wholesale DSL infrastructure, 3GPP's SGW allows independent IP PoA services to be provided by roaming partners.

Finally, Figure 1-3 shows one of the most recent advances in cellular architecture—the adoption of the home base station, in this instance, a Home ENB (HENB). The HENB uses the consumer fixed-broadband network to connect to the core cellular network. The dotted line then demonstrates the communications between the smartphone user attached to the HENB and a correspondent node on the Internet, highlighting how traffic uses a fixed-line IP service provided by the BNG before connecting to an IP PoA in the cellular domain.

Consumption Trends

In 2009, Cisco IBSG announced the latest results from its Connected Life Market Watch[6]. This program aims to provide market insight into the adoption of mobile technologies. The analysis highlighted that from an Average Revenue Per User (ARPU) perspective, mobile data already represented 25 percent of the total spending for U.S. subscribers, with revenue from data growing at an annualized rate of 40 percent, as illustrated in Figure 1-4.

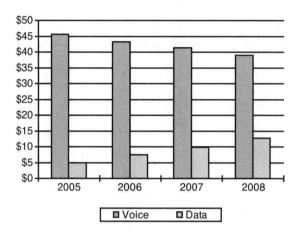

Figure 1-4   *Average Revenue per United States Mobile Subscriber*

The IBSG study also highlighted a shift in consumption habits as cellular subscribers started to consume more mobile Internet-based services. When looking at where mobile Internet consumption occurred, Figure 1-5 illustrates the findings of the Connected Life Market Watch study of U.S. mobile Internet consumption. Significantly, while occasional mobile Internet users were more likely to access services when mobile (with 56 percent of usage happening "on the go"), those regular users of mobile Internet–based services were effectively changing their behavior to consume the majority of mobile Internet services from fixed locations (35 percent from within the home and 27 percent from the office).

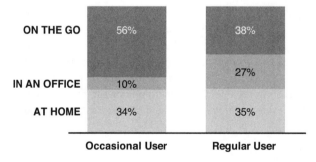

Figure 1-5   *Location of United States Mobile Internet Consumption*

Note   The shift to indoor consumption is significant because conventional macro-cellular networks need to account for the Building Penetration Loss (BPL) experienced as signals propagate through walls, floors, and windows of buildings. The BPL can result in 90–99.9 percent of the energy of wireless signal being lost, just because a user was consuming a service indoors compared to a similarly located outdoor user.

One hypothesis of why more frequent users are more likely to consume mobile Internet services in fixed locations is the increasing shift toward video-based services. To track and forecast the impact of visual networking applications on the growth of the fixed and mobile Internet, Cisco has developed the Visual Network Index (VNI) forecast[7]. VNI was developed as an annual survey to estimate global IP traffic growth and trends for both consumer and business user groups. In particular, as it relates to mobile Internet consumption, the latest VNI forecast predicts that mobile data in 2014 will be 39 times larger than the mobile data traffic in 2009, as highlighted in Figure 1-6.

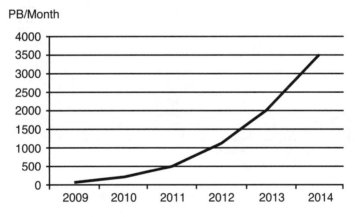

Figure 1-6   *Monthly Mobile Internet Traffic in Petabytes*

The latest VNI study also provides a forecast for the growth of mobile data traffic on a per-content-type basis. Figure 1-7 highlights the forecast growth of mobile video consumption, so that by the end of 2014, video is forecast to comprise 66 percent of all mobile data traffic, and mobile voice traffic will comprise only 4 percent of the overall total traffic.

So far, this chapter has looked at *where* users consume mobile Internet services, highlighting a shift away from truly mobile scenarios to locations that can be characterized as "in-building." You have seen *what* types of services are likely to be consumed over mobile devices in the future, with the majority of traffic being related to video services. The final piece of the puzzle is to understand *when* users access mobile Internet services. Figure 1-8 is a representation of the traffic load in a commercial cellular network offering mobile Internet services over a 24-hour period. The figure clearly illustrates the diurnal variation of traffic load within the network, showing how the data-busy hour is between 8:00 and 9:00 in the evening.

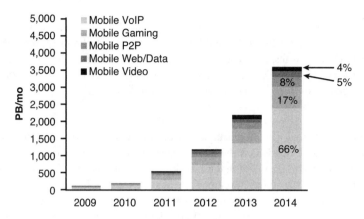

Figure 1-7   *Global Mobile Data Traffic Growth by Content*

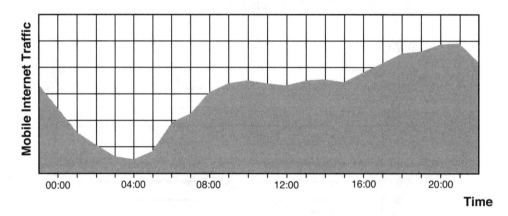

Figure 1-8   *Example Diurnal Variation of Mobile Internet Traffic Load*

Note   You can also use the information in Figure 1-8 to estimate how much of the daily traffic is consumed within the busy hour. With a throughput profile as shown, we can estimate that around 6 percent of daily mobile Internet consumption occurs in the busy hour. This compares with traditional telephony networks, which are typically dimensioned to support up to 20 percent of daily calls during the busy hour.

The final characteristic of future mobile consumption will be its "always-on" nature. Historically, while cellular network standards have had the capability to support always-on users, there were often implementation restrictions with the number of always-on users a system could support. So, cellular standards allowed mobile data–enabled devices to be attached to a cellular network without allocating them an IP address. Equally, legacy cellular networks will be typically configured to automatically deallocate a device's IP address after a period of inactivity. This can be contrasted with wireless LAN networks, which have been based on the assumption of an always-on Ethernet service. However, the next generation of cellular standards has been designed to support only always-on behavior. For example, whenever a device attaches to an all-IP LTE network, it will, by default, receive an IP address and be automatically enabled to send and receive IP packets.

Mobile Challenges

With the massive increase in forecasted consumption of mobile Internet services, it is interesting to understand how today's macro-cellular networks are positioned to accommodate this unparalleled growth in capacity. A simple way to evaluate the capacity of a conventional cellular system is to examine three key cellular characteristics:

- **Spectrum:** The amount of available radio frequency spectrum is a key factor in determining the capacity of a mobile system. The spectrum suitable for mobile networks is a scarce resource. It must be available in sufficient bandwidths to support higher-speed access while also providing good propagation characteristics required for providing wide-area coverage.

- **Spectral efficiency:** The efficiency by which spectrum is used is another critical factor in determining the capacity of a mobile system. There is an upper bound to the amount of information that can be transferred in a given bandwidth which is subject to background noise, termed the *Shannon Limit*. It is generally accepted that as more advanced signal-processing techniques are applied to mobile communications systems, they are rapidly approaching such a theoretical limit.

- **Frequency reuse:** Because of its relative scarcity, mobile systems are required to reuse their allocated radio spectrum across a particular network of cell sites. Increasing the capacity by frequency reuse typically means dividing an existing cell into multiple smaller cells.

Agilent has analyzed the growth in average macro-cellular spectrum efficiency as cellular technologies have evolved from the original GSM system to the latest LTE-A standards[8]. In parallel, the growth in available spectrum for cellular systems can be mapped. Figure 1-9 shows both of these growth lines over the period from 1990 to 2015 (with efficiency and spectrum being normalized to 1992 levels). The figure also shows the product of the two variables, indicating the estimated growth in average macro-cellular system capacity. Whereas the Cisco VNI forecast estimates that demand for mobile Internet traffic will grow 39-fold over a five-year period, Figure 1-9 illustrates that by only using better radios and more spectrum, the average capacity gains achievable by adopting a conventional macro-cellular approach will see mobile broadband capacity a supply increase by a factor of fourfold over the same five-year period. The only way that networks are going to be able to support the estimated increase in mobile broadband traffic is by increasing the adoption of smaller cells, with the chart in Figure 1-9 forecasting that the number of cells will need to increase tenfold to meet the expected demand in traffic.

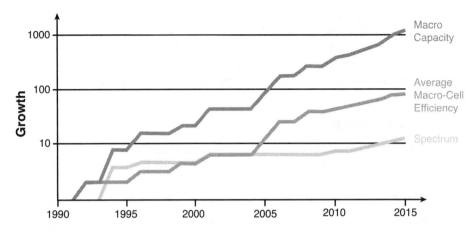

Figure 1-9   *Estimating Future Average Macro-Cellular System Capacity*

So, we can confidently predict that building the future mobile Internet will require networking technology that supports the following:

■ Scalable adoption of small-cell technologies—for example, using unlicensed IEEE 802.11 technology or licensed cellular-based home base station solutions

■ A massive number of always-on devices, including scenarios where single subscribers have access to multiple devices

■ Ubiquitous access, including nomadic access from in buildings as well as wide-area mobile access for on-the-go consumption

■ Seamless access to a range of mobile services, including video, web access, peer-to-peer, Voice over IP (VoIP), and gaming services

All of this would be easily achievable if the Internet supported native mobility. Unfortunately, the Internet is not mobile! Conventional approaches for delivering mobility have been to layer tunnels on top of the native Internet Protocol (IP). While casual observers might comment that wide-area mobility has been solved by the mobile broadband architectures developed by the cellular organizations, or even the latest all-IP mobile networks architected by the WiMAX forum, these all provide mobility functionality by tunneling packets over the Internet:

■ **GPRS Tunneling Protocol (GTP):** An overlay IP-based mobility protocol defined by 3GPP to provide mobility services for accessing the Internet by GPRS, WCDMA, and LTE-based radio access networks.

■ **Mobile IP (MIP):** An overlay mobility protocol defined by the Internet Engineering Task Force (IETF) to provide IP mobility services and adopted by 3GPP2 to provide mobility services for accessing the Internet by cdma2000-based radio access networks.

- **Control and Provisioning of Access Points (CAPWAP):** An overlay IP-based mobility protocol defined by the IETF to provide mobility services for accessing the Internet by IEEE 802.11–based radio access networks.

- **Proxy Mobile IP (PMIP):** An overlay IP-based mobility protocol defined by the IETF to provide mobility services that have been adopted by those architectures for accessing the Internet by IEEE 802.16e–based WiMAX radio access networks.

As you will see later, Mobile IPv6 does have an optimized routed mode whereby, after having originally traversed a tunnel, packets are subsequently routed directly between a mobile node and a correspondent. However, you will also see how the use of IPv6 routing headers and destination options in the operation of optimal routing simply moves the tunnel operation into the IP host; the IP applications running on a mobile node still need to be shielded from the operation of MIPv6 with route optimization.

All this complexity is caused because, when IP was first proposed in 1975, "problems of . . . mobility were many years off."[9]

Quite clearly, with the number of mobile broadband users set to eclipse the number of fixed users and with ABI Research[10] estimating that 1.15 billion handsets were sold in 2009, "problems of mobility are upon us." The industry will soon be faced with the situation that the default technique for accessing the Internet will be through a mobility tunnel. Because tunneling of traffic requires stateful tunnel gateways to be operated, services accessed through the "mobile Internet" might end up being more brittle than those accessed through the native IP networks on top of which the mobility tunnels are transported.

Summary

The next decade will see the convergence of mobility and the Internet. The various SDOs that define the next generation of wide-area mobile networks have all aligned around an "all-IP" vision, providing access to purely IP-based packet services, with networks that can be transported over converged packet-based networks.

However, we confidently predict that the mobility use cases will broaden from today's homogeneous, cellular-only view of the world:

- Devices will become more heterogeneous from an access perspective. Wi-Fi dual-mode capabilities will become widely integrated into the next generation of cellular devices.

- Users will increasingly have access to more than a single device for accessing the mobile Internet.

- Next-generation mobile networks will have to support an increasing amount of consumption from indoor locations, requiring techniques to be able to cost-effectively integrate small-cell technologies into the overall mobile network.

These transitions are triggering a reassessment of how best to build the mobile Internet, comparing alternative techniques for providing mobility in an all-IP world.

Endnotes

1. http://www.mobilemarketer.com/cms/news/content/1877.html.

2. http://www.morganstanley.com/institutional/techresearch/pdfs/Internet_Trends_041210.pdf.

3. "Mobile Devices Market Forecast Analysis," ABI Research, June 2010.

4. http://www.oecd.org/dataoecd/19/40/34082594.xls.

5. "The US Consumer PC Market In 2015," Forrester Research, June 2010.

6. http://www.cisco.com/web/about/ac79/docs/CLMW_Mobile_Internet_v20_072809FINAL.pdf.

7. http://www.cisco.com/en/US/netsol/ns827/networking_solutions_sub_solution.html.

8. M. Rumney, "IMT-Advanced: 4G Wireless Takes Shape in an Olympic Year," *Agilent Measurement Journal*, Issue 6, Sept. 2008.

9. J. Day, *Patterns in Network Architecture*, Indianapolis, Indiana: Pearson Education; 2008.

10. "Mobile Device Model Tracker," ABI Research, April 2010.

Chapter 2

Internet "Sessions"

Imagine yourself talking on your mobile phone while driving to the office. On the drive to the office, your mobile phone is connected to a number of different cell towers, and the network somehow has to make sure that the "communication session" ends up at the mobile phone regardless of its location. Apart from the fact that phoning while driving is probably not a good idea from a safety point of view, you have perhaps always taken for granted that you could keep talking without losing your connection to the person on the other end of the line. In reality it is, because of the way the Internet works, hard to enable this kind of seamless, real-time mobility. The problem becomes even harder when sessions need to be kept alive when moving across different types of access networks (for example, from cellular to Wi-Fi) or networks belonging to different operators.

This so-called session mobility is one of the more challenging issues in enabling the *mobile Internet*, a pervasive Internet Protocol–based network that links fixed and mobile nodes, whether they are sensors or servers, standalone, distributed, battery, or line powered. This chapter provides a high-level overview of the way the Internet works and explains where the difficulties lie in making session mobility possible. This background will enable you to appreciate these challenges as well as help you understand the approaches to mobility presented in Part II of this book.

The Internet and Communication

The Internet is a network consisting of many smaller networks. Hosts (a traditional term for all computers that are connected to a network) are connected to one or more of these smaller networks. Routers are a special type of hosts that are connected to more than one network and that forward data from one network to the other, as illustrated in Figure 2-1. Two hosts from different networks that want to communicate with each other do so by using the TCP/IP protocol suite, so named after two of the most important protocols in that suite, TCP and IP (explained in more detail later in this chapter). Today, TCP/IP is also used between hosts that are connected to the same network.

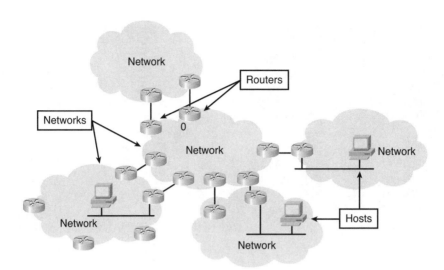

Figure 2-1   *Network Elements That Constitute the Internet*

The networks that form the Internet use many different hardware technologies, and many different applications can be used on the Internet.

Packet Switching Versus Circuit Switching

Traditional telephone networks use a technology called *circuit switching*. That is, for a given communication, a dedicated circuit is created between the two endpoints of a communication session. The advantage of this approach is that the circuit can be reserved for this one communication session; at the same time, that has a disadvantage. Even when the circuit is not used (that is, for example, when both parties are silent in a phone conversation), the capacity of the circuit is reserved.

TCP/IP networks use a different approach—connectionless packet switching. The data of a communication session here is divided into small units called *packets*, which each contain enough information to enable the network to decide how to send it to the receiving end of the communication. All packets are being sent independently to the receiver, and the receiver reassembles the packets to reconstruct the original data. Figure 2-2 illustrates this process.

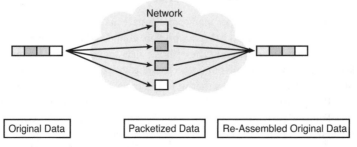

Figure 2-2   *Dividing Data into Packets at the Sender and Reassembling at the Receiver*

The benefit of this approach is that the same network communication path can be used for multiple communication sessions (multiplexing). The downside is that the order of packets might not be preserved, resulting in packets being received out of order, and that the delivery of the packets is "best effort." Other communications might use all the available resources, and thus packets might be dropped or delayed, or the connection can fail completely. For these reasons, it is difficult to provide guaranteed behavior. The cost benefits from sharing capacity, however, usually outweigh the potential problems, resulting in almost all modern networks using packet-switching technology. It is often easier and cheaper to increase capacity than to move to a connection-based model, with the exception of some mobile networks that have limited capacity because of physical limitations of the wireless spectrum.

IP over Everything, Everything over IP

The pivot point of TCP/IP-based communications is the Internet Protocol (IP) that is used to transport packets from source to destination. As illustrated in Figure 2-3, IP shields the underlying network technology from the applications that run on the network and vice versa (note that this is a simplified version of the actual protocol stack).

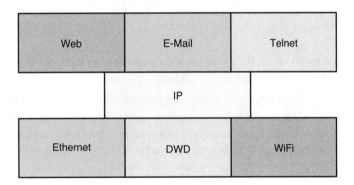

Figure 2-3   *IP over Everything, Everything over IP*

In other words, when a new data-link transport technology is developed, ensuring that IP runs on top of it will allow all existing applications to be used. Furthermore, when an application developer makes sure that his or her application uses IP packets for communication between nodes, it will automatically work on all IP networks.

This abstraction layer that IP provides between the transport layer and the applications is perhaps the single most important reason why the Internet has become so dominant. Instead of having to wait for an operator to make a certain service available to the users, every clever student can now develop his own application. At the same time, the application that worked over a slow 2-Mbps X.25 time-division multiplexing (TDM)–based network continues to work over the 10-Gbps or more optical networks that are used nowadays.

Addresses

A host on the Internet that wants to communicate with another host needs to be able to uniquely identify that host. Therefore, on the Internet, every host is associated with a globally unique address—the IP address. (Strictly speaking, this is not entirely true because of the use of Network Address Translation (NAT), as will be explained later in this chapter.) Internet communication is about sending IP packets from a source IP address to a destination IP address. The IP address is both used to identify the host itself as well as its location in the network. This means that if a host is at the same time connected to two networks, it will, by definition, also have at least two IP addresses, one for each of its network interfaces. Another important consequence of using the same identifier for both the host itself and its location in the network is that if a host that is attached to one network moves to another network, it must change its IP address.

Routers use the IP address of the destination of a communication session to determine how to forward the IP packets from the source to the destination. In its most simple form, an IP packet consists of a source IP address, a destination IP address, and some payload containing the application data. Routers use the destination IP address to forward the packets to the receiver. The receiver copies the source IP address from a received packet into the destination address to send any return packets.

IPv4 Addresses

The most commonly used addressing scheme on the Internet today is Internet Protocol version 4, or IPv4, documented in RFC 791[1].

IPv4 addresses are 32-bit binary numbers usually written in the so-called dotted decimal notation, a representation of the binary number that is easier for humans to remember. In dotted-decimal notation, the IP address is separated into four 8-bit chunks, each separated by a dot. For example, the binary representation 00001010 00000000 00000000 00000001 is written in decimal representation as 10.0.0.1.

IP addresses are composed of two parts: a network identifier (net-id) and a host identifier (host-id). The net-id is the same for all hosts on a particular network.

In the early days of the Internet, the boundary between the network and the host part of the IP address was at fixed 8-bit positions, resulting in so-called Class A networks (first 8 bits reserved for net-id, 24 bits for host-id), Class B networks (16 bits net-id, 16 bits host-id), and Class C networks (24 bits net-id, 8 bits host-id). This scheme is pretty rigid. If an organization has, for example, 300 hosts (more than the 256 addresses that can be formed with the 8 bits available for host-ids in a Class C network), the IP address registry would have to assign it a Class B network that can be used to address over 65,000 hosts, a large waste of usable addresses.

When the Internet became popular in the 1990s, this waste of usable address space resulted in a looming address shortage. To overcome this, the protocols were redesigned to allow a split between net-id and host-id at an arbitrary bit position. This system is called classless interdomain routing (CIDR), documented in RFC 1518[2]. Associated with an IP address is now a network mask that indicates how many bits of the IP address (the so-called prefix) are used to indicate the net-id and how many belong to the host-id (the suffix). So, in the example of the organization with 300 hosts, instead of moving from 256 addresses to 65,536 addresses, it can now go to 2 * 256 = 512 addresses. This together with NAT (discussed later in this chapter) has resulted in postponing the date at which all available address space will ultimately be exhausted. Figure 2-4 shows the division between net-id (here 11 bits) and host-id.

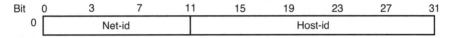

Figure 2-4   *IP Addresses Consist of a net-id and a host-id Part*

With CIDR, networks are described in the form *IP address/number of bits for net-id*. For example, 10.0.0.0/16 (pronounced as *10.0.0.0 slash 16*) indicates all IP addresses between 10.0.0.0 and 10.0.255.255. Incidentally, in this notation, the old Class A networks are designated with */8*, Class B with */16*, and Class C with */24*. Two or more networks can be combined (this is called *aggregation*) into a larger network of networks. For example, 10.0.0.0/16 and 10.1.0.0/16 together is the same as 10.0.0.0/15. Conversely, a large network can be divided into smaller subnetworks (this is called *subnetting*). Figure 2-5 illustrates network aggregation and subnetting.

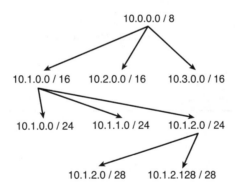

Figure 2-5   *Aggregation and Subnetting*

In essence, IPv4 packets consist of a host IP address, a destination IP address, and the payload containing the application data. Some additional fields are added to indicate the fact that it is an IPv4 packet, a checksum to detect defects caused by transporting the packet, and so on. Figure 2-6 illustrates the format of an IPv4 packet.

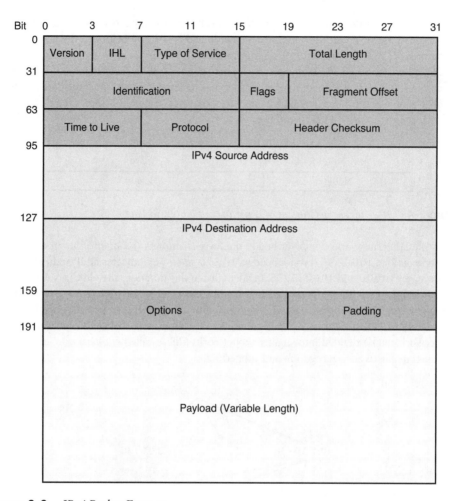

Figure 2-6   *IPv4 Packet Format*

IPv6 Addresses

Mainly because of the foreseen shortage of IPv4 address space, the Internet Engineering Task Force (IETF) has defined a new version of the Internet Protocol, Internet Protocol version 6 (IPv6), documented in RFC 2460[3]. IPv6 has a much larger address space by using 128-bit instead of 32-bit addresses. In addition to this, IPv6 contains other features to automatically assign addresses to hosts and to make routing more efficient. Figure 2-7 shows the IPv6 packet format.

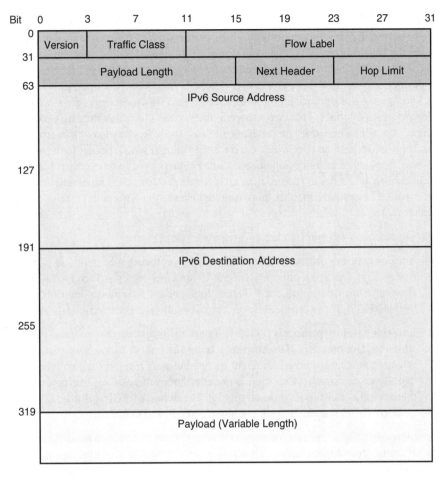

Figure 2-7   *IPv6 Packet Format*

Routing

As you saw before, all communication between endpoints on the Internet is divided into IP packets sent from a sender to a receiver. Routing is the process of discovering how to forward the packets from sender to receiver.

Routers

Routers are intermediate devices in the network that have multiple network interfaces that are connected to more than one network at the same time and that can forward packets from one network to the other. So, for the router to know what to do with a particular IP packet, it needs to have knowledge about networks that can be reached through a particular interface.

Routing Protocols

For hosts that are directly connected to the same network as the router, it is easy to configure the router to send IP packets out over the right interface. The problem is that it is, of course, impossible to know about all the hosts on the Internet and their location, not to mention the fact that this changes every second. This is where routing protocols come in. Through the use of routing protocols, routers learn which networks are reachable through which interface. That is, routers tell other routers to which they have a direct connection, which networks are reachable through them. Routers have an internal table that they use to look up over which interface they should send a packet for a particular IP address. Because of memory limitations, smaller routers usually have only a relatively small number of entries in their routing table for directly attached hosts and forward all other packets to a router that has more routing information. This path is the so-called default route.

Routing protocols fall into two broad categories:

- **Interior gateway protocols (IGP):** IGPs are the protocols used inside an administrative domain. Examples of widely used IGPs are Open Shortest Path First (OSPF), Routing Information Protocol (RIP), and Intermediate System–to–Intermediate System (IS-IS). These protocols focus on routing IP packets as efficiently as possible.

- **Exterior gateway protocols (EGP):** EGPs are the protocols that are used between administrative domains. Here efficiency is not the only criterion. One particular host is usually reachable through different routes; business relations, reputation, and past experience determine which route is preferred, or even possible. This process is therefore also called policy-based routing. The dominant EGP is Border Gateway Protocol (BGP) (currently version 4, documented in RFC 4271[4]).

The routes that IP packets take often have a large impact on the time needed to send a packet from source to destination. Therefore, a lot of research goes into ensuring that routers learn as soon as possible where to send an IP packet. Inefficient routing leads to detrimental performance of applications.

Broadcast

Sometimes all devices on a particular network need to be reached, for example, to find out which device can route packets elsewhere or to find out which device has a particular IP address. This mode of operations is called *broadcast*. For this purpose, a particular type of IP packet is used where all the bits of the host-id are set to 1. Sending a packet to this IP address (a broadcast message) is the same as sending it to all hosts in the same network as the host.

IP Multicast

Often, many thousands of hosts spread over the Internet want to receive the same application data. Think, for example, of a live TV broadcast on the Internet. The way the Internet works, this would result in many thousands of IP packets containing the exact same data, with the only difference being the destination IP address. Special protocols have been developed for this type of application called *IP multicast*. Multicast routing protocols ensure that the same payload is sent only once over a given connection. For this application, a special set of IP addresses have been reserved (224.0.0.0 through 239.255.255.255) that are not assigned to hosts for normal IP communications, but are reserved just for multicast purposes. The multicast layer can be seen as another abstraction layer on top of the physical network, and just like for regular IP where the routing layer needs to keep track of which IP addresses are associated with which physical addresses, the multicast routing layer needs to keep track of which multicast addresses are associated with which group of hardware addresses.

Network Address Translation

In the explanation about hosts on the Internet, you learned that every host could uniquely be identified and had a globally unique IP address. This is not completely true; in reality, networks often use an internal IP addressing scheme that is not exposed to the rest of the Internet (called private addresses). The reasons for this setup vary from the desire to use as few globally unique IP addresses as possible and the (perceived) security benefits of not exposing the internal network setup, to an easier network setup by using much larger address ranges than could be obtained from local Internet registries. If a host that has only a locally unique address wants to communicate with a host on the global Internet, it has to communicate through another host that does have a globally unique address and that maps the local address to a global address. This process is called *Network Address Translation (NAT)*. NAT breaks the normal communication between hosts on the Internet; however, over the years, many protocols have been adapted to be able to deal with NAT.

If the IP addresses used internally are also being used externally, problems will arise, because they are not guaranteed to be unique from the point of view of the destination. Therefore, some special ranges of IP addresses have been reserved for use as private addresses. The private address ranges are 10.0.0.0/8, 172.16.0.0/12, and 192.168.0.0/16 and cannot be used on the public Internet.

If IPv6 gains wide adoption, NAT will no longer be required for overcoming address shortages. However, NAT solutions are being proposed for coexistence of IPv4 and IPv6 during the transition to IPv6. In that case, NAT is used to translate IPv4 addresses on one network into IPv6 addresses on another network and vice versa.

TCP/IP Five-Layer Model

You are now familiar with the importance of the IP layer sitting as an abstraction layer between the application and the network layers. What has not been discussed yet is exactly how the IP packets are turned into something that the network can understand, or how applications that run on the Internet can transform their application-specific data into IP packets. As it turns out, it makes sense to further divide both the network part and the application part to separate generic functionality from specifics. The result of that is a layered model, in which the various layers each have their own functionality. For example, this allows different applications to share a generic communications layer and a protocol developer to concentrate on one layer without having to implement the complete protocol stack.

In the course of internetworking history, a number of layering approaches have been proposed, all trying to strike a balance between functional decomposition and increased complexity in having to define the interactions between the layers in a network model. A widely accepted model, and the model that will be used as a reference in this book, is the TCP/IP five-layer model, which has been described by Comer[5]. Figure 2-8 illustrates the TCP/IP five-layer model.

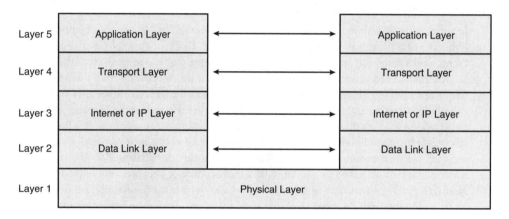

Figure 2-8   *TCP/IP Five-Layer Model*

The data of one layer is carried as payload in the packets on the layer below it. This process is called *encapsulation*, as illustrated in Figure 2-9. Data of the higher layers is largely opaque to the layers below it. A particular layer at one host "talks" to the corresponding layer at the other host.

"Largely opaque" refers to the fact that it often makes sense from an operational point of view to "leak" information from one layer to the other—for example, to optimize an application for transport over a particular type of network.

Lower layers typically refer to those layers that are below the Internet layer (also called the IP layer), and conversely, *higher layers* are those that are above the Internet layer.

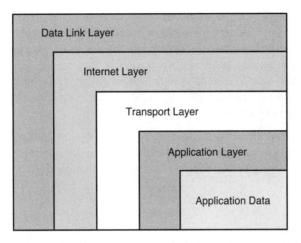

Figure 2-9   *Data from Higher Layers Encapsulated in Packets on Lower Layers*

Layer 1: The Physical Layer

The physical layer is, strictly speaking, not part of the TCP/IP model. However, because this layer carries the actual data, it is important to understand how IP packets can be transported over a physical infrastructure. There are many hardware infrastructures—fibers, copper cables, wireless, and others. These networks can span large distances (called wide-area networks [WAN]) and smaller distances (called local-area networks [LAN]). For each hardware technology, you must define an addressing mechanism to transport information over LANs or WANs. These hardware addresses must be unique inside a specific network and for a specific technology, but not necessarily globally, because IP takes care of the global communications.

Layer 2: The Data Link Layer

The data link layer, also called the network interface layer, is responsible for accepting IP packets from the Internet layer (Layer 3) and encapsulating them in a protocol that is specific for the Layer 1 network technology that is used and transmitting them over that network and vice versa.

Apart from Ethernet and Address Resolution Protocol (ARP) (discussed in the sections that follow), data link layer protocols include Layer 2 Tunneling Protocol (L2TP), Point-to-Point Protocol (PPP), digital subscriber line (DSL), Integrated Services Digital Network (ISDN), and others.

Ethernet

The most popular technology for LANs is Ethernet. Ethernet is defined in the IEEE 802.3 series of standards. Ethernet hardware addresses are 48-bit or 64-bit numbers that are assigned to network interfaces. Ethernet addresses (also called MAC addresses, hardware addresses, or Layer 2 addresses) are assigned in blocks to the manufacturers of network interface cards and are unique. The fact that the addresses are specified by the manufacturer and not the network operator also implies that they cannot be assigned in such a way that the host-id and net-id parts of the addresses can be distinguished, and thus they cannot be used for interdomain routing. The use of Ethernet addresses for routing is therefore limited to a single network domain.

The popularity of Ethernet in the LAN and the relatively low complexity of Ethernet communication resulted in Ethernet technology being used not only in LANs but also increasingly in WANs. In fact, Ethernet has become the dominant Layer 2 protocol in most networks.

ARP

The Address Resolution Protocol (ARP) (the Neighbor Discovery Protocol [NDP] serves the same purpose in IPv6) is the protocol that is used to map an IP address to a hardware address. The exact format of the ARP messages depends on the specific hardware and is implemented for many types of hardware. In its most basic form, a host sends a message to all the hosts to which it is directly connected asking for the hardware address that a given IP address is associated with. The host using the specified IP address answers with its hardware address. For efficiency reasons, these answers are cached during a specified amount of time, and hosts that change IP addresses might send a gratuitous response indicating their new IP address.

Layer 3: The Internet or IP Layer

As discussed previously, the Internet layer is responsible for handling the communication between hosts on the Internet, or to put it differently, it performs the routing function. It accepts a packet from the transport layer, turns it into an IP packet, and hands it to Layer 2 and vice versa.

Examples of Internet layer protocols (apart from IPv4 and IPv6) are Internet Control Message Protocol (ICMP), ICMPv6 (for control messages), and IPsec (for secure communications between hosts).

Layer 4: The Transport Layer

The transport layer is responsible for providing communication between applications on different hosts. The transport layer takes the data stream that comes from a program and divides it into packets. Included in the packets is information on what application transmits the data and which application at the receiving host is supposed to receive it. Instead of referring to programs with their process identifiers (that can change over time), an abstract endpoint of a communication is defined—the protocol port, which is identified by an integer. Well-known port numbers are, for example, TCP port 80 that is used for HTTP, the protocol used on the World Wide Web, and TCP port 25 that is used for Simple Mail Transfer Protocol (SMTP), the protocol used for sending email.

Transport layer protocols fall in two broad categories: reliable transport, in which it is guaranteed that the data arrives at the application on the receiving host in order and without errors, and unreliable transport, in which data transport is not guaranteed.

Examples of transport layer protocols include Datagram Congestion Control Protocol (DCCP), Stream Control Transmission Protocol (SCTP), as well as Transmission Control Protocol (TCP) and User Datagram Protocol (UDP). The latter two are discussed in more detail in the sections that follow.

UDP

UDP, documented in RFC 768[6], is the main example of a transport protocol that is unreliable. At the transport level, the receiving host will not acknowledge receipt of packets and there are no measures to limit (for example) the data rate at which packets are sent in order to take the available bandwidth into consideration. This does not mean that it is impossible to build reliable connections using UDP; it just means that if reliable connections are needed, they will have to be implemented by the applications. The advantage of using UDP is that because of the lack of overhead that is needed for providing reliability, the protocol can be very simple and therefore efficient and fast.

A UDP datagram consists conceptually of two parts:

- A UDP header consisting of four 16-bit fields containing the following:

    - A UDP source port

    - A UDP destination port

    - A UDP message length (that indicates the number of bytes in the packet)

    - A UDP checksum (to check whether the packet has been changed on the way)

- UDP data

UDP packets are encapsulated into IP packets for sending from sender to receiver. Figure 2-10 shows the structure of a UDP datagram.

TCP

The most important reliable transport protocol is the Transmission Control Protocol (TCP), documented in RFC 793[7]. When large amounts of data need to be reliably transferred between sender and receiver and vice versa, the burden on application programmers to implement delivery confirmation and error detection becomes high. TCP relieves application programmers from this burden by implementing a reliable transport protocol.

In other words, the TCP layer will make sure that the sender is informed if a packet doesn't reach its destination, will adapt the rate of sending packets to the available bandwidth, and will correct errors in transport by having the receiver ask for a packet to be retransmitted until received correctly. Because state information in the endpoints is carefully synchronized, TCP is called connection oriented. You should realize that reliable transport comes at a price, namely, increased overhead. So, for applications that don't need a reliable transport, it might be better to stick with a simple but fast protocol. Think, for example, of a voice call. If a packet is lost, it doesn't make much sense to resend it; the moment has literally passed. Reliability, rate adaptation, and error correction are implemented by having the receiver explicitly acknowledge receipt of packets from the sender to the sender.

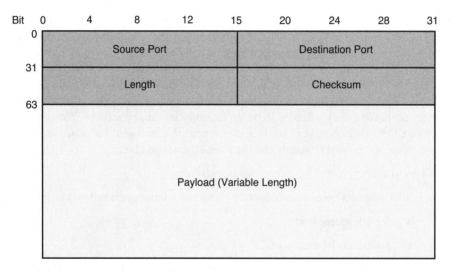

Figure 2-10 *UDP Datagram*

A TCP connection is characterized by the IP addresses of both hosts involved in the communication as well as the port numbers at both the source and destination. Because a TCP connection is identified by an IP address and port number pair, a host can communicate with multiple other hosts using the same port, as long as the combination of IP address and port number is unique.

TCP packets (called *segments*) are much more complex than UDP packets. They contain not only source and destination ports but also a sequence number (to indicate the relative position in the data stream), an acknowledgment number (to indicate the number of the next packet the sender expects), and so on. Figure 2-11 shows the structure of a TCP packet.

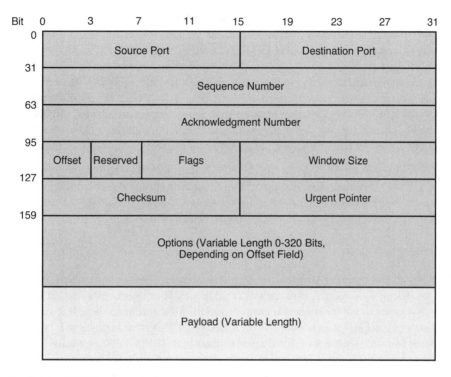

Figure 2-11   *TCP Packet*

Layer 5: The Application Layer

The application layer is the layer at which the user applications exist and that uses TCP/IP networks to communicate over. The applications interact with one of the protocols in the transport layer to send and receive data.

Examples of application layer protocols include: File Transfer Protocol (FTP), Network Time Protocol (NTP), Post Office Protocol (POP), Internet Message Access Protocol (IMAP), Session Initiation Protocol (SIP), Simple Mail Transfer Protocol (SMTP), Simple Object Access Protocol (SOAP), Secure Shell (SSH), and Telnet, as well as Dynamic Host Configuration Protocol (DHCP), Domain Name System (DNS), and Hypertext Transfer Protocol (HTTP). The latter three are examined in more detail in the sections that follow.

Socket API

If you want to create an application that connects to another application on the Internet, you need some kind of application programming interface (API) to do so. The API needs to be capable of creating connections to other hosts or wait for incoming connections from other hosts. For this purpose, most operating systems have implemented an abstraction of an endpoint for a communication session called a *socket*. The operating system or the program itself associates a socket identifier with the IP address of the host and a port. If the program wants to connect to a remote host, it has to associate a remote address and port with the socket identifier as well. The process of associating socket identifiers with IP addresses and ports is called *binding*. So, you can identify any given TCP communication session with the 5-tuple {local IP-address, local port, remote IP address, remote port, socket identifier}. For UDP, you only need the local IP address, local port, and socket identifier because UDP is not connection oriented. An important consequence of the way that applications use TCP/IP through the socket API is that if the IP address of a host changes, the identifier for the session must also change.

The socket API (for IPv4 defined in the POSIX standard[8] and for IPv6 documented in RFC 3542[9]) contains programming primitives for creating and deleting sockets, for reading and writing to sockets, as well as for operations like finding out and assigning the host name of a host, the IP address of a host, and many more.

DNS

Hosts on the Internet communicate using IP addresses; however, for humans, IP addresses are difficult to memorize, especially IPv6 addresses. For this reason, a naming scheme that is easier to use by humans is created, as well as a way to map these human-friendly names to machine-friendly addresses and vice versa. This is made possible by the Domain Name System (DNS), documented among others in RFC 1034[10]. DNS consists of a hierarchical naming scheme referred to as *domain names*. A domain name consists of a number of subnames in decreasing specificity separated by periods. For example, the domain cisco.com refers to the commercial (com) entity (less specific) called Cisco (cisco, more specific). Domain names are at the most general level organized into so-called top-level domains that either indicate a functional role (.com = commercial, .edu = education, .net = networking organization, and so on) or a country (.nl = the Netherlands, .uk = United Kingdom, .us = United States, and so on). Conceptually, the Domain Name System can be visualized as a tree with the top-level domains sharing a common root and the subdomains branching from the top-level domains, as illustrated in Figure 2-12.

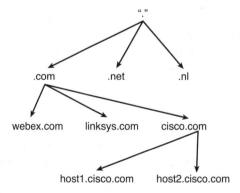

Figure 2-12   *Domain Name System Tree*

Organizations that operate a domain (like com) can delegate the operations of the subdomains of that domain (like cisco) to another entity (like to the company Cisco Systems). The responsible party for a particular (sub)domain is responsible for maintaining the mapping between host names that are of the form *name.domain* (for example, server1.cisco.com or www.cisco.com) and IP addresses.

Domain names are mapped to IP addresses through a process called *name resolution*. Associated with every domain is a server that has knowledge about the IP addresses of the hosts in that particular domain and of the subordinate server for its subdomains. These servers are called *name servers*. Client software called *resolvers* query name servers to find which IP address belongs to a particular host name by first asking the local name server and, if unsuccessful, starting from the top of the DNS tree and traversing down through the DNS tree toward the name server that holds the information for that domain name.

To find a host name that is associated with a particular IP address, a similar process is followed. IP addresses are represented in a special top-level domain in the DNS tree—the in-addr.arpa domain. The IP addresses are encoded here in decreasing order of specificity according to their dotted-decimal representation. So, the IP address 209.165.200.226 is represented in DNS as 226.200.165.209-in-addr.arpa, and the same resolution process (in this case called the *reverse lookup*) can be followed as in the case of mapping of names to addresses.

DHCP

You can manually assign an IP address to a host. However, for operational reasons (coordination is needed to make sure that IP addresses are unique) and especially when a host is mobile (and thus will need to get a new IP address all the time), it is easier to dynamically assign an IP address to a host. DHCP is a protocol that can be used by hosts to find out which IP address they have to use on the network to which they are attached (other link-layer-specific approaches exist).

To get an IP address, the host (the DHCP client) sends a broadcast message containing a hardware identifier (the MAC address). A server that is configured to administer the IP addresses replies to that message with an IP address and length of validity for that address (a *lease*). When the validity period is ended (the lease is expired) or the host moves to a new network, the host needs to ask for a new IP address.

HTTP

HTTP is an example of an application protocol (documented in RFC 2616[11]), and it is used to request and send data on the World Wide Web. HTTP is used to send web pages (documents encoded in HTML[12]) from a host running a program that serves web pages (the server) to a host (the client) being able to render the web pages in a program (the browser) that presents the web document in a user-friendly format.

Each web page is associated with a unique name called a Uniform Resource Locator (URL) (documented in RFC 1738[13]). A URL consists of the protocol used to access the page (HTTP in this case), a host, a port on that host (by default TCP port 80), a path to the page on that host, and the name of the page (default index.html) with the following syntax:

http://hostname:port/path/filename

So, the file index.html on the host www.cisco.com can be identified by the URL http://www.cisco.com:80/index.html or, by omitting defaults, as http://www.cisco.com/.

A client asks the server for a particular URL by sending a **get** command with the URL and the version of HTTP to use as parameters. The server responds by returning the web page that was requested or by sending an error message.

Sessions and Mobility

Previous sections used the term *session* rather loosely, under the assumption that you had an intuitive understanding of what was being discussed. As it turns out, things get a bit ugly when attempting to provide a definition and examine the consequences. As Internet veteran Scott Brim says:

> *"A session is instantiated by shared state for a communication that is not specific to the network path. Sessions may, but need not be, assisted by intermediaries in the network. Sessions can be one-to-one, one-to-many, many-to-one, or many-to-many."*

Intuitively that makes sense. After all, why would you care what route the bits that comprise your communication take, as long as they end up at the party with whom you are communicating? Looking at the TCP/IP five-layer model, you would expect a session to sit between the transport layer and the application layer. However, there is no session layer in the TCP/IP five-layer model. In general, sessions are considered to be "at the top" of the transport layer. For static nodes, this doesn't matter that much, but as you will see in the upcoming chapters, when nodes start moving, problems arise.

Session Persistence and the Locator-Identifier Problem

Session persistence is the notion that a communications session will be uninterrupted while one or more of the nodes engaged in the communication session move. The reason why making sure of this is a problem is that as you saw earlier in this chapter, irrespective of whether IPv4 or IPv6 is used, a communication session is partly identified by the IP addresses of the communicating hosts (the "Identifier" of the session). At the same time, the IP address of the host also indicates the location of the host in the network (the "Locator" of the session). To put it differently, the IP address is used to route packets to the right destination, so when a host gets connected to a new network, it will have to change its IP address; otherwise, packets will never reach it at its new location, and as a result of that, the session identifier changes and the session breaks.

Building the Mobile Internet

Building "the mobile Internet" is really about finding solutions for the fact that communication sessions are tied to a specific transport session and thus to a set of IP addresses. There are a number of strategies that can be followed:

- **Accept that application sessions are bound to a transport session:**

  The easiest approach is to just accept the fact that application sessions are in fact tied to a transport session and that, in a number of cases, application sessions are dropped when the point of attachment to the network changes. Actually, many applications are not or should not be that sensitive to interrupted sessions in the first place. If you think about fetching your email, it really doesn't matter that much whether the first 20 emails are fetched in one session and the next 30 in another, as long as they all end up in your inbox for you to read. Many other applications that are sensitive about session interruptions could relatively easily be made less sensitive, but until recently, the need just was not there.

  Mobile Internet access that does not require session persistence is also called *nomadic* or *roaming* access. Rather than focusing on session persistence, nomadic access focuses on seamless access to different networks. That is, the user doesn't have to go through administrative or reconfiguration hassles to get connected when arriving at a new location, but sessions will not necessarily stay "up."

- **Introduce an application layer "session persistence mechanism" that is not bound to the transport layer session:**

  A small variation on the previous approach is to introduce an application layer session persistence mechanism that is not bound to the transport layer. For example, web browsers can save the state of a communication session in the form of cookies, small pieces of data that are kept in memory or on disk and that contain the relevant information needed to continue the application session at the point where it was left when the host changed its point of attachment. Unfortunately, taking this approach requires implementing a session state in each application that needs session persistency.

  Another approach is to use the domain name of the host at the application layer instead of the IP address to identify the host. Because the actual transport of the packets will still be based on the IP address, this requires updating the DNS server when a host attaches to a new network.

- **Keep the same IP address while moving:**

  As you saw earlier in this chapter, the IP layer is an abstraction layer on top of the physical infrastructure. When a host moves to another network, it must change its IP address; otherwise, there would be no way of knowing where to route packets. Inside one (Layer 2) network, it is not necessary to change IP address; all hosts are directly connected. One technique to expand this behavior to multiple networks is to make multiple physical networks appear as one to the IP network by encapsulating

Layer 2 packets in other Layer 2 packets. This technique is called *tunneling* (and can also be used on Layer 3, as you will see in other chapters of this book). Hosts appear to be directly connected to the router, while in fact the packets are transported over a number of nodes.

■ **Introduce a "new layer":**

As you saw before, there are a number of approaches for a layered model of the Internet, and the separation between the different layers is not as strict as sometimes suggested. So, nothing stops the Internet community from "inventing" an extra layer that sits between the transport and the application layer or the transport layer and the network layer, or is a sublayer of the transport layer.

■ **Redesign the TCP/IP protocol stack to achieve separation of locators and endpoint identifiers:**

A more fundamental approach is to redesign the TCP/IP protocol stack to achieve separation of locators and identifiers; that is, to have different entities describing the location of a node and the node itself, instead of having the IP address being involved in both roles. Of course, such a fundamental change might be hard to achieve. A smooth transition from operations based on the current design is required because a "flag day" is near to impossible with the billions of connected users and devices.

The rest of this book will examine these different strategies in detail; it will explore the different approaches as well as the consequences of adopting them.

Summary

This chapter provided an overview of the Internet and the protocols that make it work. It also explained why enabling session mobility is a challenge because of the dual function of an IP address as both an identifier for the network location of a host and an identifier for the host itself. Finally, a sketch of possible approaches for session mobility was introduced that will be examined in more detail in the rest of the book.

Endnotes

1. RFC 791, "Internet Protocol," J. Postel, IETF, http://www.ietf.org/rfc/rfc791.txt, September 1981.

2. RFC 1518, "An Architecture for IP Address Allocation with CIDR," Y. Rekhter and T. Li, Eds., IETF, http://www.ietf.org/rfc/rfc1518.txt, September 1981.

3. RFC 2460, "Internet Protocol, Version 6," S. Deering and R. Hinden, IETF, http://www.ietf.org/rfc/rfc2460.txt, December 1998.

4. RFC 4271, "A Border Gateway Protocol 4," Y. Rehkter, T. Li, and S. Hares, Eds., IETF, http://www.ietf.org/rfc/rfc2460.txt, January 2006.

5.   D.E. Comer, *Internetworking with TCP/IP, 5th Edition*, Upper Saddle River, NJ: Pearson Prentice Hall; 2006.

6.   RFC 768, "User Datagram Protocol," J. Postel, IETF, http://www.ietf.org/rfc/rfc768.txt, August 1980.

7.   RFC 793, "Transmission Control Protocol," J. Postel, IETF, http://www.ietf.org/rfc/rfc793.txt, September 1981.

8.   IEEE Std. 1003.1-2001, "Portable Operating System Interface (POSIX)," Open Group Technical Standard: Base Specifications, Issue 6, December 2001.

9.   RFC 3542, "Advanced Sockets Application Program Interface (API) for IPv6," W. Stevens, M. Thomas, E. Nordmark, and T. Jinmei, http://www.ietf.org/rfc/rfc3542.txt, January 2006.

10. RFC 1034, "Domain names—Concepts and Facilities," P. Mockapetris, IETF, http://www.ietf.org/rfc/rfc1034.txt, November 1987.

11. RFC 2616, "Hypertext Transfer Protocol—HTTP/1.1," R. Fielding, J. Getty, J. Mogul, H. Frystyk, L. Masinter, P. Leach, and T. Berners-Lee, http://www.ietf.org/rfc/rfc2616.txt, June 1999.

12. "HTML 4.01 Specification," D. Ragget, A. Le Hors, and I. Jacobs, http://www.w3.org/TR/html401, December 1999.

13. RFC 1738 "Uniform Resource Locators (URL)," T. Berners-Lee, L. Masinter, M. McCahill, http://www.ietf.org/rfc/rfc1738.txt, December 1994.

Chapter 3

Nomadicity

Rather than focusing on keeping sessions alive, nomadicity is about being able to use the Internet and its services, regardless of location and time. The biggest challenge in gaining ubiquitous access is to be able to use networks and services that are not controlled by the operator that the user has a subscription with. This chapter explains the key concepts that make it possible for users and devices to gain access to IP networks and IP-based applications that are offered by others than their own operator. Nomadic or roaming use of the Internet refers to a usage pattern in which network connectivity is not available (or used) on a permanent basis, but rather intermittently and opportunistically. In other words, no session persistency at the transport layer is assumed. Therefore, this chapter does not cover Layer 2 or Layer 3 mobility, which are part of subsequent chapters. In particular, this chapter will not discuss roaming within the network of a cellular operator because that is based on Layer 2 roaming.

The basis of all Internet communications is, obviously, getting access to the Internet in the first place. In a local environment, getting access might be as simple as plugging an unshielded twisted-pair (UTP) cable into a wall outlet. As organizations grow bigger, in particular when wireless technologies are deployed or when users need to access the network from outside their own organization, security based on the ability to enter a particular building is no longer sufficient. There is a need to control access to the local network and the Internet in a scalable and efficient way.

A similar reasoning holds for application access. Users need to be able to access their networked applications, regardless of where they are. An increasingly popular phenomenon is that of offering applications "in the cloud," meaning that the application is hosted or offered by a third party somewhere on the Internet.

These are examples of the need for authentication, authorization, and accounting (AAA) mechanisms to control which persons or devices can gain access to the network and what they are allowed to do on that network. This chapter explains those mechanisms as well as the associated opportunities and challenges that come with that ability, in particular in a roaming situation.

Authentication and Authorization

A central concept for access to networks and applications is that of the digital identity—the digital representation of users or devices. The digital identity is usually associated with a unique identifier (such as a number or a name).

Authentication establishes the link between actual persons or devices and their digital representation. In other words, by successfully authenticating yourself, you prove to the network or the application that you are who you claim to be. After successful authentication, the network or the application then decides, based on policies that the operator or owner of the application has defined, what resources you get access to—the authorization.

As you can imagine, operators that often have millions of subscribers need to have sophisticated systems to keep track of all these subscribers and to provide adequate mechanisms for provisioning and deprovisioning, billing, authentication, and other services that are available to the subscribers. The servers that perform these tasks are generally referred to as AAA servers (pronounced *triple A servers*). As you will see in the sections that follow, in different domains, different types of electronic identifiers are used, which results in interoperability challenges. For example, the identifier that is used to gain access to a Long Term Evolution (LTE) network cannot be used just like that to gain access to a Wi-Fi network.

Authentication and Authorization in LTE

There are many types of cellular networks in use today. Standardization takes place in the Third Generation Partnership Project (3GPP)[1] and 3GPP2[2] (focusing mainly on the North American market). Instead of describing all the generations (1G, 2G, 2.5G, 3G, and 4G) and all the standards in those generations (CDMA, CDMA2000, EV-DO, HSDPA, GSM, UMTS, and many more) that all come with slightly different authentication methods and various roaming capabilities, this section provides a description of the LTE system for two main reasons:

- LTE is the technology that gains support from most mobile operators as the technology of choice for their future networks.

- LTE is the cellular technology that provides the most comprehensive system for roaming with other cellular but also noncellular network technologies.

Strictly speaking, LTE is only the radio access network technology. The core network architecture goes by the name System Architecture Evolution (SAE) and defines the Evolved Packet Core (EPC), the fixed part of a mobile operator network. But what is commonly referred to as LTE encompasses both the radio and the fixed network. This chapter will follow that convention.

Figure 3-1 shows the various components in an LTE network; these are defined in the list that follows. Chapter 4, "Data Link Layer Mobility," describes the EPC and its associated mobility protocol in more detail.

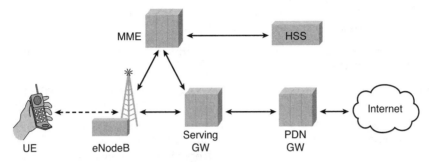

Figure 3-1   *LTE Architecture*

- The user equipment (UE) is the mobile device.

- The eNodeB is the *access point* to which the terminal connects through the wireless network and that is connected to the EPC.

- The Mobile Management Entity (MME) is the central control component in the EPC, and it is responsible for authenticating the user (by interfacing with the HSS—see the later bullet), assigning temporary identifiers to the terminals, roaming authorization, and lawful intercept.

- The Serving Gateway (Serving GW) routes packets to and from other 3GPP networks (General Packet Radio Service [GPRS], Universal Mobile Telecommunications System [UMTS]) and is a transient mobility anchor for the UE in those networks.

- The Packet Data Network Gateway (PDN GW) performs the routing to and from non-3GPP networks (like Wi-Fi, Code Division Multiple Access [CDMA] 1X, Evolution-Data-Optimized [EVDO], and WiMAX) and is the permanent mobility anchor for the UE roaming with those networks—in other words, the IP point of attachment.

- The Home Subscriber Server (HSS) contains the database with all subscriber data and is used to perform authentication and authorization as well as to provide user location.

The 3GPP specifications[3] define a number of identifiers to be used in cellular networks, the most important of which are those that identify, respectively, a user, a user subscription, and a device.

The International Mobile Subscriber Identity (IMSI) identifies users. The IMSI conforms to the ITU E.212 numbering standard and is usually 15 digits long (but can be shorter) and consists of a country code, a network operator code, and a mobile subscriber identity. The IMSI is stored in the SIM card and is used as the index key for subscriber data in the HSS, a database containing the data of all subscribers and the services they are entitled to. For privacy reasons, the IMSI is sent as little as possible over the network. Instead, after successful authentication, a temporary identifier, the Temporary Mobile Subscriber Identity (TMSI), is used.

An identifier called the Mobile Subscriber ISDN Number (MSISDN) is the phone number that corresponds with the SIM card in a mobile phone of a user. An MSISDN conforms to the ITU E.164 numbering standard and contains 15 digits that identify the country code, the network operator, and the subscriber.

Finally, the International Mobile Equipment Identity (IMEI) identifies the mobile device itself (not the SIM card inside).

Using the Authentication and Key Agreement (AKA) protocol defined in RFC 3310[4], a user authenticates to 3G and 4G networks and vice versa. The AKA procedure is a challenge-response mechanism based on a shared key that is stored on the SIM card of the terminal and in the Authentication Center (AuC) that is part of the HSS (in LTE) or HLR (in 3G). This shared key is used as input to algorithms to calculate other keys that are used for integrity (IK) and confidentiality (CK) protection of the data and for calculating the response to the challenge sent in the AKA.

Figure 3-2 and the list that follows show how the AKA procedure works in LTE. (Incidentally, UMTS networks also use the AKA.)

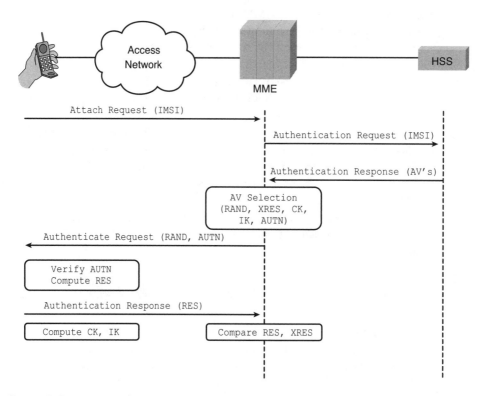

Figure 3-2   *AKA Authentication*

1.   A shared secret (Ki) is defined beforehand and stored in both the SIM card and the Authentication Center (part of the HSS).

2. The terminal sends an Attach Request to the MME containing the IMSI or TMSI of the user.

3. The MME requests authentication information from the HSS.

4. The Authentication Center function in the HSS takes a random challenge (RAND), uses the shared key Ki that is associated with the IMSI to calculate the expected response (XRES) to that challenge, as well as CK and IK, and sends an authentication vector (AV) containing RAND, XRES, CK, and IK as well as the authentication token (AUTN) used by the SIM for authenticating the network to the UE.

5. The MME then sends an authentication request to the terminal containing the RAND and AUTN. The SIM authenticates the network by verifying the AUTN and calculates the CK and IK, as well as the response (RES) to the challenge RAND using the same algorithms the HSS used.

6. The RES is sent to the MME and compared with the XRES. If the RES and XRES match, the terminal gets access.

Authentication and Authorization in Wi-Fi Networks

As described in the sections that follow, authentication for Wi-Fi networks typically comes in two flavors—captive portals and IEEE 802.1X.

Captive Portals

With the captive portal approach, the device gets access to the local wireless IP network only. Whenever the user requests a web page outside the local network, the captive portal captures that request (hence the name) and instead shows a login page in which the user enters his or her username and password or credit card details. The user credentials are verified in some kind of user database, and upon successful verification, the user then gets access to the Internet. User identifiers take the form of a username.

802.1X and EAP

The IEEE 802.1X standard defines a framework for access control to a local-area network by encapsulating Extensible Authentication Protocol (EAP) messages. Wireless security standards such as WPA (Wi-Fi Protected Access) and WPA2 use 802.1X and EAP.

Figure 3-3 illustrates an 802.1X authentication. 802.1X defines three entities:

- The supplicant is a piece of code that runs on the user device.

- The authenticator is the device that gives the device network access; in Wi-Fi, this is the access point.

- The authentication server (typically a RADIUS server) verifies the user credentials in some sort of user database and informs the authenticator of the outcome.

The user identifier usually takes the form of a Network Access Identifier[5] (NAI), an identifier of the form *username@realm*, where the realm stands for the administrative domain to which the user belongs.

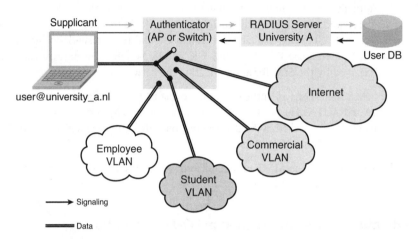

Figure 3-3   *802.1X Authentication Example of Student Gaining Access to the Campus Cetwork (Courtesy of SURFnet)*

User credentials are transported to the authentication server by using the EAP[6], a generic framework for forwarding encapsulated authentication data. EAP allows many types of credentials to be used, including username/password combinations, X.509 certificates, and others.

Figure 3-4 shows the EAP architecture. Between the supplicant and the authenticator, the EAP messages are encapsulated in Ethernet frames (EAP over LAN). Between the authenticator and the authentication server, EAP is usually encapsulated in RADIUS (or alternatively Diameter).

EAP methods define how authentication data should be encapsulated into EAP messages. Many different EAP methods exist. A number of EAP methods support confidentiality of user credentials in transit between the supplicant and authentication server. This means that neither the authenticator nor other network elements in the path between supplicant and authentication server can eavesdrop on the user credentials. In Wi-Fi networks, EAP-TTLS,[7] PEAP,[8] and EAP-FAST[9] are mainly used. All of these protect the user credentials against eavesdropping and allow mutual authentication of supplicant and authentication server. For roaming between cellular networks and Wi-Fi networks, EAP-AKA can be used, as discussed in the section "Non-3GPP Access," later in this chapter.

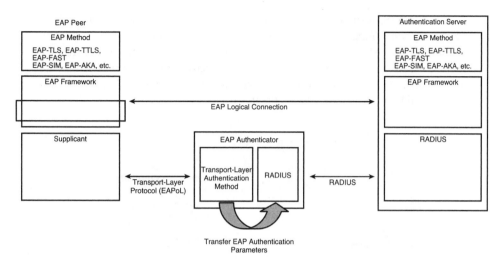

Figure 3-4   *EAP Message Communication*

Authentication and Authorization for Internet Applications

Authentication for network access is relatively difficult because there is no IP connectivity yet, so special protocols like 802.1X need to be used to transport user credentials to the authentication server. But as you saw in Chapter 2, "page 13," after you have IP connectivity, the sky is the limit. Therefore, it is hard to say anything in general about authentication for networked applications. Many different protocols exist, such as Kerberos, NT LAN Manager (NTLM), HTTP Basic Authentication, and so on. Also, every possible authentication method, ranging from username/password combinations and one-time passwords to smartcard authentication, exists and is in use. For web-based applications, the most common one is still username/password over (hopefully) a Secure Socket Layer (SSL) connection.

Federated Identity

When you cross the border into another country or when you enter a shop that offers Wi-Fi, you really don't want to have to sign up for a contract each time to connect to a network, not to mention the burden of remembering all the different usernames and passwords.

Here is where *federated identity* comes in. In the federated model, a user has a contract with only one (or a few) operators—the "home operator" that establishes the identity of the user. That one identity is then used to gain access to networks or applications managed by other operators. To make this work, the operators of the different networks need to establish a roaming or federation agreement. Such an agreement specifies under what conditions a visited network accepts an authentication statement ("this is a valid user") from the home operator, how the authentication credentials and accounting data are exchanged, and what financial arrangement is in place for visiting users.

So, in this model, as shown in Figure 3-5, the home operator (in identity lingo called the Identity Provider [IdP]) acts as a trusted third party for the serving operator, called the Service Provider (SP) or Relying Party (RP). There is no direct contractual or trust relationship between the user and the visited network, only between the user and the IdP and between the IdP and the RP. Because there is a trust relationship between the user and IdP and between the IdP and RP, the RP "trusts" the user.

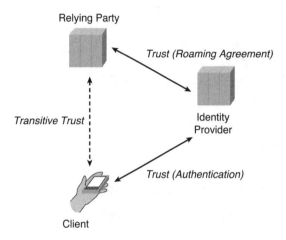

Figure 3-5 *Federated Identity*

The RADIUS[10] protocol allows forwarding of authentication requests to another RADIUS server; this is why RADIUS is widely used for network roaming. The authentication requests here are forwarded by the RP (usually also a RADIUS server) to the RADIUS server of the home operator (the IdP), and the outcome of the authentication is sent back. By combining RADIUS with EAP, the confidentiality of the user credentials can be preserved.

For access to web-based applications, a number of different protocols are used, such as Security Assertion Markup Language (SAML[11]), OpenID[12], or Open Authentication (OAuth)[13].

When users roam between networks using the same technology (that is, from one Long Term Evolution (LTE) network to another LTE or similar network), this is called *horizontal roaming*. Roaming between different types of networks, such as roaming from an LTE network to a Wi-Fi network, is called *vertical roaming*.

3GPP standardizes access to non-3GPP networks but places the LTE core network firmly in control; authentication is always performed in the LTE EPC. IEEE (the standardization body for the Wi-Fi standards) in its 802.21 standard[14] addresses vertical roaming with a more equal role for the different access technologies but does not address federated network authentication.

Federated Access in LTE

3GPP distinguishes two types of federated access:

- **3GPP access**[15]: Describes horizontal roaming.
- **Non-3GPP access**[16]: Describes vertical roaming.

In both cases, the home network needs to establish a roaming agreement beforehand (and the user's subscription should allow roaming access).

3GPP Access

3GPP access is access to an LTE network of another operator or to a UMTS or GPRS network. UMTS networks (and GPRS networks that support interworking with LTE) support AKA authentication.

Based on the IMSI (that contains a country and an operator code), the MME can ask the home HSS of the user to verify the user rather than the HSS in the serving network. The home HSS must check whether the subscription agreement with the user allows roaming, but apart from that, the authentication process is the same as for the nonroaming case.

Non-3GPP Access

Examples of non-3GPP access are CDMA-2000, WiMAX, and Wi-Fi. These networks don't use the same authentication methods, and the elements in these serving networks don't understand how to deal with an AKA authentication. So, rather than involving a network element in the serving network directly in the authentication flow with the home network, EAP is used instead. Here EAP provides the necessary abstraction from the actual authentication using AKA. For this purpose, EAP-AKA and its more secure successor EAP-AKA' (EAP-AKA Prime) have been created. The EAP identity contains the IMSI or a pseudonymous identifier that was established in a prior authentication to locate the authentication server for the user.

Figure 3-6 shows how AKA authentication can be encapsulated in EAP.

Although you can use the IP connectivity of the serving network, the typical use is to tunnel all traffic back to the home network using IPsec.

Federated Access to Wi-Fi Networks

Originally, Wi-Fi was intended to be used as a local-area network technology, typically covering an area with a radius of some 30–50 meters. Nowadays, sometimes hundreds to thousands of Wi-Fi access points together form *hotspots* that provide coverage to complete campuses or even cities. Still, the majority of the hotspot operators provide access to an area with a limited geographical scope (unlike the nationwide coverage that cellular operators provide). To provide coverage beyond the geographical region, hotspot operators need to collaborate so that subscribers of one operator can gain access to the network of another operator.

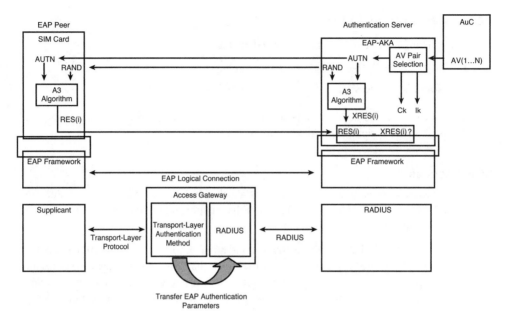

Figure 3-6   *EAP-AKA*

Roaming to Other Wi-Fi Networks

The main challenges in roaming access for Wi-Fi networks are setting up the roaming agreements and verifying the user credentials at the home network.

Because, unlike cellular networks, Wi-Fi hotspots are by virtue of the local-area character of the technology relatively small, setting up roaming agreements with a large number of Wi-Fi operators is hard to scale. To solve the scaling problem, three different types of organizational models emerge:

- The first model mimics the cellular model. A large operator acquires or leases a large number of hotspots and unifies the authentication across these hotspots. AT&T hotspots and T-Mobile hotspots are examples of this arrangement.

- In the second model, a third party acts as a broker for a large number of hotspot operators. The users have a contract with the broker and authenticate and pay for access to the broker. The broker in turn pays the hotspot operator. Examples of this arrangement are Boingo and iPass.

- The last model has individual hotspot operators join forces and agree on roaming conditions and credential verification methods. Examples of the latter are FON and the Wi-Fi roaming infrastructures that many schools worldwide participate in— eduroam. (This is further explained later in the section "Example of Wi-Fi Roaming: eduroam.")

Verification of the credentials of the users at the home network requires transporting the credentials to the home network and sending the outcome of the authentication back to the visited network. The dominant transport protocol for transporting the credentials is RADIUS.

The main advantage of the captive portal method for Wi-Fi is that it only requires a web browser on the user device. This is also why it is the most commonly used access method at public hotspots. The main downside is that because the Wi-Fi link is unprotected, simple MAC spoofing can be used by an attacker to piggyback an authenticated user's connection. Additionally, the user credentials are visible to every hotspot operator (they have to be entered in the web page that the captive portal shows) and can be observed by every RADIUS server in the path to the home RADIUS server. When 802.1X is used, the combination of 802.1X, EAP, and RADIUS allows user credential privacy. This means that users don't have to worry about giving their password to potentially thousands of hotspot operators, let alone rogue hotspot operators. An added benefit of using 802.1X is that all user traffic is encrypted over the Wi-Fi radio link, allowing the operator to be sure that every packet sent into the network originated from an authentic Wi-Fi user.

The added security features of 802.1X and better support in the most common operating systems have resulted in a slow but steady increase in use, especially in corporate environments.

802.11u

Two issues that are particularly important for Wi-Fi access are the fact that most Wi-Fi hotspots are relatively small and that there are thousands of them. In a densely populated area, a user easily often "sees" 30 or 40 different Wi-Fi networks, without knowing which of those will have a roaming agreement with the home operator and, if so, under what conditions.

This is the problem space that the upcoming IEEE 802.11u[17] standard addresses. Hotspots that are 802.11u enabled can broadcast information about the roaming consortia they belong to and under what conditions they can be used.

Example of Wi-Fi Roaming: eduroam

An example of a Wi-Fi roaming service is eduroam[18]. This service is limited to educational institutions. However, its technical setup and broad uptake (more than 500 universities in some 50 countries with over 10 million users) warrant attention.

eduroam started out in the Netherlands in 2003 and gained fast popularity in most European countries and later in Australia, Japan, Hong Kong, and Canada. Lately, U.S. schools are joining eduroam and Internet2 is supporting the initiative.

Figure 3-7 shows the European national research and education networks that participate in eduroam. (For an up-to-date overview of all participating institutions in Europe and elsewhere, refer to the eduroam website.[19])

Figure 3-7   *European National Research and Education Networks Participating in eduroam as of May 2010 (courtesy of TERENA)*

eduroam consists of a few basic elements, described in the following paragraphs.

A RADIUS hierarchy is set up consisting of a set of institutional (redundant, for failover purposes), national, and continental RADIUS servers. All institutional RADIUS servers connect to the national servers in their country. All national servers connect to the top-level servers for their continent, and the continental servers (Europe, America, and Asia-Pacific) connect to each other.

Figure 3-8 shows the RADIUS hierarchy that constitutes eduroam. The top-level servers that are fully meshed know which top-level servers serve what national domains. The national servers are connected to all institutional servers in their country and to the top-level servers in their continent. The institutional servers are connected to their national servers.

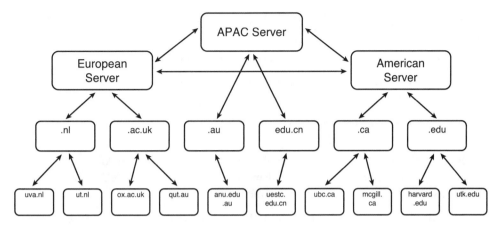

Figure 3-8   *The eduroam Hierarchy*

802.1X is used for secure access to the institutional Wi-Fi networks.

EAP is used to protect user credentials. EAP identities are of the form anonymous@*domain-name-of-institution* or, instead of anonymous, a pseudonymous identifier. Users' authentication requests are forwarded through the RADIUS hierarchy based on the domain name of the institution to which the user belongs.

In other words, the home institution authenticates the user and the serving institution authorizes the user for access. The home institution of the user can decide which authentication method and what EAP method to use.

Figure 3-9 shows a typical eduroam authentication, which is described in further detail in the list that follows.

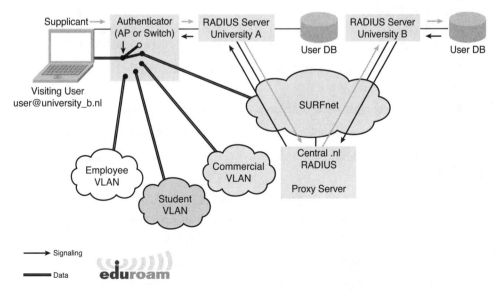

Figure 3-9   *The eduroam Basic Operation (Courtesy of SURFnet)*

1. A user from University B in the Netherlands tries to gain access to the network at University A, also in the Netherlands.

2. The authenticator asks the user (or rather the supplicant) to authenticate.

3. The user sends the authentication credentials encapsulated in EAP with an EAP identity of anonymous@university_b.nl to the authenticator.

4. The authenticator at University A forwards the EAP message to the RADIUS server of University A.

5. The University A RADIUS server observes that the EAP identity does not belong to University A and forwards the EAP message to the national RADIUS server for the Netherlands operated by SURFnet, the Dutch research and education network.

6. The SURFnet RADIUS server for the .nl domain sees that the EAP identity belongs to University B and forwards the EAP message to the University B RADIUS server. (If the EAP identity were not for the .nl domain, the EAP message would be forwarded to the European top-level server.)

7. The University B RADIUS server deencapsulates the EAP message and verifies the credentials.

8. University B sends the result of the authentication back along the same route.

9. The RADIUS server at University A instructs the authenticator to allow access to the user (and possibly to assign the user to a specific VLAN for guests).

Federated Access to Applications with SAML

When you assume that more and more applications will be offered "in the cloud," it is imperative that scalable mechanisms exist for federated identity. The most widespread systems for federated identity to (mainly) web-based application make use of the Security Assertion Markup Language (SAML) protocol suite. SAML is an XML-based markup language for transporting authorization assertions between IdPs and RPs.

Figure 3-10 shows a typical SAML (version 2.0) flow, which is further described in the list that follows:

1. The user uses his browser to try to access a resource under control by the RP.

2. The RP issues an authentication request to the browser (plus a redirect to the IdP).

3. The browser sends the authentication request to the IdP and asks for an authentication statement.

4. The user (if not already authenticated) authenticates at the IdP.

5. The IdP issues an authentication statement to the browser stating that the user is successfully authenticated (plus a redirect back to the RP).

6. The browser presents the authentication statement to the RP.

7. The RP gives the user access to the resource (assuming that the user satisfies the RP's policies and a roaming arrangement exists between the IdP and RP).

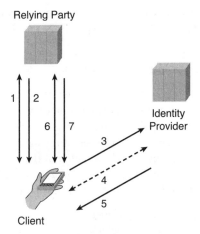

Figure 3-10   *SAML 2.0 Authentication Flow*

Location Information and Context Awareness

One particular characteristic of the mobile Internet is obviously that users are mobile—that is, not bound to a particular location. The location of users can be used for a number of location-based services, ranging from finding the nearest pizza parlor through turn-by-turn driving directions to finding a person that makes an emergency call.

Many modern devices contain a Global Positioning System (GPS) chip for providing location information. GPS is, however, not very accurate indoors or in the presence of buildings. Therefore, in many networks, additional ways of positioning a mobile terminal are used.

Location information is, however, just one example of the broader issue of context awareness. Knowledge about the network, the device that accesses the network, the user, and the applications can all be leveraged to offer the user a tailor-made user experience. But that is beyond the scope of this book.

The following paragraphs explain how location is determined in LTE and Wi-Fi networks.

Location Information in LTE

Nowadays many mobile devices contain a GPS receiver. This allows the applications to acquire the location of the device and offer services based on that location. In addition to that, many devices are able to use so-called assisted GPS (A-GPS) to overcome the inaccurate indoor positioning of GPS. With A-GPS, the network supplies location information (based on the position in relation to cell towers) or information about the geo-orbital position of the GPS satellites. This allows devices to acquire fast and reliable positioning information in all circumstances, even indoors. This is of particular importance in emergency situations (like 911 or 112 calls in, respectively, the United States and Europe).

Location Information for Wi-Fi Networks

Unlike in cellular systems, where there are relatively few radio towers of which the position is well known, for Wi-Fi networks, the location of all access points is not always well known and might change. This makes it comparatively harder to use the location of the access points to reliably determine the position of the mobile equipment. If the location of the access points is stable, however, the location of the access point can be used to determine the location of a mobile terminal accurate to typically about 50 meters, even better if triangulation is used between multiple access points.

An example of a Wi-Fi positioning system is the Cisco Wireless Position Appliance[20] that is part of the Cisco Context-Aware Mobility solution and that can be used to track assets and users.

Privacy and Security

Privacy concerns develop when user data is spread across many locations. Personal Identifiable Information (PII), such as street addresses, IP addresses, first and last names, and login credentials, can be traced back to an individual or a small group of individuals. Privacy regulations often dictate the amount of PII data that can be exchanged.

At the same time, users need to be properly authenticated when they are trying to access another network, and users often want to share their location to get location-based services.

Law enforcement requires the ability to track crime suspects and monitor their transactions and conversations. For that purpose, operators need to be able to redirect and monitor traffic of particular users without their knowledge. These Lawful Intercept (LI) requirements complicate roaming agreements, traffic offload, and other route optimization functions, because the easiest way to comply with these requirements is to direct all traffic through a central location, where it can be monitored.

A useful concept in federated access is that of a "pseudonym," an identity that is unique for a specific user and often for a specific access network but that can only be linked to an individual user by the home network operator. The extent to which pseudonymity can be used varies from one access technology to another and from implementation to implementation.

From a security point of view, a benefit of the federated model is the fact that the sensitive user data is not distributed over many systems, but concentrated in the IdP.

Another benefit of having a centralized authentication server is that it is possible to introduce stronger authentication means (like smartcards) without the need to change all applications to support this type of authentication.

Apart from authentication and authorization data, the user traffic and the control traffic between the various elements in the network often need to be protected against eavesdropping and tampering. For this purpose, a wide variety of cryptographic means are used.

Privacy and Security in LTE

In LTE (unlike UMTS), a great deal of effort has gone into making sure that compromising the security of one network element will not imply compromising the security of the system as a whole. As an example of that, a complex system for the generation of cryptographic keys has been developed that is being used for securing the communication between the various other network elements. In particular, all keys inside a visited network are derived from a "master" key, which is specific for that serving network. This means that if the security in the serving network is breached, this will not have any implications for the home network and the integrity of the user credentials.

Traffic between the serving network and the home network is protected using IPsec.

In the initial AKA authentication, the IMSI is sent to the serving network, but after that, a temporary identifier is used. This means that the serving network is still capable of observing the IMSI, but at least the casual eavesdropper is unable to monitor the point of attachment of that particular IMSI.

Privacy and Security in Wi-Fi Networks

For captive portals, it is by the nature of that technology very difficult to provide location privacy and credential protection, the users submit their credentials after all at that specific location and to the captive portal that is used by the hotspot operator. These problematic security properties are worsened by the fact that users are in a way "trained" to submit their username and password or other authentication credential to every web page that remotely looks like a plausible hotspot page, instead of sharing their credentials only with their home network operator. Furthermore, unlike with 802.1X, typically all users get IP access to the local LAN that the hotspot is connected to, even before authentication. So, it is relatively easy to eavesdrop on the wireless traffic.

Using 802.1X in combination with EAP in contrast, it is possible to use pseudonymous identifiers for the users (identifiers such as anonymous@*homeprovider* or pseudonym12345@*homeprovider*), and in addition to that, 802.1X sets up a secure association between mobile equipment and access point, thereby protecting the user traffic against eavesdroppers on the wireless network.

Privacy and Security in SAML

SAML-based identity federations have been designed with user privacy and confidentiality in mind. Users are redirected to their own IdP to perform authentication so that the user credentials don't have to be shared with the RP. Instead of using the actual user identity for interacting with the RP, it is possible to use a pseudonymous identifier that is unique for the user and on a per-RP basis (a so-called *targeted identity*).

From a privacy aspect, there is one concern that has to do with the nature of SAML-based federations. The SAML model is geared toward an enterprise-centric model. That is to say, the IdP is always a party in a transaction, and therefore the IdP has a good insight in all the transactions that a user performs. In answer to this concern, there has been a lot of interest in what is called *user-centric identity*. In this model, the user uses an IdP for initial identity proofing and goes on wielding that proof of identity without having to involve the IdP in every transaction. So the Identity Provider does not need to know what services the user accesses. Examples of user-centric identity approaches are OpenID, OAuth, and Infocard.

DynDNS

So far, this chapter has concentrated on the user gaining access to the network or application. There is, however, another important issue to consider—how to find the mobile equipment if the other side initiates the communication. As you will see in future chapters, there are a number of solutions that provide a stable *anchoring point* that can be used to find the current point of attachment or to direct all traffic to, but they require changes in the protocol stack. The standard way of informing "the Internet" where a certain host resides is by using the Domain Name System (DNS). DNS, after all, contains mappings from host names to IP addresses. So, if the entry in DNS is updated every time a host changes its point of attachment (and thus IP address), DNS information can be used to find the target IP address of a connection.

This is precisely what Dynamic DNS (DynDNS) is—a DNS server that is optimized for frequent updates of the mapping information. A number of implementations of DynDNS exist, often provided for free. For this to work, a DNS client that updates the current name to IP address mapping every time the host changes IP address is required.

Because of the distributed nature of DNS (it takes some time before DNS resolvers become aware of a change), DynDNS is not practical when DNS changes occur very frequently, in the order of magnitude of seconds.

Another point of concern is that rogue DNS updates can be used to redirect traffic. Unless the DNS updates can be authenticated—for example by using DNS Secure (DNSSEC)—this is a security problem. DNSSEC, however, is not yet widely in use.

Summary

Nomadic use refers to a usage pattern of the Internet with intermittent access. Key to a user experience of anytime, anywhere access to the Internet and its applications are scalable, secure, and seamless access methods. Federated identity plays an important role in providing such a user experience in the presence of multiple-access networks and applications offered by different operators. Nomadic use requires some form of context awareness to provide services that are tailored to location, access method, and device.

Endnotes

1. The 3D Generation Partnership Project, http://www.3gpp.org.

2. The 3D Generation Partnership Project 2, http://www.3gpp2.org.

3. TR 21.905, "Vocabulary for 3GPP Specifications," http://www.3gpp.org/ftp/Specs/html-info/21905.htm.

4. RFC 3310, "HTTP Digest Authentication Using AKA," A. Niemi, J. Arkko, and V. Torvinen, http://www.ietf.org/rfc/rfc791.txt, September 2002.

5. RFC 4282, "The Network Access Identifier," B. Aboba, M. Beadless, J. Arkko, and P. Eronen, http://www.ietf.org/rfc/rfc4282.txt, December 2005.

6. RFC 5247, "Extensible Authentication Protocol Key Management Framework," B. Aboba, D. Simon, and P. Eronen, http://www.ietf.org/rfc/rfc4282.txt, August 2008.

7. RFC 5281, "Extensible Authentication Protocol Tunneled Transport Layer Security Authenticated Protocol Version 0," P. Funk and S. Blake-Wilson, http://www.ietf.org/rfc/rfc5281.txt, August 2008.

8. "Protected Extensible Authentication Protocol," http://en.wikipedia.org/wiki/Protected_Extensible_Authentication_Protocol.

9. RFC 4851, "The Flexible Authentication via Secure Tunneling Extensible Authentication Protocol Method," N. Cam-Winget, D. McGrew, J. Salowey, and H. Zhou, http://www.ietf.org/rfc/rfc4851.txt, May 2007.

10. RFC 2138, "Remote Authentication Dial In User Service," C. Rigney, A. Rubens, W. Simpson, and S. Willens, http://www.ietf.org/rfc/rfc2138.txt, April 1997.

11. "SAML V2.0 Executive Overview," P. Madsen, et al., http://www.oasis-open.org/committees/download.php/13525/sstc-saml-exec-overview-2.0-cd-01-2col.pdf, April 2005.

12. OpenID, http://openid.net.

13. OAuth, http://oauth.net.

14. IEEE 802.21, http://www.ieee802.org/21.

15. TS 33.401, "3GPP System Architecture Evolution: Security Architecture," http://www.3gpp.org/ftp/Specs/html-info/33401.htm.

16. TS 33.402, "3GPP System Architecture Evolution: Security Aspects of non-3GPP Accesses," http://www.3gpp.org/ftp/Specs/html-info/33402.htm.

17. IEEE 802.11u, http://en.wikipedia.org/wiki/IEEE_802.11u.

18. K. Wierenga and L. Florio. "eduroam: Past, Present and Future." *Computational Methods in Science and Technology*, Vol. 11, No. 2: February 2005.

19. eduroam website, http://www.eduroam.org.

20. "Cisco Location Solution Overview," https://www.cisco.com/en/US/solutions/collateral/ns340/ns394/ns348/ns753/net_brochure0900aecd8064fe9d_ps6386_Products_Brochure.html.

Chapter 4

Data Link Layer Mobility

The fundamental architecture of the Internet is built upon a foundation of associating an IP address, not with a host, but with an interface of a host. Associating an IP address with a host would certainly have facilitated mobility, but as John Day describes[1], when IP was first proposed in 1975, "problems of multicast and mobility were many years off."

These architectural issues are compounded by the way in which the upper layers, dealing with applications, are coupled to lower layers, dealing with IP transport. Chapter 2, "Internet 'Sessions'," has introduced the concept of Internet sockets that are used to allow communications between remote application processes on different hosts. An Internet socket is identified with a local socket address that includes the local IP address.

As a consequence, with application processes running on a host being bound to an Internet socket, which is in turn bound to an individual interface on that host, you can easily see why solving mobility below the IP transport layer is an attractive proposition. Mobility for any existing host or application can be supported by augmenting the data link layer with mobility functionality.

Approaches to data link layer mobility "hide" mobility from the IP layer and consequently require the IP Point of Attachment (PoA) to remain static throughput a communications session. A by-product of such approaches is that any mobility events are hidden from the correspondent node (CN), and hence the CN cannot determine that it is communicating with a mobile host. Furthermore, because the data link layer domain might well cover a significant geographic area (and indeed might cover an entire country in the case of packet data–based cellular networks, as you will see later in this chapter), the correspondent node might be unable to derive significant user location information from the associated IP PoA address. Such characteristics might be important for addressing user location privacy issues introduced in Chapter 3, "Nomadicity."

This chapter describes different use cases that have caused specific data link layers to be enhanced with mobility functionality.

Mobility Across an Ethernet-Bridged Domain

Before delving into the advanced data link layer mobility architectures that provide wide-area mobility, you first need to take a look at Ethernet bridging and determine what local mobility functionality is inherently supported by the baseline data link layer technology.

Ethernet bridging controls data flows within a network, with individual bridges forwarding traffic only to the interface(s) that need to receive the traffic. IEEE 802.1d[2] defines five bridging processes for determining what to do with an Ethernet frame:

- **Learning:** When the bridge receives an Ethernet frame from a device, it records the source MAC address and the source interface.

- **Flooding:** When a bridge receives an Ethernet frame with an unknown destination MAC address, it *floods* the frame by forwarding it to all forwarding interfaces except for the one on which it received the frame.

- **Filtering:** When the bridge receives an Ethernet frame with a destination MAC address on an interface that it has previously recorded the address as a source MAC address, the bridge will *filter* the frame by discarding it.

- **Forwarding:** When the bridge receives an Ethernet frame with a destination MAC address that it has previously recorded and the associated interface is different from the one on which the frame was received, the bridge *forwards* the frame out of the recorded interface.

- **Aging:** When the bridge records a source MAC address and associated interface, it will timestamp the record. If the bridge doesn't see another frame from the source MAC address before an aging timer expires, the record is deleted.

You can now see that basic bridging supports mobility, as further illustrated in Figure 4-1. Suppose that hosts H1 and H2 have an ongoing application section active. Bridge B1 has previously learned that host H2 is reachable through interface 1, so normal communication proceeds.

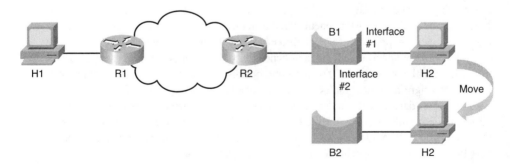

Figure 4-1   *Example Bridged Network*

Now, suppose that host H2 subsequently moves from being attached to bridge B1 to bridge B2. The Internet socket of host H1 is oblivious to the move and sends packets to the H2 destination address. These frames are received at bridge B1, which continues to forward them out of interface 1. Only after the MAC record for host H2 has aged out will the bridge B1 start to flood frames destined to host H2 out of interface 1 and interface 2. These frames will be received by bridge B2, which will similarly flood frames out of its interfaces toward the attached host H2.

As you can see, if the Internet socket associated with the application is unidirectional, there can be a significant interruption in the communication between hosts H1 and H2 before the MAC table in bridge B1 ages out.

Note   The default timer for aging out MAC entries in Cisco switches is 5 minutes.

The previous description assumes that host H2 had been configured with a static IP address. We have already described how an Internet socket is tied directly to an IP address, and hence the following section will look at how the interactions triggered by dynamic IP address allocation can help in implementing mobility solutions.

Interaction Between Mobility and Dynamic IP Address Allocation

When we discuss advanced-use cases involving wireless networks, we often overlook how delivering basic mobility across an enterprise was challenged before the introduction of dynamic IP address allocation. Manually configuring static IP addresses and Domain Name Servers (DNS) was a clear inhibitor to mobility across hierarchical enterprise networks.

The administrative burden of managing static IP addresses was removed with the introduction of dynamic IP addresses by the deployment of Dynamic Host Configuration Protocol (DHCP) on the endpoints and corresponding server functionality in the network. Figure 4-2 shows the operation of DHCP, which is described further in the list that follows:

1.   The client first broadcasts a DHCP DISCOVER message, which, in this example, is received by a router that has been configured with DHCP relay functionality. The router unicasts the DHCP message to its configured DHCP server. This allows a single server to provide DHCP services to clients on many subnets.

2.   The DHCP server responds with a DHCP OFFER message that includes an offered IP address as well as subnet mask information. Because more than one DHCP server might have received and responded to the DHCP DISCOVER message, the IP address is only reserved and not allocated to the client.

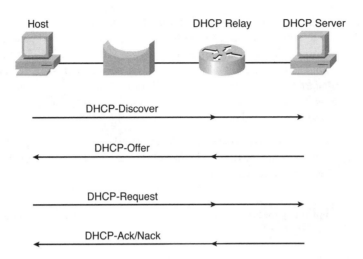

Figure 4-2   *DHCP Operation*

3.   The client then responds with a DHCP REQUEST message, containing the IP address from the selected DHCP OFFER message.

4.   The server responds with a DHCP ACK message that confirms the IP address has been temporarily allocated to the client for a certain lease interval.

If a client has previously been leased an IP address, the preceding four-step process is simplified to a two-step process, whereby the client can skip the discover process and directly broadcast a DHCP REQUEST message containing the previously allocated IP address. If the previous IP address information has been recovered after a restart, the client might have changed subnets, in which case the DHCP server cannot allocate the requested IP address, and it will respond with a DHCP NACK message.

While DHCP was not designed to provide host mobility, you can see how the preceding procedures enable "plug-and-play" nomadic connectivity within a single Layer 2 subnet. When a client changes Ethernet ports, the DHCP process will trigger the broadcast of a DHCP REQUEST message. Each switch receiving the Ethernet frame containing the broadcast message will flood the frame out of all its interfaces. Consequently, the specification by DHCP to use an IP broadcast message for the DHCP DISCOVER and REQUEST messages ensures that all MAC tables in the bridged domain are suitably updated with the new location of the client's MAC address, hence supporting mobility for upper-layer IP applications across the Layer 2 subnet.

Mobility Using Wireless LAN Technology

While DHCP supported basic "plug-and-play" operation, the introduction of mobility in the enterprise is most often associated with deployment of wireless LAN technology. Originally specified in 1999, IEEE 802.11[3] standardized wireless Ethernet networking defining how a wireless LAN access point (AP) can provide wireless service to associated clients (termed *stations* in IEEE 802.11), with the combination of access points and stations being referred to as a Basic Service Set (BSS). In addition to single AP deployments, IEEE 802.11 defined the means by which several BSSs can be connected through a local-area network (LAN) and then appear as a single BSS to the Logical Link Control (LLC) layer of any station associated with one of the constituent BSSs (termed Extended BSS in IEEE 802.11).

The previous section demonstrated how mobility across a Layer 2 bridged domain can be supported but that the updating of the MAC tables in the bridged domain required the client to reinitialize the DHCP process on its Ethernet interface. In an IEEE 802.11 wireless LAN (WLAN) environment, the movement between APs in an Extended BSS does not trigger a reinitialization of the DHCP process, resulting in the MAC tables not being updated with the clients' new Point of Attachment to the Ethernet-bridged domain.

To accommodate basic mobility in an IEEE 802.11 environment, IEEE 802.11f[4] Inter-Access Point Protocol (IAPP) was defined to enable mobility across access points. IEEE 802.11f recommendations included the broadcasting of a Layer 2 Update frame by the AP when a new client associates with it. The Layer 2 Update is an IEEE 802.2 eXchange IDentification (XID) Update Response frame sent using the MAC source address equal to the MAC address of the client that has associated with the AP. This ensures that any Layer 2 devices (for example, bridges and switches) update their forwarding tables with the correct port to reach the new client location.

> **Note**   In addition to Layer 2 Update frames, IEEE 802.11f defined associated messages sent between access points for supporting mobility between multivendor APs. After a client had associated with an AP, a message was sent to an IAPP multicast address that was used to inform all APs of the MAC address of the client. If there was a preexisting AP with the same MAC address listed in its associations, the message allowed such an AP to remove the client from its list of associations, leading to optimized operation.
>
> IEEE 802.11f was defined as *Trial-Use Recommended Practice* and did not receive wide industry support, due in part to its lack of support for fast interaccess point mobility use cases. In 2006, the IEEE withdrew the recommendation.

Fast Wireless LAN Local Mobility

As more real-time IP applications are adopted, the requirement to support fast seamless mobility across a subnet is becoming increasingly important. However, support for fast mobility is hampered by the equally important deployment of WLAN security.

Initial attempts at securing WLAN infrastructure using Wired Equivalent Privacy (WEP) have been shown to be extremely weak. As a result, WEP authentication has been dropped from the IEEE 802.11 specification and has been replaced with IEEE 802.11i[5]. IEEE 802.11i uses the Extensible Authentication Protocol (EAP), defined in RFC 5247, for providing an end-to-end framework for supporting authentication methods between clients and the network.

Rather than providing a specific authentication method, the EAP framework was designed to support both current and future authentication methods. The framework has evolved to support multiple wireless and point-to-point methods, including the following:

- EAP Subscriber Identity Module (EAP-SIM)

- EAP for UMTS Authentication and Key Agreement (EAP-AKA)

- EAP Transport Layer Security (EAP-TLS)

- EAP Tunneled Transport Layer Security (EAP-TTLS)

- EAP Flexible Authentication through Secure Tunneling (EAP-FAST)

Whereas EAP provides the authentication framework, IEEE 802.1X[6] provides the functionality to associate that authentication operation with an individual port. Figure 4-3 shows the operation of IEEE 802.11i.

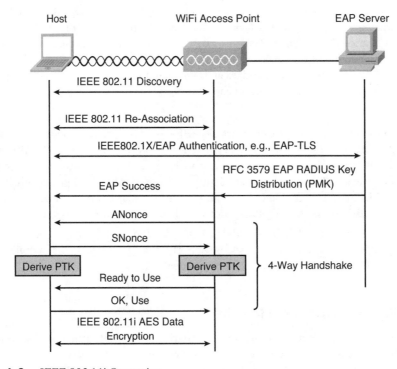

Figure 4-3   *IEEE 802.11i Operation*

You can see that IEEE 802.1X is used to encapsulate EAP messages and send them over the wireless Ethernet infrastructure. Typically, a common authentication server is used to provide service to a number of IEEE 802.1X–protected ports, so communication between the WLAN access point and authentication server is supported using EAP-over-RADIUS (as specified in RFC 3579). This allows the EAP method to run end to end between the client and the authentication server. RADIUS is then used to deliver Pairwise

Master Keying (PMK) material generated by the EAP authentication method to the WLAN access point. Finally, this master keying material is used by the client and access point in a four-way handshake that is used to derive Pairwise Temporal Keys (PTK) that are subsequently used to key the Advanced Encryption Standard (AES) algorithm. The port connecting the client to the AP is then unblocked, and packets can be securely sent between the client and access point over the Wi-Fi network.

You can see that the operation of IEEE 802.11i impacts the deployment of mobility solutions because, as described previously, keying material derived from an agreed EAP method needs to be delivered to the access point before the wireless link can be secured. The time spent during the EAP method needs to accommodate multiple round-trip signaling exchanges between the client and EAP server, key calculation, as well as possible smart-card access. For example, analysis of the EAP-SIM method[7] indicates that over 2 seconds is required to perform the EAP negotiation. Obviously, an interruption interval of over 2 seconds is unacceptable if the WLAN network is being used to support real-time services to mobile users.

Note   To improve roaming performance, IEEE 802.11i introduced the Proactive Key Caching (PKC) feature. This enables a client station to cache the PMK derived during successful EAP authentication using a particular AP. If, after having left the coverage of this particular AP, the client subsequently moves back into coverage, the client can reuse the cached keying material, avoiding performing a second EAP authentication with the same AP.

Instead of running a complete EAP authentication exchange to derive keying material, an alternative approach is to allow the client to perform an initial signaling exchange with the target access point to allow the calculation of the temporal keys in advance. These keys can then be applied after the client associates with the target access point. This is the basic operation of the IEEE 802.11r[8] Fast Transition standard, which defines these initial signaling exchanges as either *Over-the-Air*, where the client signals the target AP using IEEE 802.11 authentication, or *Over-the-Distribution System*, where the client signals the target AP through the current AP.

You can see from Figure 4-4 how the IEEE 802.11r Fast Transition Authentication signaling between the client and the target AP is used to enable the target AP to derive the Pairwise Temporal Keying material. In addition, the reassociation signaling is enhanced to signal that full IEEE 802.1X/EAP authentication is not necessary, allowing the target AP to directly transition the port to the unblocked state and secure the wireless link between it and the client. Experimental results[9] have demonstrated that the transition time using IEEE 802.11r can be decreased to under 50 ms, sufficient to enable mobility to be supported for real-time services.

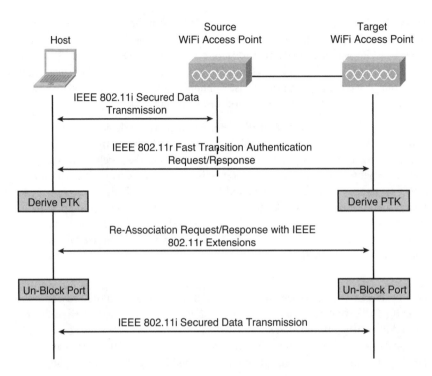

Figure 4-4   *Fast Transition Using IEEE 802.11r*

Note   With IEEE 802.11r, only the initial AP communicates with the AAA server. Subsequent fast transitions to a new AP will trigger this new AP to interact with the initial AP to recover keying material, rather than directly with the AAA server. However, the scope of IEEE 802.11r does not include the method by which the new AP communicates with the initial AP.

Wireless LANs and Mobility Across a Layer 3 Domain

The previous section described how wireless LAN technology has been enhanced to enable fast, secure mobility across a Layer 2 subnet. While such approaches are perfectly adequate for providing mobility to consumers around a residential property, or even scenarios dealing with small branch deployments, the same techniques are challenged at delivering mobility across a typical enterprise campus deployment.

Over the years, the Cisco-recommended, three-tier hierarchy to designing enterprise networks has been widely deployed. The three tiers are as follows:

■ **Access:** The access layer is the first tier or edge of the campus. It is used to attach hosts (PCs, printers, servers, IP phones, and WLAN access points) to the wired portion of the campus network.

■ **Distribution:** The distribution layer in the campus design provides an aggregation point for all the access switched in the network.

- **Core:** The core layer provides a highly available backbone that is ultimately responsible for providing the connectivity between the wide variety of hosts and the computing and data storage services located in the data center.

You can see that the baseline wireless LAN technology is therefore ideal at providing mobility when a user moves within an access domain, for example, a user moving between AP1 and AP2 in Figure 4-5. However, whenever the user moves between access domains—for example, a user moving between AP2 and AP3 in Figure 4-5—the new WLAN AP belongs to a different subnet, so the user's device needs to obtain a new IP address before services can continue on AP3.

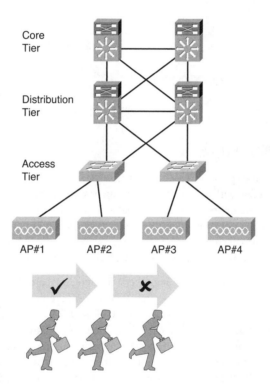

Figure 4-5 *WLAN Mobility Across a Campus Network*

What is needed is a technique to be able to abstract the Point of Attachment of the WLAN user from the physical access point equipment connected to the access tier and move this into the distribution tier. Such functionality has been specified by the IETF Control and Provisioning of Wireless Access Points (CAPWAP) working group.

One of the goals of the CAPWAP working group was to define an architecture that would allow the "centralization of authentication and policy enforcement functions for a wireless network."[10] To achieve its objectives, the CAPWAP architecture allows the functionality of a conventional "fat" access point to be decomposed between a Wireless Termination Point (WTP) or "lightweight access point" and an Access Controller (AC) or "wireless LAN controller (WLC)," as shown in Figure 4-6. Importantly, the client stations are unaffected by such a decomposition and continue to operate oblivious to the repartitioning of access point functionality.

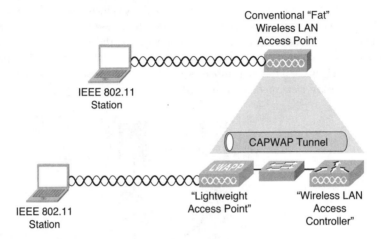

Figure 4-6   *CAPWAP Architecture*

CAPWAP essentially splits the MAC termination for a particular WLAN client between the AP and the controller, with a CAPWAP tunneling protocol linking the two functions. All the AAA state, including the PMK keying material, is maintained by the centralized controller instead of being distributed in the APs. One of the obvious benefits of such an architecture is that when a client moves between access points managed by the same controller, it is a simple task to update the client's state with the CAPWAP tunnel to the new AP.

CAPWAP supports deployments where the WTP and AC share the same Layer 2 domain, but also supports deployments where the WTP and AC are in different subnets. DHCP extensions have been specified in RFC 5417 to allow a WTP to be dynamically configured with the IP address of its CAPWAP AC. Using such techniques, the wireless LAN controller can be relocated from the access tier to the distribution tier, effectively providing mobility for users moving between different subnets in the access tier. Because the Layer 2 PoA is at the WLC, a change of client IP address is no longer required as the WLAN user moves from AP2 to AP3 in Figure 4-5.

Note   In the CAPWAP architecture, the WLC is responsible for providing centralized authentication services for attached WLAN clients, acting as the AAA authenticator. Because the WLC can cache credentials, the architecture therefore supports IEEE 802.11r fast mobility without the need to define how the new AP communicates with the initial AP.

Interwireless LAN Controller Mobility

In medium- and large-scale deployments of the CAPWAP architecture, there might be multiple WLCs used to manage a large number of APs. In such scenarios, mobility might be required to be supported when a user moves from being attached to a source AP managed by a first WLC to being attached to a target AP managed by a second WLC. Whereas inter-AC communications were defined as being strictly outside the scope of the CAPWAP protocol specification, this has not prevented vendors from delivering such functionality, whereby a set of WLCs cooperate to provide seamless mobility services. This then allows a mobile client to seamlessly maintain its Layer 3 PoA within a network infrastructure, even while moving between APs managed by different discrete WLCs.

The Cisco WLC includes such functionality using the concept of a mobility group. Controllers that are part of the same mobility group cooperate to support seamless mobility. An inter-WLC mobility protocol is defined to allow sharing of important mobility-related information.

In medium-size installations, multiple WLCs might be required to scale an AP deployment. In such cases, the controllers are typically connected to the same upstream distribution switch in "local connection" configuration. Figure 4-7 shows how the WLAN system can be configured so that the same APs are part of the same Extended BSS. In this case, the two WLCs are part of the same mobility group, and mobility is supported as the client moves from AP1, managed by controller 1, to AP2, managed by controller 2.

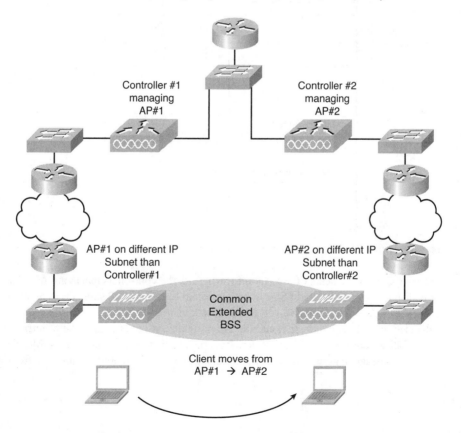

Figure 4-7   *Inter-WLC Mobility on Same Subnet*

All the WLCs in a group will be configured with identical information describing the mobility group. Each WLC is responsible for sending repeated keepalives to other WLCs in the mobility group using the unicast Switch-Announce message, as shown in Figure 4-8. At point 1, a client first associates with an AP managed by controller 2. This controller sends a Mobile-Announce message to all controllers in the mobility group, including information necessary to identify the client and Extended BSS. Assuming that the client was previously associated in an AP managed by controller 1 at point 2, this controller will match the client identity in the Mobile-Announce message and will respond with a unicast Mobile-Handoff message. The old controller will then delete information for the client session.

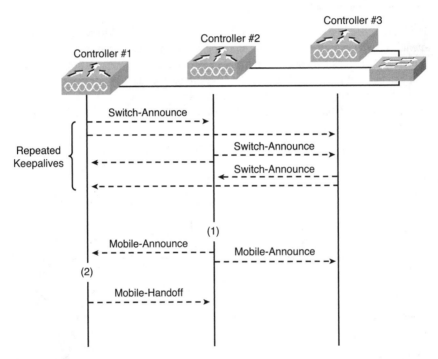

Figure 4-8 *Inter-WLC Message Exchange with Local Connection*

In larger-size deployments of WLAN infrastructure, the controllers managing APs that provide a common Extended BSS can be connected to different IP subnets. To allow the client's IP PoA to remain unchanged in this case, the inter-WLC functionality needs to be enhanced to support intersubnet mobility. In particular, whereas in the case of intrasubnet mobility, controller 1 in Figure 4-8 deletes the client state after sending the Mobile-Handoff message, Figure 4-9 shows the signaling flow for intersubnet mobility. After the mobile client has authenticated itself to controller 2, there is still a Mobile-Announce/ Mobile-Handoff message exchange used to allow controller 1 to forward the client state to controller 2 (including IP address, default gateway, and DHCP server IP address), but now controller 1 retains the client state and provides IP PoA services for the mobile client. Any packets that are received by controller 1 destined to the mobile node are tunneled toward controller 2, which then forwards the packets toward the mobile node. Similarly, controller 1 will provide proxy ARP functionality, responding with its own MAC address for ARP requests targeting the mobile node's IP address.

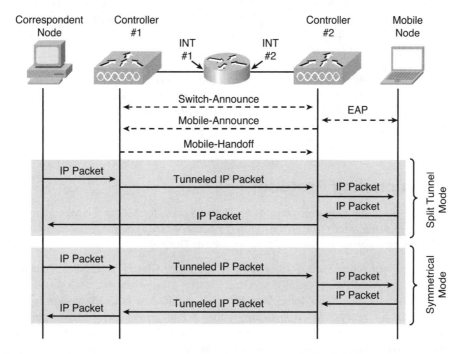

Figure 4-9   *Inter-WLC Message Exchange with Intersubnet Mobility*

When it comes to forwarding packets between a correspondent and mobile nodes, two options are supported, as shown in Figure 4-9:

- **Split tunnel mode:** In split tunnel mode, when controller 1 receives a packet for the mobile node, it is tunneled toward controller 2, where it is forwarded to the mobile client. In the reverse direction, upstream packets are switched directly from controller 2. The issue with such an approach is if Unicast Reverse Path Forwarding (URPF) is enabled in the network, the routers will drop such upstream traffic.

- **Symmetrical mode:** To allow operation in networks with URPF enabled, conventional split tunnel mode is enhanced with the capability to tunnel uplink packets from controller 2 to controller 1, where they are deencapsulated and forwarded to the wired network.

> **Note**   URPF is used to reduce the amount of malicious traffic on a network by enabling routers to verify the reachability of the source address in packets being forwarded and can be used to limit the ability to send IP packets with spoofed IP addresses into the network. If the source IP address is not valid, the packet is simply discarded. URPF can operate in *strict mode*, whereby a packet must be received on the interface that the router would use to forward the returning packet.
>
> In Figure 4-9, because controller 1 is the IP PoA, the router should be configured to forward packets destined to the source IP address of the mobile node out of interface INT1. Consequently, if the router receives an uplink packet from the mobile node on interface INT2, URPF will cause the router to discard such packets.

As you can see, the decomposition of the enterprise WLAN access point into a two-level hierarchy comprising a wireless LAN controller and lightweight access point has significantly facilitated the deployment of advanced enterprise mobility functionality, including being able to support mobility across Layer 3 domains and also across large campus networks, scaling to multiple IP Points of Attachment.

GPRS Tunneling Protocol

3GPP specifications have evolved from the Global System for Mobile (GSM) communication specification, which in 1997 introduced a packet-based system optimized for bursty traffic patterns and asymmetrical flows, termed the General Packet Radio System (GPRS).

The GPRS architecture needed to coexist with the legacy Circuit Switched (CS) architecture used to provide voice and SMS services. Figure 4-10 shows how the CS core network comprises a Gateway Mobile Switching Center (MSC), which is always located in a subscriber's home network and is effectively the CS Point of Attachment to the public switched telephone network (PSTN) for mobile terminating calls. The subscriber can be roaming and consequently the CS architecture introduces the concept of a Visited MSC that is responsible for authenticating users as well as providing voice services to attached subscribers.

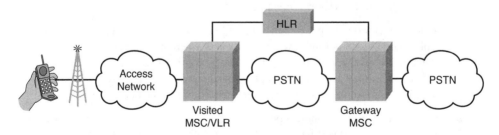

Figure 4-10   *3GPP Circuit-Switched Core Network Architecture*

As its name suggests, the Home Location Register (HLR) is located in the subscriber's home network and is a database containing subscriber information related to services as well as the current location of each active user. When a subscriber first activates his phone in a network, the Visited MSC will contact the subscriber's HLR to recover challenge/response information, which it subsequently uses in authenticating the subscriber's device. During this procedure, the HLR will store the address of the Visited MSC where a subscriber is located. Now, when a mobile-terminated call is made, the call signaling will be received by the Gateway MSC in the user's home network. The Gateway MSC will then query the HLR to recover the address of the Visited MSC, which it then signals to enable completion of the call.

Because GPRS needed to support similar functionality (in other words, with the IP PoA being in the subscriber's home network, while a subscriber was roaming in a visited network), when 3GPP defined the architecture for the Packet Switched (PS) core network, a similar functional split was selected. A Gateway GPRS Support Node (GGSN) is defined to provide the IP PoA for GPRS subscribers, and a Serving GPRS Support Node (SGSN) is defined to authenticate GPRS subscribers and to provide a transient aggregation point for GPRS subscribers attached to a particular visited access network, as shown in Figure 4-11. The GPRS Tunneling Protocol (GTP) is defined as the protocol used between the SGSN and GGSN network elements. Because GTP allows the IP PoA to remain static while the client devices move, from the mobile device's perspective, the entire cellular network can be viewed as a simple point-to-point connection.

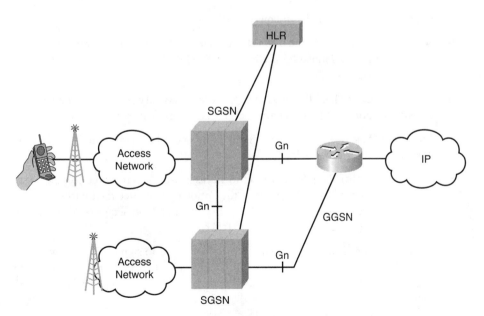

Figure 4-11   *3GPP Packet-Switched Core Network Architecture*

GPRS Tunneling Protocol

GTP essentially comprises two protocols:

- GTP-U, which is used for encapsulating user data within the GPRS core network

- GTP-C, which is used to signal between the SGSN and GGSN network elements

Not only does GTP-C support tunnel management operations establishment/modifications/termination, but it is also used for context transfer capability and to support quality of service (QoS) negotiation.

The GPRS Tunneling Protocol (GTP) is a UDP-based tunnel protocol that provides mobility based on a Packet Data Protocol (PDP) Context and has been specified by 3GPP in 29.060[11]. GTP-U has been allocated UDP port 2152 by the International Assigned Number Authority (IANA).

Before a mobile device can receive services from the PS core network, it must first activate a Packet Data Protocol (PDP) context. GTP tunnels are identified by a Tunnel Endpoint Identifier (TEID) and are used to carry encapsulated Tunneled Protocol Data Units (T-PDU). The T-PDU typically corresponds to an IP packet to/from a mobile user, with the maximum size of a T-PDU being 1500 bytes.

Figure 4-12 shows the 32-bit TEID in the GTP header fields. This should be a random number, dynamically allocated by the receiving-side entity.

The other fields are described as follows:

- **Version:** The original version 0 of GTP has been replaced with GTP version 1. GTP version 2 has been defined for use in the Evolved Packet Core (EPC), but only for control messages (GTP-C).

- **Protocol Type (PT):** GTP is used to support both mobility procedures and charging record transport. The latter is termed GTP' and is signified by having the PT set to 0.

- **Extension Header Flag (E):** When set to 1, this is used to signify the presence of the Next Extension Header field.

- **Sequence Number Flag (S):** When set to 1, this is used to signify the presence of the Sequence Number field. GTP supports the option to guarantee the transmission order of T-PDUs, in which case the S flag is set to 1 and the Sequence Number field is increased for each T-PDU sent over GTP-U.

- **N-PDU Number Flag (PN):** When set to 1, this is used to signify the presence of the N-PDU Number field. The Network Protocol Data Unit (N-PDU) number is used to support packet delivery following mobility events when operating in acknowledged mode.

- **Length:** The length of the packet following the mandatory portion of the header.

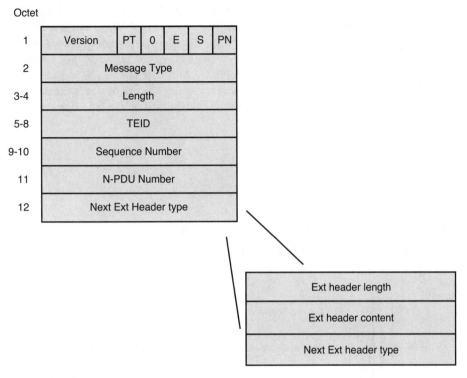

Figure 4-12 *GTP Header Fields*

GTP supports the ability of a user to have multiple GTP tunnels (corresponding to multiple TEIDs) simultaneously active. These GTP tunnels can terminate on different IP PoAs; for example, allowing a mobile device to be multihomed to different Packet Data Networks (PDN) by having multiple IP addresses assigned over a single access network. 3GPP refers to this concept as multiple Access Point Name (APN) support. For example, this capability can allow a single GPRS device to have one IPv4 address allocated to allow access to a corporate network and a second IPv4 address allocated to allow access to a service provider network.

Alternatively, the multiple GTP tunnels can be associated with a single IP PoA, in which case there is a single primary PDP context associated with a single IP address and up to eight supplementary GTP tunnels that are associated with secondary PDP contexts. Besides the unique TEID, each PDP context can be associated with a particular QoS configuration, which then allows the mapping from the GTP tunnel to an Access Network–specific QoS mechanism, for example, using different Radio Access Bearers (RAB) for supporting the transport of T-PDUs sent over different GTP tunnels. The mobile device uses an identifier called the Network Services Access Point Identifier (NSAPI) to uniquely identify a particular GTP context. The NSAPI value is included in the signaling between the mobile and SGSN and incorporated into the TEID exchanged between the SGSN and GGSN.

When multiple GTP tunnels are associated with a single IP address, an access control list (ACL) is required by the GGSN to determine which downlink TEID to use to send the T-PDU. In GTP, this is referred to as a *Traffic Flow Template (TFT)*, which is used by the GGSN for classification of downlink T-PDUs into Conversational, Streaming, Interactive, and Background traffic classes, as shown in Figure 4-13. The TFT can be provided by the mobile device when the secondary PDP context is established or by a separate policy function that interfaces to the GGSN. Filtering can be based on the following attributes:

- Remote IPv4/IPv6 address

- Protocol Number/Next Header type

- Destination port or port range

- Source port or port range

- Type of service/traffic class type or IPv6 flow label

- IPsec Security Parameter Index (SPI)

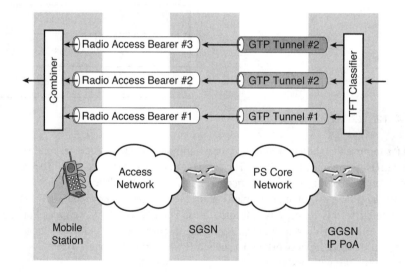

Figure 4-13 *GTP QoS Support*

In addition to mobile unicast services, GTP supports the definition of a multicast service tunnel as part of the Multimedia Broadcast and Multicast Service (MBMS). MBMS is a downlink point-to-multipoint service with modes for multicast and broadcast data. The technology transmits a multicast and broadcast stream from a single source, which is then replicated to a group of mobile users.

A single MBMS-GTP tunnel can be used for delivering all packets to those users who have joined a particular multicast service. Two options are defined for delivering the multicast traffic over the GTP tunnels:

- **IP unicast:** Sending multicast traffic into a unicast GTP tunnel, in which case multiple MBMS-GTP tunnels will need to be established to each access network serving users who have joined the multicast service.

- **IP multicast:** Sending multicast traffic into a multicast GTP tunnel, in which case a single MBMS-GTP tunnel can be used to serve all users who have joined the multicast service.

3GPP Mobility Using GTP

As described in the preceding section, GPRS mobility is based on PDP contexts, so after attaching to the network, the mobile device needs to first establish a PDP context. Unlike in the CS world, where a user's context was fixed throughput the duration of a voice session at the first visited MSC where the call is handled, the 3GPP PS core network defines the ability to transfer the active contexts of a user between SGSNs using the inter-SGSN Gn interface, as shown previously in Figure 4-11.

The other key architectural difference between the CS and PS core networks is that in the CS network, voice services are executed by the MSC in the visited network, whereas in the PS core, the GGSN is most likely to be in the home network, even when a subscriber is roaming.

Note   The PS core network architecture does not preclude GGSN deployment in a visited, roamed-to network. However, operators have been keen to offer differentiated services through service portals in the home network. Deploying the GGSN in the home network ensures that the subscriber's operator has full visibility of all packets and is consequently able to provide differentiated services, for example, prepaid-based data roaming services or mobile Virtual Private Network (VPN) access, whereby users' packets are "tunneled switched" at a home GGSN, switching from GTP encapsulation into a tunnel used for delivering the corporate VPN service (for example, IPSec).

Access Point Name

An Access Point Name (APN) identifies a Packet Data Network (PDN) that is configured on and accessible from a GGSN. A PDN corresponds to particular routing domain, and APNs can be configured to use overlapping IP addresses. The APN corresponds to a DNS name of a GGSN and is comprised of two parts:

- **The APN network identifier:** Defines the external PDN to which the GGSN is connected.

- **The APN operator identifier:** Defines in which operator PS core network the GGSN is located.

For example, the APN used to access a Cisco corporate VPN service can be of the form cisco.mnc150.mcc310.gprs, where 310 is the Mobile Country Code and 150 is the Mobile Network Code in which the GGSN is located.

The APNs to which a subscriber can access are downloaded from the HLR as part of the GPRS Attach Procedure. The APN is also provided by the mobile node when it activates a PDP context, and the SGSN is responsible for checking that the APN is valid; otherwise, the PDP Context request will be rejected.

Note   You might have noticed that 3GPP has defined the use of the .gprs top-level domain (TLD). There is no .gprs TLD in the public DNS system. Instead, the mobile operators have agreed to operate a private DNS system that can be used to resolve APNs to GGSN IP addresses on the inter-Public Land Mobile Network (PLMN) IP backbone network.

PDP Context Activation

To send and receive IP packets, the mobile device must first establish a PDP context. Figure 4-14 shows the signaling procedures involved with context activation, which is initiated by the mobile sending an Activate PDP Context Request message to the network. The message will typically include the APN to which the PDP context should be established as well as the requested QoS parameters.

The SGSN will then use the APN to query its local DNS to derive a GGSN IP address. The SGSN will then send a GTP-C Create PDP Context Request message to the GGSN. Table 4-1 shows some of the key information elements in this message.

Table 4-1   *Create PDP Context Request Message*

Information Element	Description
TEID data	TEID that SGSN expects to receive GTP-U messages for this user
TEID signaling	TEID that SGSN expects to receive GTP-C messages for this user
Access Point Name	APN for this PDP context
SGSN address for signaling	IP address for GTP-C messages
SGSN address for user traffic	IP address for GTP-U messages
QoS profile	QoS to apply to this PDP context, including traffic class and bit rates

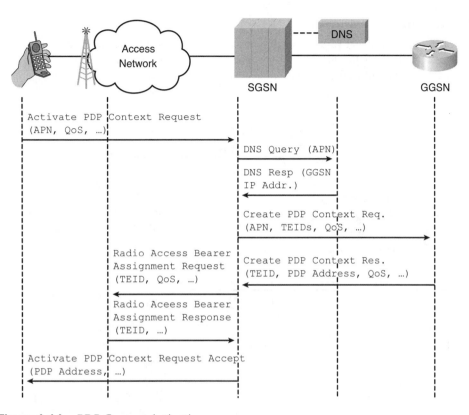

Figure 4-14   *PDP Context Activation*

The GGSN will allocate a PDP address to the context, which can be an IPv4 or IPv6 address, and will respond with a GTP-C Create PDP Context Response message, including the data and signaling TEID, mobile device IPv4 address or IPv6 prefix, possibly down-negotiated QoS, and GGSN IP addresses for use by the SGSN.

At this stage, the SGSN will trigger the establishment of a Radio Access Bearer (RAB) for transporting the PDP context in the access network. The procedure ends with the SGSN signaling the mobile device that the PDP Context Request has been accepted, including providing the mobile device its PDP address for use on this PDP context.

The same procedure can be used to establish a secondary PDP context using the same PDP address, in which case the request will include the QoS for the secondary context as well as the TFT, which allows the GGSN to forward downlink packets into individual GTP-U tunnels.

Established PDP context can subsequently be modified. For example, the QoS associated with a PDP can be downgraded and upgraded by either the GGSN, SGSN, access network, or mobile device.

Mobility and Context Transfer

The GTP PS core network supports access network mobility triggered, for example, by the mobile device moving into a new routing area. In such cases, the mobile device signals the move by sending a Routing Area Update Request message, as shown in Figure 4-15.

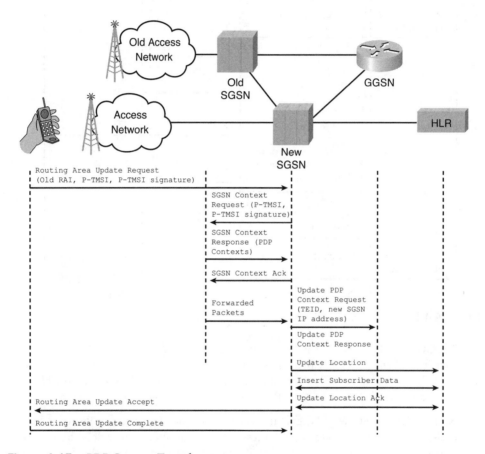

Figure 4-15   *PDP Context Transfer*

This request includes old Routing Area Identifier (RAI), the identity of the mobile node previously allocated by the old SGSN know as the Packet Temporary Mobile Subscriber Identity (P-TMSI), as well as a P-TMSI signature generated by the old SGSN.

Note   A temporary identifier (P-TMSI) is used to avoid identity tracking. Chapter 3 provides other examples where pseudonyms are used in authentication signaling procedures.

The new SGSN needs to recover the PDP context information from the old SGSN, so it uses the old RAI to determine which SGSN holds the existing contexts. The new SGSN sends an SGSN Context Request message to the old SGSN, which is a GTP-C message, including the P-TMSI and P-TMSI signature provided by the User Equipment (UE). The old SGSN, which previously allocated these identities, can then authenticate the request as being from valid UE.

The old SGSN then responds to the new SGSN with PDP context information and mobility management information, including cached authentication information that the new SGSN acknowledges. The old SGSN then signals the old access network that buffered and unacknowledged downlink PDUs need to be sent back to the old SGSN, which forwards these to the new SGSN for subsequent sending to the UE. The new SGSN then updates its location with the HLR, triggering the PS Subscriber Profile to be downloaded. The new SGSN then signals the mobile device that its routing area update has been accepted, providing new P-TMSI and P-TMSI signature, which the UE acknowledges with a Routing Area Update Complete message.

As you can see, GTP provides more than the simple network-based mobility of the GTP-U protocol. Critical GTP-C functionality includes the following:

- QoS control/context modification

- Context transfer capability (allowing keying material to be transferred between SGSNs)

- Transient forwarding of data between a source SGSN and a target SGSN to ensure that packets in flight are not lost during handover interruptions

Proxy Mobile IPv6-Based Mobility

As highlighted in the introduction to this chapter, the benefit of handling mobility at the link layer is that conventional hosts can continue to use traditional socket interfaces and mobility is hidden below the IP layer. Conversely, handling mobility at the network layer, as discussed in Chapter 5, "Network Layer Mobility," requires hosts to be mobility aware.

The IETF had traditionally looked to support mobility at the network layer using Mobile IP. However, the lack of wide-scale adoption of such technologies by native IP hosts triggered the IETF to form a new working group (WG) focused on Network-based Local Mobility Management (NetLMM). The NetLMM WG was tasked with defining a protocol where IP mobility is handled without the involvement from the mobile node, where mobile functionality in the network is responsible for tracking the user and triggering signaling on its behalf.

Note   In many respects, this was a recognition that the majority of mobile subscribers were being supported using network-based mobility through the GTP protocol defined by 3GPP. While GTP continued to be a network-based mobility protocol applied to 3GPP access networks, the mobile industry was calling for a network-based mobility protocol that could be integrated with non-3GPP access networks.

IETF Network-Based Mobility

The network-based mobility protocol selected by the NetLMM WG is based on Proxy Mobile IPv6 (PMIPv6) and specified in RFC 5213[12]. As its name suggests, PMIPv6 uses the MIPv6 concepts that are described in Chapter 5, but now, instead of a mobile host performing the mobility signaling, a proxy mobility agent performs signaling of behalf of a mobile device attached to the network.

Note   The *network* in the IETF network-based mobility does not signify that the network layer is responsible for mobility, rather that the network is responsible for providing mobility services to hosts that are unaware of mobility operations. The NetLMM WG defined PMIPv6 to hide mobility from attached hosts.

Two new network functions are defined in PMIPv6:

■   **The Local Mobility Anchor (LMA):** Provides the home agent function within a PMIPv6 domain, being the topological anchor point for the mobile node's care-of address.

■   **The Mobile Access Gateway (MAG):** A function of an access router responsible for triggering the mobility-related signaling on behalf of the attached mobile device.

Figure 4-16 shows the signaling exchanges involved with PMIPv6 network-based mobility. The following list describes the operation of network mobility using PMIPv6 based:

1. A Mobile Node (MN) enters the network and attempts to configure its IP interface by sending a Router Solicitation message to the access router. As part of the network attachment procedure, the MAG will have received an MN identity—for example, as part of the EAP exchange, as described in Chapter 3.

2. The MAG forms a Proxy Binding Update (PBU) message including the MN Identifier Option and sends this to the LMA.

3. When the LMA accepts this binding, it sends a Proxy Binding Acknowledgment (PBA) message back to the MAG, including the mobile node's home network prefixes, and triggers the establishment of a bidirectional tunnel between the LMA and the MAG.

4. On receiving the PBA, the MAG confirms the tunnel setup and advertises the home prefixes toward the mobile node with a Router Advertisement message.

5. The mobile device will then configure its IP address using the home prefixes supplied by the LMA, creating an IP address that topologically belongs to the LMA.

6. The MAG now acts as the default gateway for the mobile node, ensuring that any packet sent by the mobile node will be received by the MAG and reverse-tunneled toward the LMA. Similarly, when the LMA receives packets destined toward the mobile device, it will tunnel these to the MAG, where they are deencapsulated before forwarding on to the mobile node.

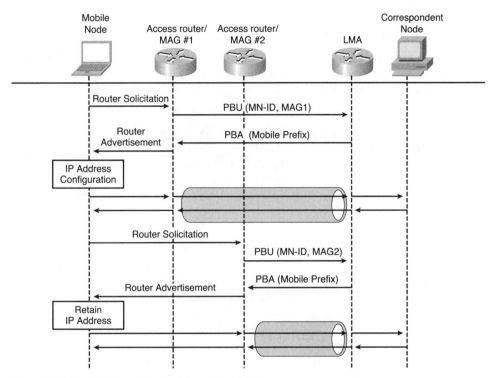

Figure 4-16   *PMIPv6-Based Network Mobility*

If the mobile device now moves areas so that it is covered by a new MAG, the same PBU/PBA signaling exchange occurs as shown in Figure 4-16. Now, because the home prefix signaled and advertised by the new MAG is identical to the old prefix, the mobile device will retain its IP address configuration, and all established communications sockets are able to seamlessly continue operation.

> **Note**   Although the preceding description details operation with IPv6-enabled hosts using State-Less Address Auto-Configuration (SLAAC, RFC 2462), network mobility provided with PMIPv6 is also compatible with IPv4 hosts as well as IPv4 transport networks and stateful address configuration.

WiMAX Mobility Using Proxy Mobile IP

As we have highlighted earlier in this chapter, previous attempts to leverage IEEE technology in mobile systems have used the IEEE 802.11 family of standards, which were primarily aimed at leveraging LAN functionality for providing hotspot coverage. The Worldwide Interoperability for Microwave Access (WiMAX) communication system is an end-to-end, all-IP wireless system designed to provide *wide-area mobile* access to broadband IP services using IEEE-defined wireless technology. The WiMAX architecture defines the use of the IEEE 802.16-2005[13] standard, also known as IEEE 802.16e, for providing the physical and MAC layer support.

Compared to IEEE 802.11 technology, which has been defined for use with unlicensed radio bands—for example, the 2.4-GHz unlicensed Industrial Medical and Scientific (ISM) band—WiMAX has been primarily designed for operation in the licensed spectrum, for example, at 2.3 GHz, 2.5 GHz, and 3.5 GHz.

While the IEEE 802.16e group defined the WiMAX radio interface, it was left to the WiMAX Forum to define the system architecture[14], which integrates the WiMAX radio into an all-IP network capable of supporting micro- and macro-mobility. The WiMAX system architecture comprises the Subscriber Station (SS), the Base Station (BS), the Access Service Node Gateway (ASN-GW), and the Connectivity Services Network (CSN), as shown in Figure 4-17.

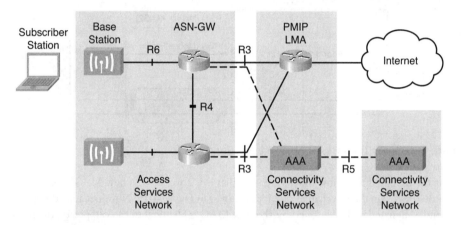

Figure 4-17　*WiMAX System Architecture*

As illustrated in Figure 4-17, a number of key reference points are defined, including R6 between the ASN-GW and the Base Station and R3 and R5 between the ASN and CSN and between two CSNs, respectively. The R3 interface is used to support AAA, policy enforcement, and mobility management capabilities, including the tunneling techniques used to transfer data between the ASN and CSN. The inter-CSN R5 interface is defined to be used in a roaming scenario when IP egress occurs in a visited network, but users still need to be authenticated and authorized by their home service provider.

The WiMAX core network is architected to support macro-mobility using CSN-anchored mobility. In this case, both the ASN and CSN are involved with mobility management. Whereas two different mobility management architectures are supported by the

WiMAX core network—namely, Client Mobile IP (CMIP) based and Simple IP client with Proxy Mobile IP (PMIP) based—this chapter will focus on the latter, describing how PMIPv6 is used to hide macro-mobility from attached WiMAX devices.

Note   When the first release of WiMAX was specified, the NetLMM WG had not completed its standardization of PMIPv6. Instead, informational RFC 5563[15] was used to support link layer mobility using PMIPv4.

WiMAX Session Establishment

WiMAX uses EAP authentication, and information concerning the PMIPv6 operations is piggybacked on top of the AAA exchange, including the following:

- **IP address options:** The ASN-GW includes information on whether it supports IPv4 and/or IPv6 host addressing as well as whether IPv4 transport of PMIPv6 is supported. The home AAA responds with authorized IP address options for the user, including DHCP server information.

- **PMIP parameters:** The home AAA server provides the ASN-GW with the address of the designated LMA selected for handling a particular client's PMIPv6 session. In addition, the PMIPv6 security bootstrapping parameters are also provided.

Optionally, the home AAA server can be used to allocate the IPv4 MN-HoA or the IPv6 Home Network Prefix. Alternatively, the LMA can be used to allocate such, within its Proxy Binding Acknowledged message.

When using data link layer mobility, the client is not presumed to include additional mobility functionality; hence address management and host configuration are typically performed using DHCP. In such cases, the ASN will include a DHCP Proxy, and PMIPv6-based address allocation can be triggered by the receipt of a DHCP-Discover message, as shown in Figure 4-18. In this example, the IPv4 MN-HoA has not been received during the AAA exchange, and hence no address is included in the PMIPv6 PBU message.

The PMIPv6 LMA HA responds with the PBA message, including the IPv4 MN-HoA address. If a DCPHv4 server address has been received during the AAA exchange, the ASN-GW operates as a DHCP relay, forwarding the DHCP-Discover message but now populating the IPv4 MN-HoA address in the "requested IP address" option, and the standard DHCP exchange continues. The session is now established, and the core network is configured to tunnel packets between the PMIPv6 MAG and LMA.

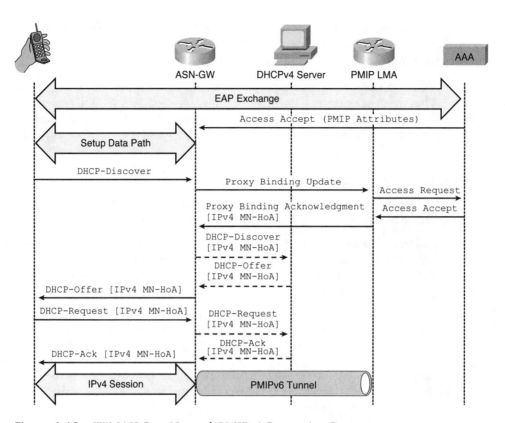

Figure 4-18   *WiMAX Core Network PMIPv6 Connection Setup*

PMIPv6-Based WiMAX Session Mobility

The trigger for WiMAX macro-mobility operation typically occurs when the mobile device moves to a base station covered by a different ASN-GW. The trigger can originate from the new target ASN-GW or from the old source ASN-GW, as shown in Figure 4-19 and described in the list that follows.

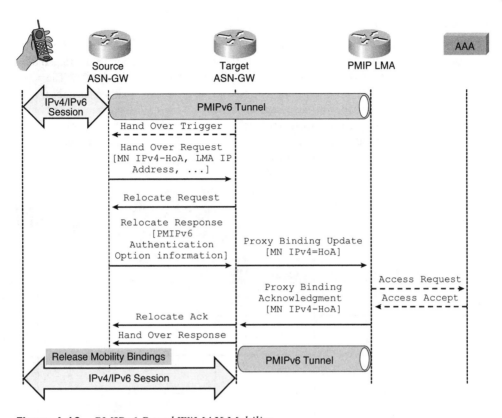

Figure 4-19   *PMIPv6-Based WiMAX Mobility*

1. The source ASN-GW needs to provide the target ASN-GW with the client's PMIPv6 configuration, including Home Network Prefix or IPv4 HoA, LMA IP address, DHCP configuration, as well as PMIPv6 security mode configuration information.

2. The target ASN-GW then requests the PMIPv6 handover by sending a Relocate Request message. If the PMIPv6 session requires authentication options, the source ASN-GW will return these with the Relocate Response message. The receipt of the Relocate Response message will trigger the target ASN-GW to perform a binding update toward the LMA.

3. The LMA updates the binding cache entry with the new location of the client. The LMA then establishes a new PMIPv6 tunnel toward the new ASN-GW and simultaneously tears down the tunnel toward the source ASN-GW.

4. Finally, the target ASN-GW indicates to the source ASN that relocation has been successfully completed, allowing it to remove the mobility and DHCP contexts.

PMIPv6-Based Session Termination

When the client finally terminates its session, it will typically trigger a release of its allocated IP address. Figure 4-20 shows an example of session termination being triggered by the client sending a DHCP-Release message to the DHCP relay in the ASN-GW. The ASN-GW sends a PBU message to the associated LMA, signaling that the client has detached from the network by including the client's MN IPv4-HoA and a requested binding lifetime of 0. The LMA processes the message, removes bindings for the MN IPv4-HoA as well as any other resources, and responds with a PBA as well as signaling the AAA with an Accounting Stop message.

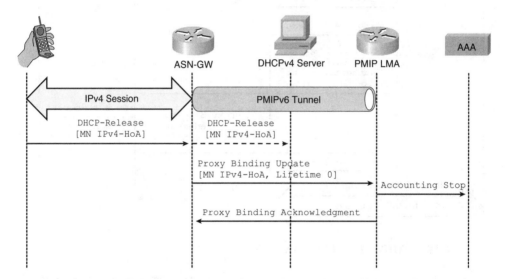

Figure 4-20   *PMIPv6-Based Session Termination*

3GPP Mobility Using Proxy Mobile IP

The previous section covering 3GPP described how GTP is used to provide data link layer mobility for 3GPP access networks. The most recent activity within 3GPP has been to define a new radio access technology, termed Long-Term Evolution (LTE), which is able to support significantly increased data rates. This new radio technology has triggered a rearchitecting of the packet core network, with the Evolved Packet Core (EPC) being defined to support IP services to LTE-enabled mobile hosts. In a departure from the legacy 3GPP core (comprising SGSN and GGSN), the EPC was designed to support mobile services over non-3GPP-defined radio access technologies, such as wireless LAN, WiMAX, as well as cdma2000-based radio access technologies.

To support link layer mobility between 3GPP and non-3GPP access networks, the EPC has been designed to support GTP and PMIPv6-based mobility. Figure 4-21 shows the Evolved Packet Core elements comprising a serving gateway, which is a transient user-plan anchor for 3GPP access networks, and a PDN gateway, which is the IP PoA for the user. GTP is used as the link layer mobility protocol between the serving GW and the PDN GW. Figure 4-21 also shows how non-3GPP access networks are integrated into the EPC. The PDN GW is augmented with PMIPv6 LMA functionality, and the non-3GPP access network is assumed to include the definition of an access gateway, which implements the PMIPv6 MAG function—for example, the ASN-GW in the case of WiMAX. Hence, PMIPv6 is used for intersystem handovers between 3GPP and non-3GPP radio access technologies.

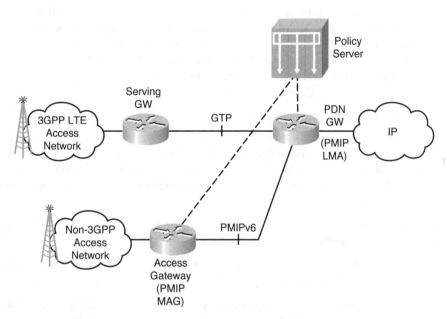

Figure 4-21   *3GPP PMIPv6 Architecture for Non-3GPP Access Networks*

Delivering Equivalent GTP Functions with PMIPv6

As you have already seen, GTP provides more than simple data link layer mobility functionality, including transport of QoS information as well as support for multiple PDP contexts to allow bearer binding to be performed by the IP PoA (as shown previously in Figure 4-13) and APN concepts that allow users to attach to different routing domains. Because PMIPv6 is being used for 3GPP–to–non-3GPP intersystem handovers, the equivalent functionality was required by 3GPP to be realized using PMIPv6. Instead of simply duplicating the functional split as defined with GTP, 3GPP instead opted to redefine the functionality, in particular for differentiated QoS support. 3GPP has defined a single PMIPv6 tunnel between the access gateway and PDN gateway instead of the multiple GTP tunnels between the serving gateway and PDN gateway. This means that, whereas the policy server interfaces to the PDN GW for GTP bearer binding, the same policy server needs to interface to the access gateway for binding bearers to QoS flows, as shown in Figure 4-21.

Note   The binding of the radio bearers to QoS flows does not mean that the intermediate IP network is not involved in supporting end-to-end QoS. The PMIP-MAG and PMIP-LMA functions are responsible for ensuring consistent Differentiated Services Code Points (DSCP) operation—for example, by ensuring that the DSCP markings from inner IP packets are copied into the outer IP packet used to transport the PMIPv6 tunnel.

To support PMIPv6 to different routing domains with possibly overlapping IP addresses, generic routing encapsulation (GRE) key extensions for tunneling packets between the access gateway and PDN gateway are used[16]. The GRE packet header allows uniquely identifying packets associated with different Packet Data Networks (PDN), even when those PDNs that have allocated overlapping IP addresses.

Intertechnology Handover

The 3GPP standard supports intertechnology handover between non-3GPP access networks that are connected to the EPC using PMIPv6 and 3GPP access networks that are connected to the EPC using GTP. Figure 4-22 shows the signaling flows when a device first attaches to the EPC using non-3GPP access technology, which is described further in the list that follows:

1. The non-3GPP access GW triggers the sending of the PBU message to the PDN GW, establishing the PMIPv6 tunnel.

2. When the device decides to perform a handover to a 3GPP access network, it signals a handover in the L2/L3 attach procedure.

3. This signal triggers the 3GPP access gateway—for example, an MME/serving GW or SGSN—to recover the PDN GW address during access authentication.

4. The 3GPP access gateway then triggers the establishment of a GTP tunnel using a Create Session Request/Response message exchange with the PDN GW.

5. At this time, the 3GPP Radio Access Bearer is established, which is then signaled to the PDN-GW using a Modify Bearer Request/Response message exchange.

6. The PDN GW now can route downlink packets destined toward the device using the GTP tunnel.

7. Finally, the PMIPv6 binding is revoked, which triggers the removal of the PMIPv6 tunnel and the non-3GPP access bearer.

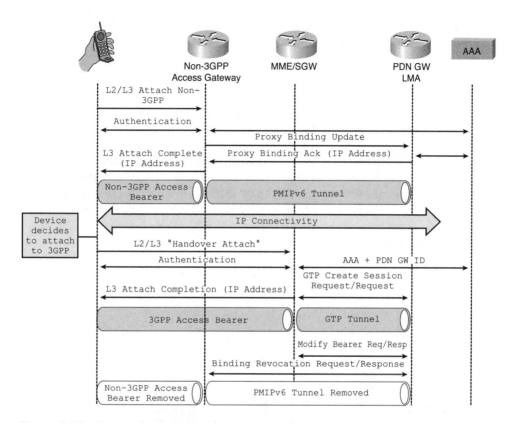

Figure 4-22   *Intertechnology Handover Between PMIPv6 and GTP*

Data Link Layer Solutions to Providing Mobility Across Heterogeneous Access Networks

Chapter 5 provides examples of mobility solutions that can be used for supporting Layer 3–based mobility across heterogeneous access networks. Although using data link layer techniques to provide mobility solutions across different data link layers corresponding to heterogeneous access networks can be viewed as a dichotomy, the clear benefits to solving mobility at the data link layer has motivated the development of solutions that use IP tunneling to extend the cellular data link layer to be accessible over any IP network.

3GPP Generic Access Network

While this book examines techniques for providing mobility functionality for IP services, the primary motivation for providing data link layer solutions for mobility across heterogeneous access networks was to allow access to cellular data link layer circuit-switched functionality over IP access networks. With the majority of cellular revenue still coming from legacy voice services, and with the rapid adoption of smartphones with dual-mode capabilities enabling access to both cellular and Wi-Fi access networks, the industry moved to standardize techniques for accessing GSM data link layer services over IP networks.

The Generic Access Network (GAN) is the standardized version of Unlicensed Mobile Access (UMA) specified by 3GPP[17]. The GAN architecture defines a client-initiated IPsec tunnel, but instead of simply using the IPsec tunnel to transport native IP packets from the WLAN-enabled device, GAN defines a complete access system including the use of a new network element, the GAN Controller (GANC). Communication with the GANC allows control messages to be sent over a TCP socket, instead of the cellular data link layer, as illustrated in Figure 4-23. Although originally defined only for GSM and GPRS access, GAN has been subsequently enhanced with a 3G mode of operation, allowing dual-mode 3G devices to access legacy services over WLAN access networks.

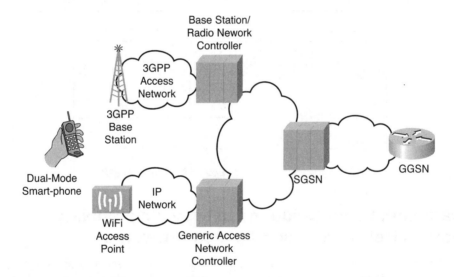

Figure 4-23 *Generic Access Network Architecture*

The GAN Controller appears to the rest of the network like a standard 2G Base Station Controller (BSC) or 3G Radio Network Controller (RNC), hence allowing standardized 3GPP data link layer mobility techniques to be used for providing seamless access to IP services as the user moves between native cellular networks and IP-enabled Wi-Fi access.

Because the GANC peers with 2G BSC and 3G RNC elements, conventional handover can be supported if the dual-mode phone is able to report "measurements" performed on the WLAN network. Assuming that a dual-mode phone has the ability to support simultaneous communications over cellular and WLAN, the GAN-enabled device will first establish an IPsec tunnel to the GAN Controller and then register with the GANC, during which it receives system information, including a dummy neighbor cell identity. The cellular network will have been configured to broadcast include the same dummy cell in its neighbor list. While native phones will recover this information, they will fail to decode GSM information using the dummy cell identity and hence not report any information to the network. However, a GAN device, which prefers WLAN coverage and recovers the same cell information it received during GANC registration, will start to report the dummy neighbor cell at an artificially high value. This will trigger normal 3GPP procedures for BSC or RNC-to-GANC handover, including the use of GTP for SGSN-based mobility.

Host Impacts of Data Link Layer Mobility

One of the key drivers for defining mobility events to be hidden from the IP layer is that all existing applications can be easily supported. However, when the protocol supports handoff between different access technologies, as is the case with PMIPv6, although the IP address is guaranteed to be preserved as the host switches access technologies, the operation of the host when switching network interfaces in the middle of a session is currently undefined and could still result in the session being disconnected when access technologies are changed.

Note   3GPP has defined different access networks for supporting link layer mobility using 2.5G systems based on Time Division Multiple Access (TDMA) radio technology, 3/3.5G systems based on Wideband Code Division Multiple Access (WCDMA) radio technology, and most recently with the Evolved Packet System (EPS) based on Orthogonal Frequency Division Access (OFDMA) technology. Importantly, these systems have been defined to operate using a single radio (to allow lower-cost handsets to be developed) but that also presents a single network interface to the host. Hence, handovers between different cellular access technologies are guaranteed to be masked from upper layers in the cellular host.

For multi-interface hosts to support data link layer mobility, the fundamental design principle of associating IP addresses with individual interfaces needs to be resolved. As with other problems, this one can be solved by introducing a level of indirection between the IP layer and the physical interfaces. One such approach is to introduce an intermediate logical interface or Virtual Interface Adaptor (VIA) to hide the link layer mobility from the IP layer.

Figure 4-24 shows the host architecture supporting such an approach where the VIA is implemented as a logical interface decoupled from the physical interface. The VIA is then bound to multiple physical interfaces that provide the transmit and receive functionalities for sending packets over the individual physical links.

The VIA then enables address continuity during intertechnology handovers, with the change in interface being hidden from the various applications.

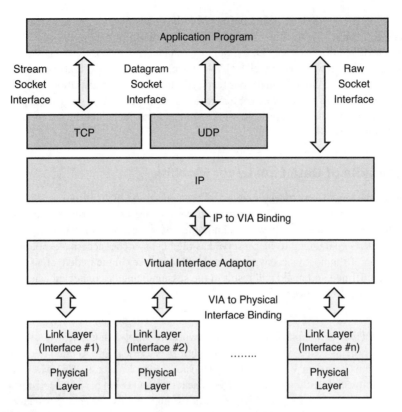

Figure 4-24 *Virtual Interface Adaptor Architecture*

Summary

The rationale for attempting to solve mobility at the data link layer is clear. Application processes are bound to Internet sockets, which in turn are bound to individual interfaces on that host. Solving mobility below the IP transport layer ensures that mobility for any existing host or application can be supported by augmenting the data link layer with mobility functionality. Indeed the increasing adoption of IP services on 3GPP-based mobile devices demonstrates how data link layer mobility can be defined to support seamless service across nationwide coverage areas.

Given the clear benefits of link layer mobility, this chapter first looked at native Ethernet architectures and demonstrated how Ethernet bridging with hosts enhanced with DHCP capability can be used to provide "plug-and-play" nomadicity across an enterprise Layer 2 network. The introduction of mobility in the enterprise is most often associated with deployment of wireless LAN technology, so we have shown how the introduction of hierarchy into the enterprise wireless LAN architecture has enabled the support of fast, secure mobility across Layer 3 domains.

This chapter then described those protocols that have been specifically designed to deliver data link layer mobility in wide-area wireless environments. The use of PMIPv6, as defined between the WiMAX ASN-GW and CSN-GW as well as toward 3GPP's PDN gateway for supporting non-3GPP radio technologies, has been described, together with the more widely deployed GTP protocol. Both approaches allow mobility to be hidden from the network layer.

Finally, this chapter concluded with the unfortunate limitations of link layer mobility schemes. While the advantages of such techniques are clear when dealing with a homogeneous access technology, the binding of a socket to an IP address on a host's interface means that Virtual Interface Adaptor architectures need to be deployed if intertechnology handover is to be supported. The rationale for solving mobility below the IP layer was that this would allow any existing host running any existing application to support mobility. The necessity to augment host functionality with VIA technology then opens the possibility of adding other host functionality to provide alternative means to support mobility. Such approaches will be described in greater details in the following chapters.

Endnotes

1. J. Day, *Patterns in Network Architecture*, Indianapolis, Indiana: Pearson Education; 2008.

2. IEEE 802.1D-2004, "IEEE Standard for Local and Metropolitan Area Networks: Media Access Control (MAC) Bridges."

3. IEEE 802.11-1999, "Part 11: Wireless LAN Medium Access Control (MAC) and Physical Layer (PHY) Specifications."

4. IEEE 802.1F-2003, "IEEE Trial-Use Recommended Practice for Multi-Vendor Access Point Interoperability via an Inter-Access Point Protocol Across Distribution Systems Supporting IEEE 802.11 Operation."

5. IEEE 802.11I-2004, "Part 11: Wireless LAN Medium Access Control (MAC) and Physical Layer (PHY) Specifications Amendment 6: Medium Access Control (MAC) Security Enhancements."

6. IEE 802.1X-2004, "IEEE Standard for Local and Metropolitan Area Networks: Port Based Access Control."

7. J. Korhonen, "Performance Implications of the Multi-Layer Mobility in Wireless Operator Networks," 4th Berkley-Helsinki Ph.D. Student Workshop on Telecomms. Software Arch., June 2004.

8. IEEE 802.11R-2008, "Part 11: Wireless LAN Medium Access Control (MAC) and Physical Layer (PHY) Specifications—Amendment 2: Fast Basic Service Set (BSS) Transition."

9. S. Bangolae, C. Bell, and E. Qi, "Performance Study of Fast BSS Transition Using IEEE 802.11r," Int. Conf. on Comms. and Mobile Computing, 2006.

10. RFC 5415, "Control and Provisioning of Wireless Access Points (CAPWAP) Protocol Specification," P. Calhoun, et. al., March 2009.

11. 3GPP TS 29.060, "General Packet Radio Service (GPRS); GPRS Tunneling Protocol (GTP) across the Gn and Gp Interface."

12. RFC 5213, "Proxy Mobile IPv6," S. Gundavelli, K. Leung, V. Devarapalli, K. Chowdhury, and B. Patil, Aug. 2008.

13. IEEE 802.16e-2005, "IEEE Standard for Local and Metropolitan Area Networks. Part 16: Air Interface for Fixed and Mobile Broadband Wireless Access Systems."

14. WiMAX Forum Network Architecture, "Stage 3 Detailed Protocols and Procedures."

15. RFC 5563, "WiMAX Forum/3GPP2 Proxy Mobile IPv2," K. Leung, G. Dommety, P. Yegani, and K. Chowdhury, Feb. 2010.

16. draft-ietf-netlmm-grekey-option, "GRE Key Option for Proxy Mobile IPv6," A. Muhanna, M. Khalil, S. Gundavelli, and K. Leung, work in progress.

17. draft-yokota-netlmm-pmipv6-mn-itho-support, "Virtual Interface Support for IP Hosts," H. Yokota, S. Gundavelli, T. Trans, Y. Hong, and K. Leung, work in progress.

Chapter 5

Network Layer Mobility

As discussed in Chapter 2, "Internet Sessions," Layer 3 (the Internet, or network layer) is responsible for the transmission of datagrams from source to destination. The network layer is responsible for routing functions and fragmentation/reassembly while maintaining any quality of service (QoS) required by the transport layer. This section provides a brief overview of the network layer to illustrate the challenges that arise because of mobility.

The Internet Protocol (IP) is the most commonly known example of a Layer 3 protocol, and it provides the foundation upon which the Internet itself was built. IP is responsible for connectionless transfer of packets from an end node, through a network, to another end node.

For the network to identify a specific node, an addressing scheme (IP addressing) is used. The IP address uniquely identifies an endpoint connected to the network, and all packets are sent across the network indicating both the source IP address and destination IP address. In addition, TCP, which resides at the transport layer, creates connections, identified by a 4-tuple (source IP address, source port, destination IP address, destination port), used to identify the transmission session.

If neither endpoint is mobile, sending traffic from source to destination is trivial. Routers use the hierarchical structure of Internet addressing to locate a path from the source endpoint to the destination endpoint, and the packet is sent to the next hop in that path.

The IP address assigned to the endpoint, in essence, serves two purposes. For TCP, the IP address serves as an endpoint identifier upon which sessions can be established and maintained. At the network layer, however, the IP address is used in making routing decisions. Figure 5-1 illustrates how IP addresses are assigned and used at the network layer.

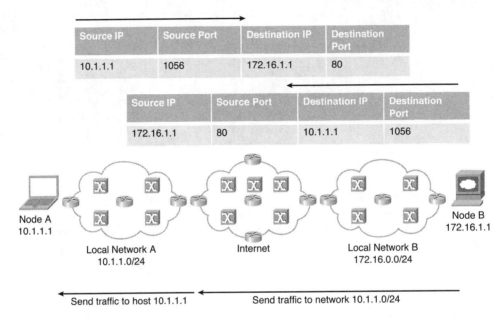

Source IP	Source Port	Destination IP	Destination Port
10.1.1.1	1056	172.16.1.1	80

Source IP	Source Port	Destination IP	Destination Port
172.16.1.1	80	10.1.1.1	1056

Node A
10.1.1.1

Node B
172.16.1.1

Local Network A
10.1.1.0/24

Internet

Local Network B
172.16.0.0/24

Send traffic to host 10.1.1.1   Send traffic to network 10.1.1.0/24

Figure 5-1   *Network Layer Connectivity*

For this reason, mobility presents a unique problem to the network. Layer 3 mobility refers to an end node that changes point of attachment in a way that is visible to Layer 3. Layer 3 creates a two-dimensional challenge:

■   The mobile node keeps its IP address. If this were the case, the hierarchical structure of Internet addressing is no longer aligned with real Internet topology, and the network cannot properly route to the mobile node. Figure 5-2 illustrates the problem presented by mobility at the network layer.

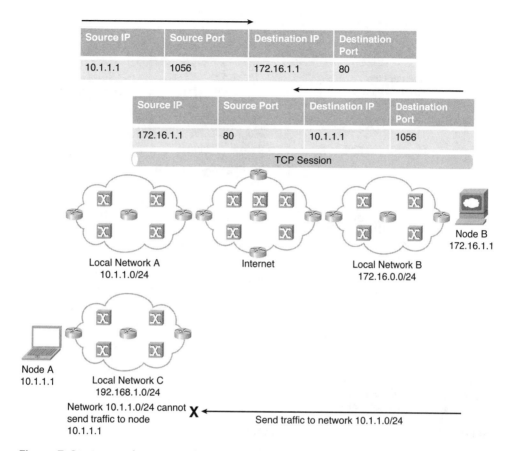

Figure 5-2   *Network Layer Mobility Problem*

- The mobile node changes its IP address. If this were the case, all TCP sessions built on the original IP address can no longer continue and are broken. Figure 5-3 illustrates the problem presented by network mobility at the transport layer.

Because this chapter covers the topic of network layer mobility, you will learn about seamless mobility—that is, persistence of the TCP session as an endpoint changes point of attachment. Because it is unreasonably complex to expect that the network routing decisions and topology can adapt to reflect the mobility of every endpoint, it is necessary to preserve the endpoint's original IP address, regardless of point of attachment. More specifically, it is necessary to preserve the endpoint's original IP address, as perceived by the other node communicating over the established TCP session.

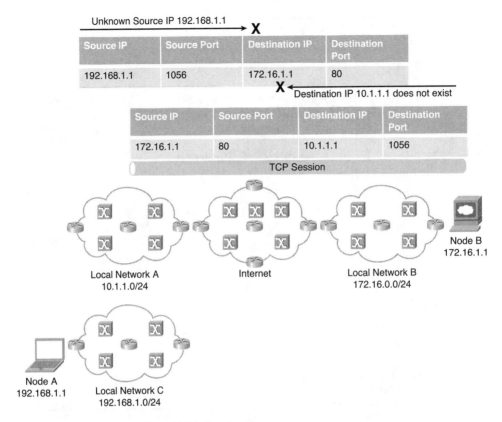

Figure 5-3   *Transport Layer Mobility Problem*

A number of mechanisms have been standardized to provide seamless mobility. Each of these methods have one thing in common—they utilize a separate IP address for endpoint identification than for routing.

This chapter will discuss four mechanisms designed for network layer mobility as well as the associated architectures, deployment examples, and use cases for each:

- Mobile IPv4

- Mobile IPv6

- Dual Stack Mobile IP (DSMIP)

- IKEv2 Mobility and Multihoming (MOBIKE) Protocol

Mobile IPv4

Mobile IPv4 was first standardized by the IEEE in RFC 2002, published in 1996. Subsequent RFCs have updated the original RFC 2002, and the current Mobile IPv4 RFC is 3344. With the growth of cellular systems, it was recognized that there was a need to support some mechanism of mobility in which the mobile node could continue to communicate with either a static or another mobile node without forcing new session establishment.

> **Note**   All RFCs are available at http://www.ietf.org/rfc/rfc*xxxx*.txt, where *xxxx* is the number of the RFC.

Mobile IPv4 provides this mechanism while imposing no requirements on static nodes. That is, a static node has no awareness that the node with which it is communicating has changed point of attachment. This has allowed Mobile IPv4 to be deployed as an overlay on top of the existing IP/Internet model without any impact to the routing and addressing structure.

Mobile IPv4 Technology Overview

Mobile IPv4 uses numerous mobility-specific terms and definitions to address mobility, and also introduces a number of new elements into the IP network architecture. This new terminology can broadly be classified as:

■ Network-specific terms

■ Network element-specific terms

■ Addressing-specific terms

Network-Specific Terms

For the purpose of understanding, Mobile IPv4 has employed numerous network reference points to better clarify where the mobile node is located:

■ The *home network* has a network prefix matching that of the mobile node's home address. (See the section "Addressing-Specific Terms," later in this chapter, for more detail.) Traffic will be routed normally to the mobile node's home address when the node is attached to the home network.

■ The *virtual network* typically resides on the home agent (see the following section for more detail), but might also reside as a nonphysical entity on any router in the home network. The router that hosts the virtual network advertises reachability to the virtual network to foreign networks.

■ A *foreign network* is any network other than the mobile node's home network. The mobile node might be communicating with a node residing in a foreign network when it changes point of attachment. Mobile IPv4 allows the mobile node to move transparently without any node in the foreign network being aware.

A visited network is a foreign network to which the mobile node is connected.

Figure 5-4 illustrates the domains of a Mobile IPv4 network.

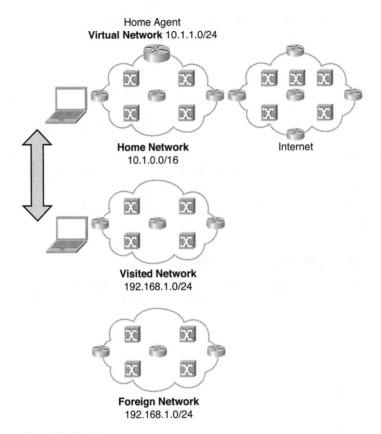

Figure 5-4   *Mobile IPv4 Domains*

Network Element–Specific Terms

Mobile IPv4 networks consist of four network entities:

■ The *mobile node* refers to the device that changes its point of attachment across multiple networks. This point of attachment change might or might not result in the change of IP address, depending on whether link layer connectivity can be maintained. The mobile node can be a host device or a router.

■ The *foreign agent* is a router in a mobile node's visited network. The foreign agent provides Layer 3 routing functions to the mobile node during the life of the node's association. For traffic originated from the mobile node, the foreign agent also acts as the default gateway. For traffic destined to the mobile node, the foreign agent establishes a tunnel to the home agent.

■ The *home agent* is a router in the mobile node's home network. The home agent provides tunneled delivery of mobile-destined traffic through the established tunnel to the foreign agent when the mobile node is outside the home network. The home agent also maintains a database that contains the current location information for any mobile node that has previously registered.

■ The *correspondent node* is any node (static or mobile) with which the mobile node is communicating. The function of Mobile IPv4 is to allow the mobile node to change point of attachment without the correspondent node being aware. This allows TCP sessions to continue to functional normally.

Figure 5-5 builds on Figure 5-4, illustrating the elements of the Mobile IPv4 network.

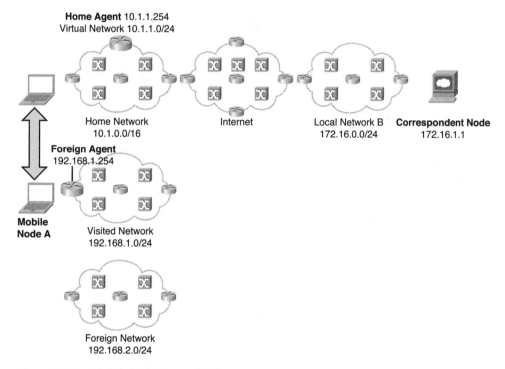

Figure 5-5 *Mobile IPv4 Network Elements*

Addressing-Specific Terms

To facilitate the routing of packets to the mobile node, both within and outside the home network, Mobile IPv4 relies on multiple IP address assignments:

■ The *home address (HoA)* is assigned by the home agent to the mobile node. This address is maintained by the mobile node for the entire length of its session. The home address does not change, regardless of the mobile node's point of attachment to the network.

■   The care-of address (CoA) is the termination point of the tunnel from the home agent. The CoA can refer to an address on the foreign agent itself, known as the foreign agent CoA, or to an address assigned locally to an interface on the mobile node, known as the colocated care-of address (CCoA).

Figure 5-6 builds on Figure 5-5, illustrating the addressing components of the Mobile IPv4 network.

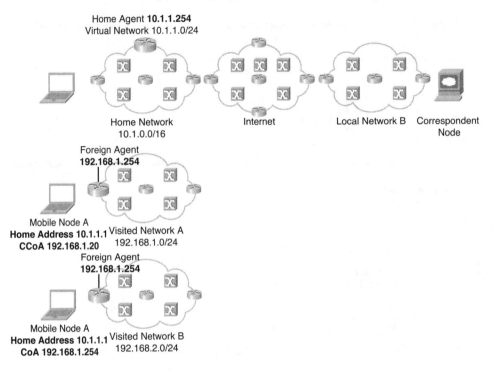

Figure 5-6   *Mobile IPv4 Addressing*

Mobile IPv4 Operation

As discussed earlier in the chapter, a home agent relies on an internal database to track a mobile node location and determine the appropriate way to route traffic to the mobile node. The Mobile IPv4 protocol has a number of processes that take place to populate the database in the home agent. These processes can be characterized into three functions:

■   Mobile IPv4 Agent Discovery

■   Mobile IPv4 Registration and Authentication, Authorization, and Accounting (AAA)

■   Mobile IPv4 Tunnels, Bindings, and Datagram Forwarding

The sections that follow cover these three functions in more detail.

Mobile IPv4 Agent Discovery

Mobile Agent Discovery is the method used by the mobile node to determine the network to which it is currently connected. This discovery takes place when a mobile node is first turned on or when a mobile node changes network point of attachment. There are two ways that the mobile node can discover its location—advertisement or solicitation.

Agent Advertisements

Agent Advertisement is the method used by the mobility agents to advertise which services it has available. When the mobile node first connects to a new network, it listens for Agent Advertisement messages. Agent Advertisements are unauthenticated multicast messages sent to the "all systems on this link" multicast address (224.0.0.1) or the "limited broadcast" address (255.255.255.255).

The Agent Advertisement messages are actually extensions of the Internet Control Message Protocol (ICMP) Router Advertisement message. These ICMP Router Advertisement messages are defined in the ICMP Internet Router Discovery Protocol (IRDP), defined in RFC 1256.

Figure 5-7 illustrates the ICMP Router Advertisement message format.

Type = 9	Code	Checksum
Number of Addresses	Address Entry Size	Lifetime
Router Address 1		
Preference Level 1		
...		
Router Address N		
Preference Level N		

Figure 5-7 *ICMP Router Advertisement*

The extension includes information on registration lifetime, whether the advertising router is a home agent or foreign agent, and the tunnel encapsulation type. In addition, if the mobility agent is a foreign agent, the Agent Solicitation message also includes whether reverse tunneling (see the section "Tunneling and Reverse Tunneling," later in this chapter) is supported, the foreign agent CoA, and whether the foreign agent has available capacity to accept new registrations.

Figure 5-8 illustrates the format of the Agent Advertisement message.

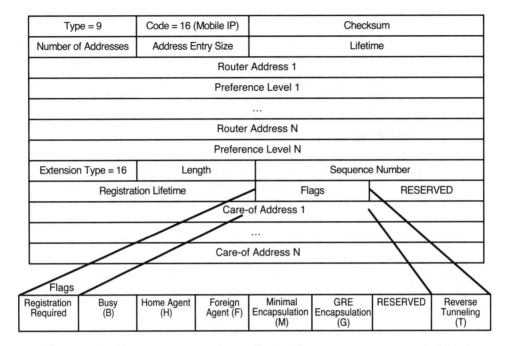

Figure 5-8   *MIPv4 Router Advertisement Extension*

Agent Advertisement messages are required when a mobile node cannot discover, through a Layer 2 protocol, both its own local IP address and a local mobility agent. 3rd Generation Partnership Project 2 (3GPP2) and other mobility standards rely on link layer mechanisms, such as Point to Point Protocol (PPP), to establish connectivity and Internet Protocol Control Protocol (IPCP) to configure IP over the PPP link. The IP address contained in the IPCP negotiation can be used to determine the network to which the mobile node is connected—home or foreign. After the PPP session is established, Agent Advertisements can be sent over the PPP session. More information on Mobile IPv4 in practice can be found later in this chapter.

Agent Solicitations

Because multicast and broadcast Agent Advertisements consume network bandwidth, the rate at which these messages are sent is often limited so as not to consume a significant amount of bandwidth. If the mobile node does not receive any Agent Advertisements for a period of time, it can optionally send an Agent Solicitation message to discover a CoA. Solicitation is a method by which the mobile node solicits an Agent Advertisement message. This Agent Advertisement message can be sent unicast to the mobile node.

The Agent Solicitation message is identical to the ICMP Router Solicitation message defined in the IRDP standard. Figure 5-9 illustrates the format of the Agent Solicitation message.

Type = 10	Code = 0	Checksum
RESERVED		

Figure 5-9   *Mobile IPv4 Agent Solicitation Message*

Mobile IPv4 Registration and AAA

After Agent Discovery has been completed, the mobile node has successfully determined whether it is connected to its home network or a foreign network. While mobile nodes might use regular IP when in the home network, and Mobile IPv4 when in a foreign network, mobile standards organizations, such as 3GPP2, treat all networks as foreign networks and therefore require Mobile IPv4 to be used at all times.

RFC 3344 defines three registration events for the mobile node:

- Registration

- Deregistration

- Reregistration

The sections that follow describe these registration events in more detail.

Mobile IPv4 Registration

A mobile node initiates a Registration Request (RRQ) when either the outcome of its Agent Discovery process concludes that it is connected to a foreign network or a link layer mechanism results in network layer establishment. This RRQ allows the mobile node to request service from a foreign agent (optional), inform the home agent of its current CoA (registration), renew a registration that is about to expire (reregistration), or deregister.

RRQ messages originate from a mobile node and are destined for a mobility agent. The mobility agent might be a foreign agent or a home agent, depending on both the mobile node's preference for CCoA and the foreign agent's preference for registration. Table 5-1 includes the different scenarios that determine whether the mobile node registers through a foreign agent relay or directly with a home agent.

Table 5-1   *Policy Enforcement Interaction Descriptions*

Mobile Node Preference	Foreign Agent Preference	Registration Interaction
CoA	CoA	The mobile node registers through the foreign agent.
CCoA	CoA	The mobile node registers through the foreign agent.

continues

Table 5-1 *Policy Enforcement Interaction Descriptions* *(continued)*

Mobile Node Preference	Foreign Agent Preference	Registration Interaction
CCoA	CCoA	If the foreign agent explicitly requests that the mobile node register by setting the R bit in the Agent Advertisement message, the mobile node registers through the foreign agent. If the foreign agent does not explicitly set the R bit, or if no Agent Advertisement is received, the mobile node registers directly to the home agent.

When registering directly with the home agent, RRQs and RRPs are exchanged directly between the mobile node and home agent.

When registering with the foreign agent, all RRQs originated by the mobile node are sent to the foreign agent, which acts as a relay to the home agent. The home agent replies with a Registration Reply (RRP) message. The foreign agent also acts as a relay for the RRP toward the mobile node. Figure 5-10 illustrates the foreign agent's role in the Mobile IPv4 registration process.

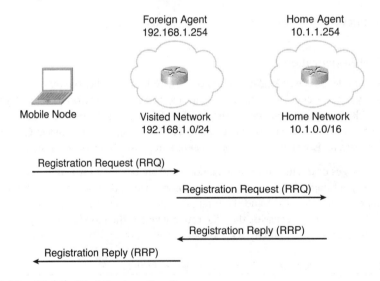

Figure 5-10 *Mobile IPv4 Registration Process*

The registration process also has several other optional capabilities:

- Allowing the mobile node to discover its home address

- Maintaining multiple registrations simultaneously for tunneling multiple copies of the same IP packet to each registered CoA

- Deregistering specific CoAs

- Discovering the home agent address dynamically (see the following sidebar, "Dynamic Home Agent Assignment")

Dynamic Home Agent Assignment

Some link layer establishment protocols require that the end node include a topologically significant IP address at establishment/registration. As noted earlier in this chapter, PPP IPCP, for example, requires that the registering node be assigned a unique IP address prior to identifying a foreign agent CoA. This ultimately creates a scalability issue for mobile nodes, because the intent of the foreign agent CoA is to allow multiple mobile nodes to share a single CoA.

RFC 2290, "Mobile IPv4 Configuration Option for PPP IPCP," is one of many standards defined to extend link layer mechanisms for support of Mobile IPv4 endpoints. The inclusion of these options using the IPCP IP Address Configuration Option allows the mobile node to determine what IP address to use as the CoA when registering with the home agent.

RFC 2794, "Mobile IP Network Access Identifier (NAI) Extension for IPv4," extended the flexibility of RFC 2290 by allowing a mobile node to be identified by an NAI. In addition to allowing mobile nodes to be authenticated through standard AAA methods (discussed in the next section), this RFC also extended the Mobile IPv4 RRQ process.

This extension allows the NAI to be used to determine the mobile node's home address. A mobility agent includes this message in the RRP. The extension also enables the RRQ to include a "zero" (0.0.0.0) or "all" (255.255.255.255) address for the home agent. This value allows the mobility agent—either directly or through AAA interaction—to dynamically allocate the mobile node's home agent address.

This process is known as *dynamic home agent assignment*.

RRQ and RRP Messages

RRQ and RRP messages in Mobile IPv4 use the User Datagram Protocol (UDP) as the transmission protocol. UDP relies on a simple transmission model that does not involve session establishment, guarantee reliability, or ensure data integrity. UDP, therefore, provides an unreliable transport mechanism for the Mobile IPv4 registration process. The Mobile IPv4 protocol itself provides reliability with the inclusion of retransmission capabilities, validity checksums, and session identification.

Figure 5-11 illustrates the format of an RRQ message. Table 5-2 identifies the message fields and their usage.

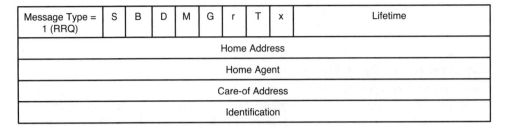

Figure 5-11   *RRQ Message Format*

Table 5-2   *RRQ Message Fields and Usage*

Message Field	Definition
Simultaneous Bindings (S)	As discussed earlier in this chapter, a mobile node can maintain multiple bindings, or tunnels, with the home agent simultaneously. This bit notifies the home agent that the mobile node intends to establish a new binding while keeping the existing bindings.
Broadcast Datagrams (B)	A home agent can be advised, by the mobile device, to either allow broadcast traffic through the Mobile IPv4 tunnel or to prohibit broadcast traffic through the Mobile IPv4 tunnel.
Decapsulation by Mobile Node (D)	This bit notifies the home agent as to whether the mobile node is operating in CoA or CCoA mode. When operating in CCoA mode, the mobile node is the endpoint for the mobile IPv4 tunnel and is therefore responsible for decapsulation of all packets sent to the CoA. When operating in CoA mode, the foreign agent is the endpoint for the mobile IPv4 tunnel.
Minimal Encapsulation (M)	The mobile node can request which type of encapsulation the home agent uses. This bit requests that the home agent use minimal encapsulation.
GRE Encapsulation (G)	The mobile node can request which type of encapsulation the home agent uses. This bit requests that the home agent use GRE encapsulation.
Reverse Tunneling Requested (T)	See the "Tunneling and Reverse Tunneling" section, later in this chapter.
Lifetime	This value indicates the number of seconds that the registration is valid. A registration expires if not replied to prior to the expiration of the Lifetime timer.
Home Address	This is the address of the mobile node. If set to "zero" (0.0.0.0), the mobile node expects the IP address to be returned.
Home Agent	This is the address of the home agent. If set to "zero" (0.0.0.0) or (255.255.255.255), the mobile node expects the IP address to be assigned dynamically. See the sidebar "Dynamic Home Agent Assignment," earlier in this chapter.

Message Field	Definition
Care-of Address	This is one of the endpoints for the Mobile IPv4 tunnel. The other endpoint is the home agent. This CoA is either an address on the foreign agent or an address on the mobile node.
Identification	Because UDP does not provide sequencing, the Mobile IPv4 registration process uses a unique identification value to match RRQs from the mobile node to RRPs from the mobility agent. This identification value is constructed by the mobile node, sent to the mobility agent in the RRQ and included by the mobility agent in the RRP.
Extensions	Mobile IPv4 extensions can be added to the RRQ. See the "Authentication and Accounting" section, later in this chapter, for more information on authorization-enabling extensions.

A mobility agent uses the RRP message in response to a RRQ. The RRP is sourced from the mobility agent and destined to the mobile node. The RRP message notifies the mobile node whether the registration request was accepted and for what length of time.

Figure 5-12 illustrates the format of an RRP message. Table 5-3 identifies the message fields and their usage.

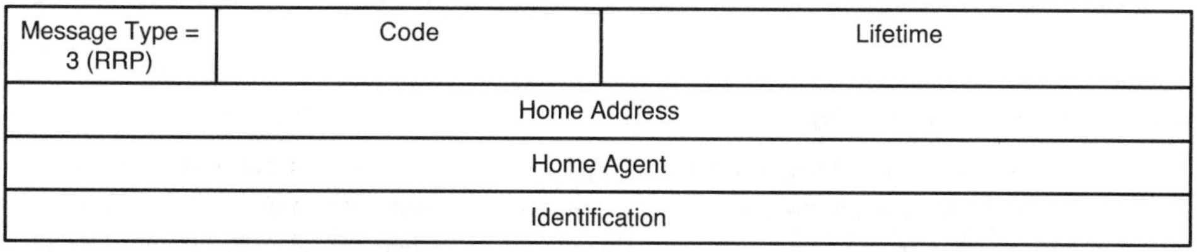

Message Type = 3 (RRP)	Code	Lifetime
Home Address		
Home Agent		
Identification		

Figure 5-12 *RRP Message Format*

Table 5-3 *RRP Message Fields and Usage*

Message Field	Definition
Code	The mobility agent notifies the mobile node as to the status of the registration request using a code value. This code value falls into three categories: ■ Accepted ■ Accepted, but simultaneous bindings not supported ■ Denied The mobility agent can deny the registration request for numerous reasons. RFC 3344 maintains a full list of registration denied codes.

continues

Table 5-3 *RRP Message Fields and Usage* *(continued)*

Message Field	Definition
Lifetime	This value indicates the number of seconds that the registration is valid. This value can differ from the value requested by the mobile node in the Lifetime field of the RRP. The mobility agent can assign any number of seconds equal to or less than that requested by the mobile node, including "zero" (which indicates deregistration) or 0xffff (which indicates infinity).
Home Address	This value identifies the IP address of the mobile node.
Home Agent	This value identifies the IP address of the mobile node's home agent.
Identification	Because UDP does not provide sequencing, the Mobile IPv4 registration process uses a unique identification value to match RRQs from the mobile node to RRPs from the mobility agent. This identification value is constructed by the mobile node, sent to the mobility agent in the RRQ, and included by the mobility agent in the RRP.
Extensions	Mobile IPv4 extensions can be added to the RRQ. See the "Authentication and Accounting" section, later in this chapter, for more information on authorization-enabling extensions.

Authentication Extensions

For security purposes, Mobile IPv4 messages rely on shared authentication values, known as *message authentication codes*, for authenticating messages sent from the mobile node to a mobility agent, and between mobility agents. These authentication values, derived through Hash-based Message Authentication Code (HMAC) with Message Digest algorithm 5 (HMAC-MD5), are used to protect the UDP payload, including all extensions.

HMAC-MD5 uses an iterative cryptographic hash function along with the key defined in the security context to create the message authentication code.

Security contexts are established between nodes in the Mobile IP network. Each security context contains a shared key or public/private key pair, an authentication algorithm, and a style of replay protection.

All security contexts between two nodes are collectively known as a *Mobility Security Association*. Each security context within the Mobility Security Association is indexed using a *Security Parameter Index (SPI)* value. When receiving a message that requires authentication, the mobility node uses the SPI value to determine which security context is to be used, and therefore which key is applicable, for the derivation and verification of the authentication value.

Mobile IPv4 includes the authenticator in RRPs and RRQs as extensions. There are three types of authentication extensions:

- **MN-HA authenticator:** The MN-HA authenticator is used to authorize and validate messages between the mobile node and home agent. This authentication extension is mandatory in all RRQs and all RRPs generated by the home agent. The mobile node and the home agent are required to maintain a security association.

- **MN-FA authenticator:** The MN-FA authenticator is used to authorize and validate messages between the mobile node and foreign agent. This authentication extension is optional in all RRQs and RRPs, because the mobile node and foreign agent are not required to maintain a security association.

- **FA-HA authenticator:** The FA-HA authenticator is used to authorize and validate messages between the foreign agent and home agent. This authentication extension is optional in all RRQs and RRPs, because the foreign agent and home agent are not required to maintain a security association.

Mobile IPv4 AAA Interactions

As you have seen in Chapter 3, "Nomadicity," AAA services have historically been used on the Internet to provide a mechanism by which a network can verify and validate a node attempting to access network services, as well as a means to account for the consumption of those services. AAA relies on credentials communicated by the connecting node to the network access gateway, which can be authenticated prior to allowing access to the network. These credentials can include some form of identification (subscriber or node), other unique data, or digital signature.

AAA servers are typically used to interact with the network access gateway by providing credential verification services. The RADIUS protocol, defined in RFC 2865, and the Diameter Base protocol, defined in RFC 3588, are the two most prevalent methods of providing these authentication services.

With the growth of Mobile IPv4 as a mechanism to provide network services, RFC 2977, "Mobile IP Authentication, Authorization, and Accounting," was developed to provide AAA functions to mobile nodes requesting Mobile IPv4 services.

Note   RFC 2977, "Mobile IP Authentication, Authorization, and Accounting," is applicable to both Mobile IPv4 and Mobile IPv6 protocols.

In the Mobile IPv4 AAA architecture, the mobility gateways are the network access gateways contacting either a foreign or home AAA server to validate the credentials provided by the mobile node. The AAA server core functions include the following:

- Enabling authentication for Mobile IP registration

- Authorizing the mobile node

- Initiating accounting

The AAA server can also be responsible for obtaining an IP address for the mobile node. Figure 5-13 illustrates the generic Mobile IPv4 AAA architecture.

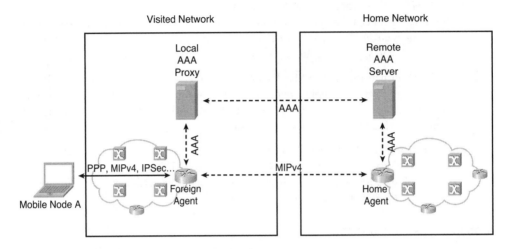

Figure 5-13   *Mobile IPv4 AAA Architecture*

As discussed earlier, RFC 2794 provides a mechanism by which a mobility agent can interact with the AAA server and validate a mobile node using the unique NAI value. This allows a mobile node to be authenticated to the network, authorized for connection, and assigned an IP address through AAA interaction.

Mobile IPv4 Challenge/Response Extension

RFC 4721, "Mobile IPv4 Challenge/Response Extensions," provides an additional optimization for AAA interaction by creating the Mobile-AAA Authentication extension for both Mobile IPv4 RRQ messages.

The AAA Authentication extension includes information relevant for the mobility node to create a request to the AAA server for authentication.

These extensions also allow the foreign agent to use a challenge/response mechanism in the Agent Advertisement message to verify the mobile node.

> **Note**   Challenge/response authentication methods are common in remote-access networks. These methods allow one node in the authentication process to present a challenge to the other node. The other node must provide the expected response to the challenger to be authenticated. The challenge/response mechanism can take on two forms:
>
> ■   **One-way authentication:** With this form of authentication, one node is authenticating itself to the other. In effect, the network element (server, network access gateway, and so on) ensures that the client is a trusted entity.
>
> *continues*

■   **Mutual authentication:** With this form of authentication, each node is required to authenticate itself to the other node, in a "handshake" model. In effect, the network element and the client ensure that the other is a trusted entity. Mutual authentication ensures that the both the client and network element are trusted entities, which protects against rogue network elements responding to client traffic.

Mobile IPv4 relies on one-way authentication in which the mobile node replays the challenge presented by the mobility agent. The mobility agent is responsible for rotating challenges to ensure limited lifetime. The foreign agent can send a challenge to the mobile node in Agent Advertisement messages. The mobile node includes the response in an MN-FA challenge extension of the RRQ. This challenge is used to ensure that the mobile node is not replaying an earlier RRQ. This provides local assurance that a legitimate mobile node is attempting to connect to the network, instead of a node that has intercepted an earlier RRQ.

Mobile IPv4 AAA Key Distribution

The AAA server can optionally play a critical role in the Mobile IPv4 registration authorization process. The AAA server can maintain a key distribution function for the Mobile IPv4 nodes, including the following:

■   Identification and creation of a security association between the mobile node and home agent so that the mobile node can create the MN-HA authenticator

■   Identification and creation of a security association between the mobile node and foreign agent so that the mobile node can create the MN-FA authenticator

■   Identification and creation of a security association between the foreign agent and home agent so that the home agent can create the FA-HA authenticator

RADIUS Interactions

The RADIUS protocol, defined in RFC 2865, has already been introduced in Chapter 3 and is the most widely deployed AAA technology to date. This protocol has been deployed in dialup, cable, DSL, and wireless networks. As the most prevalent AAA technology, Mobile IPv4 mobility agents are capable of communicating with AAA servers using the RADIUS protocol through a standardized set of Mobile IPv4 RADIUS attributes.

Figure 5-14 illustrates how a mobility agent provides RADIUS AAA support for Mobile IPv4 RRQs.

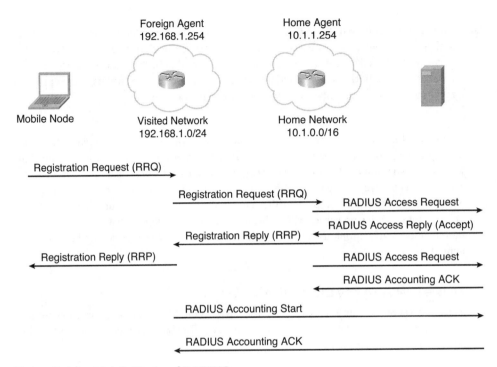

Figure 5-14   *Mobile IPv4 and RADIUS*

RFC 5030 provides guidelines for Mobile IPv4 RADIUS attributes. The RADIUS proto-col supports Vendor-Specific Attributes (VSA), which permit vendors to use the RADIUS protocol to communicate information between the network access gateway and the RADIUS server that is not addressed through any standard. While VSAs accelerated Mobile IP RADIUS interaction by allowing vendors to create their own RADIUS attrib-utes, these solutions were not interoperable.

RFC 2865 defines standard attributes communicated between a network access gateway and a RADIUS server, but there is no standardized set of RADIUS attributes for commu-nication between a mobility agent and the RADIUS server within the technology-agnos-tic Internet Engineering Task Force (IETF). However, many mobility standards organiza-tions, such as 3GPP2, have adopted their own RADIUS vendor ID (5535). This provides a technology-specific standard for implementing RADIUS communication.

Diameter Applications

The Diameter protocol, defined in RFC 3588, provides another AAA framework, and was designed to be a more robust protocol than RADIUS. Diameter provides the following functions, above and beyond the RADIUS protocol[1]:

- **Transmission-level security:** The RADIUS protocol provides only application layer authentication and validation, while Diameter provides transport security with optional IPsec encryption.

- **Failover capability:** Diameter supports application layer acknowledgments and failover algorithms.

- **Reliable transport:** By relying on TCP or Stream Control Transport Protocol (SCTP) as the transport protocol, as opposed to UDP, Diameter leverages the transport layer reliability mechanisms. As discussed earlier, UDP does not provide an assured delivery of packets. TCP and SCTP, by contrast, provide sequencing, retransmissions, and flow control algorithms design to guarantee delivery of packets.

- **Capability negotiation:** RADIUS peers do not have knowledge as to the other's capabilities. This capability allows Diameter peers to determine a mutually acceptable service.

- **Peer discovery and configuration:** RADIUS configuration requires manual assignment of servers and clients. Diameter peers can dynamically discover peers through Domain Name System (DNS).

In addition to these Diameter capabilities, RFC 4004 defines a Mobile IPv4 application that allows a Diameter server to provide AAA functions for Mobile IPv4 services.

During Mobile IPv4 registration, the Diameter server provides the derivation and transport of mobility security associations, namely, the MN-HA, MN-FA, and FA-HA keys. The Diameter server is also an integral component in interrealm mobility, including providing authentication and accounting for a mobile node.

Figure 5-15 illustrates how a mobility agent provides Diameter AAA support for Mobile IP RRQs.

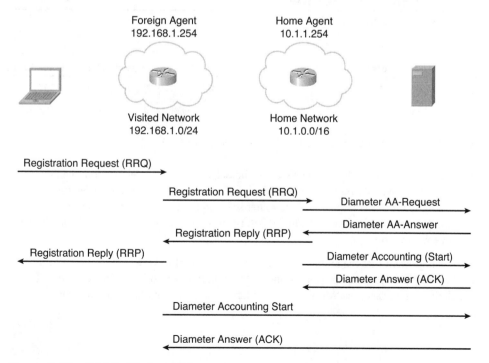

Figure 5-15 *Mobile IPv4 and Diameter*

Mobile IPv4 Tunnels, Bindings, and Datagram Forwarding

Upon successful registration to the mobility agent, the mobile node is then able to send traffic to a corresponding node. From a mobility perspective, the challenge is no longer related to identifying the point of attachment and signaling layer process, but instead a bearer plane problem—delivering all packets from correspondent nodes to the CoA of the mobile node. This traffic is encapsulated between the CoA and the home agent in either IP in IP, generic routing encapsulation (GRE), or minimal encapsulation.

The mobile node routes traffic to its default router. When using a foreign agent CoA, the default router might be the foreign agent CoA or be selected from the list provided in the ICMP Router Advertisement portion of the Agent Advertisement message. Figure 5-16 illustrates the bearer plane functions of Mobile IPv4 with foreign agent CoA.

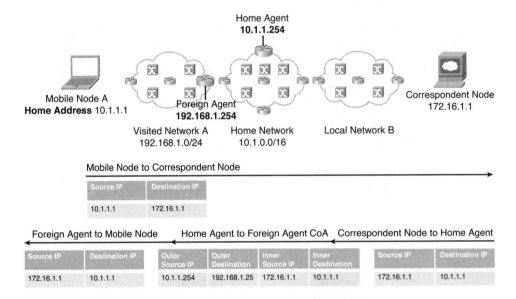

Figure 5-16   *Mobile IPv4 Routing with Foreign Agent CoA*

When the mobile node is using a CCoA, the default router is selected from the list provided in the ICMP Router Advertisement portion of the Agent Advertisement message, as long as the network prefix of the router selected matches the network prefix of the mobile node CoA message. Figure 5-17 illustrates the bearer plane functions of Mobile IPv4 with CCoA.

It is important that the mobile node does not issue any broadcast Address Resolution Protocol (ARP) messages while connected to a foreign network. This restriction is further clarified in the section "Mobile IPv4 and Layer 2 Interactions," later in this chapter.

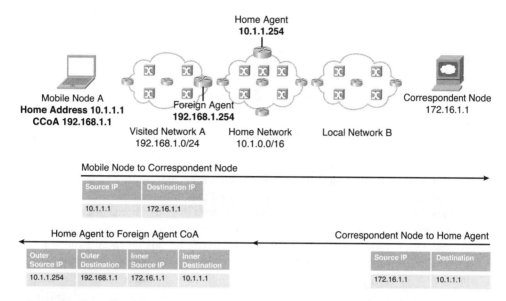

Figure 5-17 *Mobile IPv4 Routing with CCoA*

Tunneling and Reverse Tunneling

By default, the Mobile IPv4 tunnel established between the CoA and home agent is unidirectional. The mobile node sends traffic directly to a correspondent node, while the correspondent node sends traffic to the home agent. Figure 5-18 illustrates triangular routing.

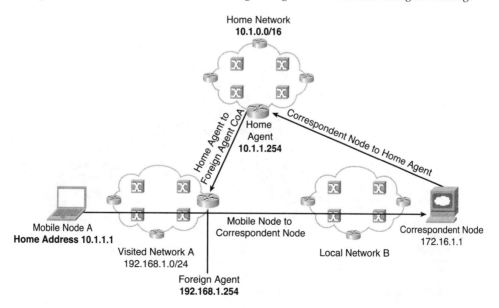

Figure 5-18 *Mobile IPv4 Triangular Routing*

As you can see in Figure 5-18, the routing path forms a triangle with the following vertices:

■   Traffic from the mobile node to the correspondent node is sent directly through the foreign agent.

■   Traffic from the correspondent node to the mobile node is first sent to the home agent.

■   The home agent then encapsulates the traffic and forwards the traffic to the mobile node CoA.

Triangular routing is not just inefficient, but it also causes problems for many network elements that rely on bidirectional communication flows or topologically accurate source/destination address pairs. For example, firewalls and other border routers at network ingress points can discard flows destined for the home agent because the mobile-initiated connection originally exited the network through a different border gateway. Chapter 4, "Data Link Layer Mobility," describes issues with triangular routing in more detail.

To resolve the triangular routing problem, Mobile IPv4 reverse tunneling, standardized in RFC 3024, is used. Reverse tunneling forces traffic to be routed symmetrically, through the home agent, in both the forward and reverse paths. The mobile node, when configured for reverse tunneling, uses the foreign agent as its default gateway, and the foreign agent encapsulates all traffic and sends it to the home agent. In this way, the home agent essentially acts as the border router for the Mobile IPv4 domain. Figure 5-19 illustrates Mobile IPv4 reverse tunneling.

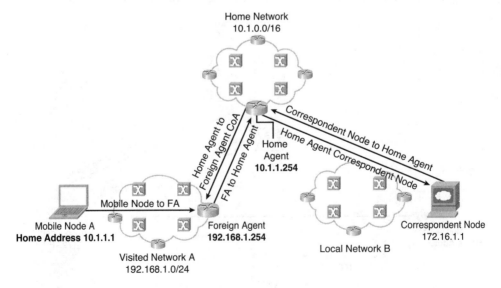

Figure 5-19   *Mobile IPv4 Reverse Tunneling*

Mobile IPv4 and Layer 2 Interactions

While Mobile IPv4 does resolve mobility at the Internet Layer of the TCP/IP stack, it actually creates additional challenges at the lower layers. Chapter 1 discusses how ARP works in a network.

Mobile IPv4 networks present a unique challenge for ARP. When a packet is routed into a network, the Mobile IPv4 home agent intercepts all packets destined for a mobile node and tunnels this traffic to the CoA. However, when a local corresponding node on the same network attempts to send a packet to the mobile node, the correspondent node does not need to route the packet. Because both the mobile node and correspondent node are on the same network, the correspondent node issues an ARP request to determine the hardware, or link layer, address of the mobile node. If the mobile node responds to this ARP request, the home agent would never see the packet. Figure 5-20 illustrates a local correspondent node forwarding packets to a mobile node under standard ARP functionality.

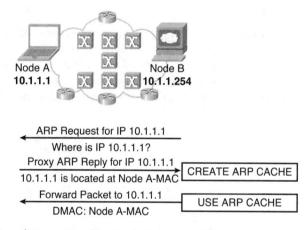

Figure 5-20 *Local Correspondent Node Standard ARP Functionality*

This presents a challenge because the correspondent node does not need to understand or be aware of the Mobile IPv4 session on the mobile node. If the mobile node changes point of attachment, the local correspondent node would not be aware and will continue to use its local ARP table to determine how to forward the packet. Figure 5-21 illustrates the mobility challenge that arises while communicating with a local correspondent node.

For this reason, Mobile IP4 adopted specific ARP rules that both mobile nodes and mobility agents must follow, including the following:

- The mobile node must not issue broadcast ARP messages while away from its home network.

- The foreign agent must not issue broadcast ARP messages to determine the MAC address of the mobile node. Instead, the foreign agent must obtain the MAC address from either an Agent Solicitation message or RRQ message.

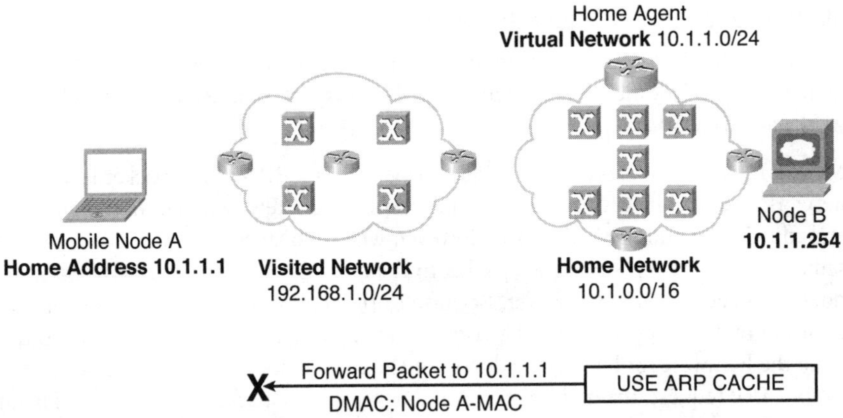

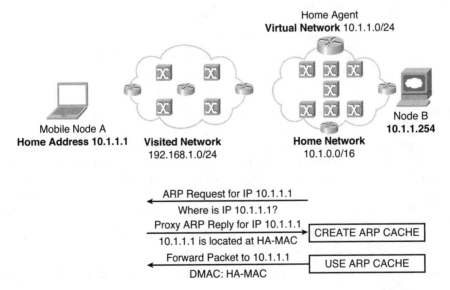

Figure 5-21   *Mobility Challenge with Local Correspondent Node*

■   The foreign agent's ARP cache for a mobile node must be as long as the RRP lifetime.

■   When the mobile node is away from the home network, the home agent uses Proxy ARP messages to reply to ARP requests for a mobile node's link layer address. A Proxy ARP message is an ARP reply sent by one node (the home agent) on behalf of another node (the mobile node). Figure 5-22 illustrates how Proxy ARP messages issued by the home agent solve the forwarding challenge that arises by communicating with local correspondent nodes.

Figure 5-22   *Home Agent Proxy ARP*

■ When the mobile node changes IP point of attachment, the home agent issues a gratuitous ARP message. This gratuitous ARP message updates local nodes as to the link layer address of the mobile node. This link layer address points to the home agent, and local nodes associate the mobile node's link layer address with the IP address of the home agent. Figure 5-23 illustrates how gratuitous ARP messages issued by the home agent solve the mobility challenge that arises by communicating with local correspondent nodes.

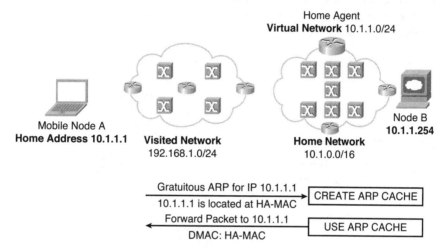

Figure 5-23   *Home Agent Gratuitous ARP*

Mobile IPv4 in Practice

Mobile IPv4 is one of the most-implemented mobility protocols and the most-implemented network layer mobility protocol to date. Mobile IPv4 is standardized in the IETF and leveraged across numerous organizations, including both 3GPP2, the standards organization for today's Code Division Multiple Access (CDMA) Evolution Data Only (EVDO) networks and WiMAX Forum Network Working Group (NWG).

While Mobile IPv4 has numerous deployment examples in both service provider and enterprise networks, the following sections discuss specific implementations of Mobile IPv4 relative to mobile standards organizations. These sections will look at a specific example of Mobile IPv4, as implemented in CDMA networks standardized by 3GPP2.

3GPP2 Implementation of Mobile IPv4

3GPP2 X.S011 defines the usage of Mobile IPv4 to provide mobility services in a CDMA network environment. A CDMA data network includes four main elements:

■ **Base Transceiver Station (BTS):** The BTS is the radio frequency (RF) node in the CDMA architecture.

- **Packet Control Function (PCF):** The PCF is both a packet-routing node between the BTS and Packet Data Serving Node (PDSN) as well as a radio node that provides intelligence and channel assignment to the mobile node.

- **PDSN:** The PDSN provides the network access gateway function to the packet data network. The PDSN terminates PPP sessions from the mobile node and provides the foreign agent function for the Mobile IPv4 session.

- **Home Agent (HA):** The HA provides Mobile IPv4 standards-compliant functions for the packet data network, ensuring that the mobile node can seamlessly hand off between CDMA BTSs.

Figure 5-24 illustrates a CDMA network architecture.

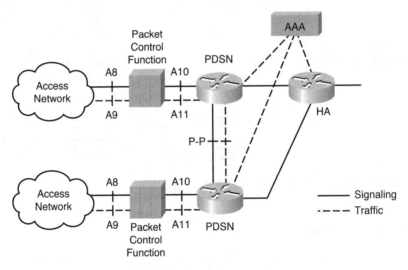

Figure 5-24 *CDMA Network Architecture*

Figure 5-25 illustrates the call flow for establishing a Mobile IPv4 connection in a CDMA network.

When a mobile node attempts to connect to the CDMA network, it attempts to establish a connection over the A10 interface, which is a PPP interface used to authenticate the mobile subscriber for network access.

The PPP session typically does not use Challenge Handshake Authentication Protocol (CHAP) authentication. This is done to reduce the call setup time. Instead, the PDSN will send Agent Advertisement messages that include the Agent Advertisement Challenge extension after the PPP session is successfully negotiated.

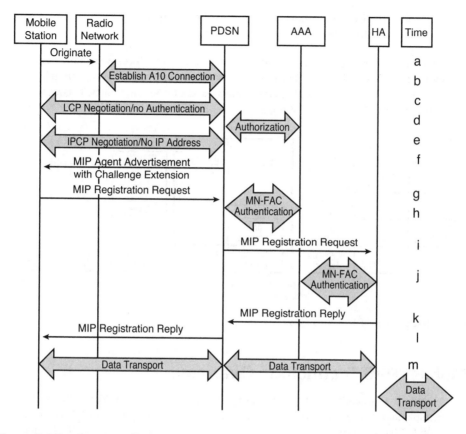

Figure 5-25 *CDMA Call Flow*

After the PPP has been completed, the mobile node initiates an RRQ to the PDSN. The foreign agent function in the PDSN communicates with a AAA server to authenticate the subscriber, retrieve a home agent IP address (if a dynamic home agent is required), the FA-HA SPI. The PDSN then proxies the RRQ message to the home agent, including the MN-FA challenge extension, NAI, and MN-AAA authentication extension.

The home agent interacts with the AAA server again to authenticate the mobile node for mobile services. After it is successfully authenticated, the home agent sends an RRP message to the PDSN/FA.

The mobile node home IP address can be assigned at many different steps within the call flow, including the following:

■ **Mobile IPv4 RRQ:** The mobile node can request a specific home IP address, known as a static IP address, from the mobility agents.

■ **FA-CHAP response from the AAA server:** If configured for CHAP authentication, the AAA server can assign a home IP address to the mobile node during authorization by the PDSN.

■   **Mobile IPv4 RRP:** The home agent can assign a home IP address, based on NAI, in the Mobile IPv4 RRP message.

After it is established, the mobile node can communicate with corresponding nodes using reverse tunneling. All packets both to and from the mobile node are sent through the home agent. Figure 5-26 illustrates the protocol stack for sending traffic between a mobile node and correspondent node.

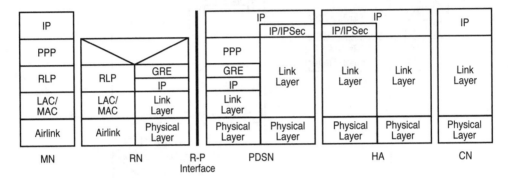

Figure 5-26   *CDMA End-to-End Protocol Stack*

Mobile IPv6 Technology Overview

Mobile IPv6 is standardized in RFC 3775. Much like Mobile IPv4, Mobile IPv6 provides transparent mobility support for mobile nodes communicating across IPv6 networks. Mobile IPv6 shares many of the same features and capabilities as Mobile IPv4 while leveraging the advantages that the IPv6 protocol itself provides. The major differences between Mobile IPv4 and Mobile IPv6 include the following:

■   Mobile IPv4 foreign agents provide local mobility agent function for a mobile node that has roamed into a foreign network. Mobile IPv6 does not require a local mobility anchor, so no foreign agent exists in a Mobile IPv6 network.

■   Because no foreign agent exists, route optimization and reverse tunneling options are not required for Mobile IPv6. The Mobile IPv6 route optimization capability allows the Mobile IPv6 protocol to coexist with ingress filtering devices located at border gateways.

■   The IPv6 protocol supports neighbor unreachability. This detection can be used in Mobile IPv6 to assure symmetric routing between the mobile node and its default router in the foreign network.

■   Rather than using IP in IP or other encapsulation techniques, the majority of traffic sent to a mobile node is done so using the IPv6 routing header.

■   Mobile IPv6 does not create the same challenges with link layer interactions. (See the section "Mobile IPv4 and Layer 2 Interactions," earlier in this chapter.) Instead of relying on ARP, Mobile IPv6 relies on IPv6 neighbor discovery.

Mobile IPv6 Operation

Mobile IPv6 operation is similar to that of Mobile IPv4. The mobile node is always reachable through its HoA, regardless of point of attachment. The mobile node registers its CoA with a home agent in the home network whenever it changes point of attachment within foreign networks.

While the binding between the mobile node's CoA and home address allows any node corresponding with the mobile node to continue communication, traffic is routed in a nonoptimal manner. Mobile IPv6 resolves this by allowing the correspondent node to participate in the Mobile IPv6 process. The two nodes (mobile and correspondent) communicate through two different methods—bidirectional tunneling and route optimization—as explained in the sections that follow.

Note   As you will see later in this chapter, the operation of route optimization requires that the Correspondent Node supports additional Mobile IPv6 functionality.

Bidirectional Tunneling Mode

Bidirectional tunneling mode does not require the correspondent node to support Mobile IPv6. In this mode, traffic is routed similarly to a reverse tunneling mode in Mobile IPv4. Figure 5-27 illustrates bidirectional tunneling mode in Mobile IPv6.

Packets from the mobile node toward the correspondent node are tunneled to the home agent and then routed from the home network to the correspondent node. Packets from the correspondent node are routed to the home agent and then tunneled to the mobile node.

Bidirectional tunneling mode requires IPv6 neighbor discovery capability in the home agent.

IPV6 neighbor discovery, defined in RFC 2461, is an important function in Mobile IPv6. IPv6 neighbor discovery allows a network node to discover the link layer address of nodes residing on the same network and a network host to find a default router. The IPv6 neighbor discovery capability allows Mobile IPv6 to function over any link layer technology and disassociates the home agent from taking part in any link layer communications.

When a mobile node moves outside the home network, it registers with the home agent. The home agent uses proxy neighbor discovery to notify link-adjacent nodes that all traffic destined for the mobile node should be sent to the home agent.

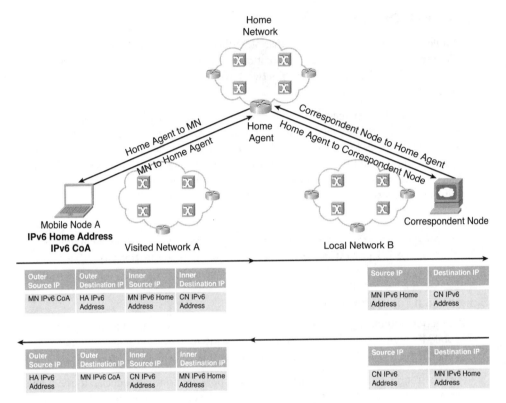

Figure 5-27   *Mobile IPv6 Bidirectional Tunneling Mode*

Route Optimization Mode

Route optimization mode in Mobile IPv6 allows the IPv6 network to use standard short-est-path (or policy-based) algorithms to determine how packets are routed from the corre-spondent node to the mobile node. This mode requires the correspondent node to sup-port the Mobile IPv6 protocol.

Figure 5-28 illustrates route optimization mode in Mobile IPv6.

To populate the bindings database on the correspondent node, the mobile node sends Binding Update messages, similar to those sent to the home agent. The correspondent node maintains a bindings database that maps the mobile node's home address and CoA.

Packets from the mobile node toward the correspondent node are sent directly to the cor-respondent node. Packets from the correspondent node are routed directly to the CoA of the mobile node.

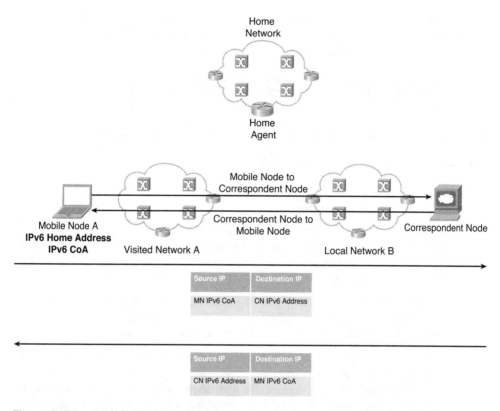

Figure 5-28   *Mobile IPv6 Route Optimization Mode*

IPv6 Destination Option Header

In Mobile IPv6 route optimization mode, the mobile node sources all packets from its CoA. This is required to conform with reverse path forwarding (RPF), a technique for preventing IP address spoofing.

TCP sessions, as discussed in the introduction to this chapter, are bound to both source and destination IP addresses. Under normal circumstances, the TCP layer would break when the mobile node's source IP address (CoA) changed, because the correspondent node's TCP stack would no longer have an associated flow. The Mobile IPv6 Destination Options header resolves this problem.

In Mobile IPv6, the Destination Options header is used in packets sent by the mobile node to notify the correspondent node of its home address. The inclusion of the home address in this Destination Options header makes the use of the CoA for transport transparent above the network layer.

The correspondent node replaces the IPv6 source address in the IPv6 header with the home address provided in the Destination Options header. The replacing of the address with that recovered from the Options header ensures that the operation of route optimization is masked from the upper layer applications. Figure 5-29 illustrates how a correspondent node uses the home address provided in the Destination Options header.

Next Header = 60 (Destination Header)	Hdr Extension Length	Option Type	Option Length
Home Address			

Figure 5-29   *Mobile IPv6 Destination Options Header*

IPv6 Type 2 Routing Header

In Mobile IPv6 route optimization mode, the correspondent node uses the mobile node CoA as the destination for all packets. By ensuring that all packets are sent to the mobile node's CoA, ingress filtering devices or devices that require topologically accurate source/destination address pairs continue to operate normally.

Under normal circumstances, the TCP layer would break when the mobile node changes point of attachment because the mobile node's TCP stack would no longer have an associated flow. The Mobile IPv6 Type 2 Routing header resolves this problem.

In Mobile IPv6, the Type 2 Routing header is used in packets sent by the correspondent node to the mobile node. The correspondent node puts the mobile node's home address in this header. The mobile node replaces the IPv6 destination address in the IPv6 header with the home address provided in the Type 2 Routing header. Figure 5-30 illustrates how a mobile node uses the home address provided in the Type 2 Routing header.

Next Header = 43 (Routing Header)	Hdr Extension Length	Routing Type = 2	Segments Left = 1
RESERVED			
Home Address			

Figure 5-30   *Mobile IPv6 Type 2 Routing Header*

Mobile IPv6 Messages and Message Formats

Although it relies heavily on standard IPv6 extensions and protocols, the Mobile IPv6 protocol does define a number of IPv6 header extensions and protocol extensions. The most notable Mobile IPv6 changes are the inclusion of a Mobility header in IPv6 packets and the creation of four new ICMPv6 messages.

Mobile IPv6 Mobility Header

The Mobility header is an extension header used by any node participating in the Mobile IPv6 process. This extension can be added by the home agent, mobile node, or correspondent node (when route optimization mode is used). The Mobility header is used for the creation and management of mobility bindings. Figure 5-31 illustrates the structure of the Mobility header. Table 5-4 provides additional information on the Mobility Header (MH) type value.

Next Header = 59 (Mobility Header)	Hdr Extension Length	Mobility Header Type	RESERVED
Checksum		DATA	

Figure 5-31 *IPv6 Mobility Header Structure*

Table 5-4 *MH Type-Value Functions*

MH Type	MH Message	MH Message Function
0	Binding Refresh Request (BRR) message	This message is sent by the mobile node to update its binding information in either the home agent or correspondent node.
1	Home Test Init (HoTI) message	This message is sent by the correspondent node to the mobile node's home address to initiate the return routability procedure. The HoTI message is routed through the home agent.
2	Care-of Test Init (CoTI) message	This message is sent by the correspondent node to the mobile node's CoA to initiate the return routability procedure.
3	Home Test (HoT) message	This message is sent from the mobile node to the correspondent node in response to the HoTI message.
4	Care-of Test (CoT) message	This message is sent from the mobile node to the correspondent node in response to the CoTI message.
5	Binding Update (BU) message	This message is sent by the mobile node to notify either the home agent or a correspondent node that it has changed network point of attachment and has a new CoA.
6	Binding Acknowledgment (BA) message	This message is sent either by the home agent or by a correspondent node to acknowledge that it has received a BU message.

continues

Table 5-4   *MH Type-Value Functions   (continued)*

MH Type	MH Message	MH Message Function
7	Binding Error (BE) message	This message is sent by a correspondent node to a mobile node indicating a mobility error; for example, if the mobile node sends a message to a correspondent node with the Destination Options header indicating a home address, but the correspondent node does not have the CoA in its binding database.

The BU and BA messages are illustrated in Figure 5-32.

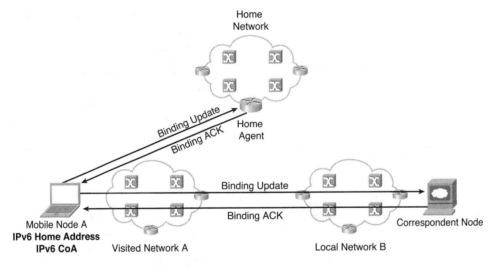

Figure 5-32   *Mobile IPv6 Binding Procedure*

Note   To ensure that the mobile node sending the binding update is the same mobile node that is sending data packets, the *return routability procedure* is used.

The return routability procedure allows the correspondent node to verify both the CoA and home address of the mobile node. The correspondent node sends two test messages using the IPv6 Mobility header (see the section "Mobile IPv6 Messages and Message Formats," earlier in this chapter)—one to the CoA and one to the home address, simultaneously. The message destined for the CoA is routed directly to the mobile node. The message destined for the home address is initially routed through the home agent. Upon successful reply by the mobile node to both messages, the correspondent node establishes an entry in its binding database, and no subsequent verification traffic needs to be sent to the mobile node. Figure 5-33 illustrates the return routability procedure.

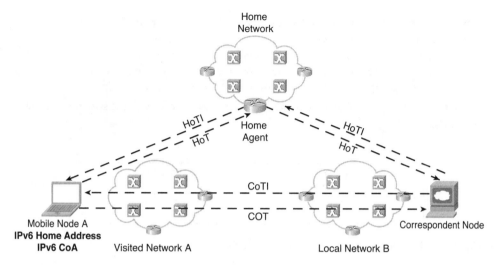

Figure 5-33 *Mobile IPv6 Return Routability Procedure*

Mobile IPv6 ICMP Message Types

Mobile IPv6 introduces four new ICMP message types, as summarized in Table 5-5. These messages are used during dynamic home agent address discovery (see the next section), network renumbering, and address configuration on the mobile node.

Table 5-5 *MH Type-Value Functions*

Message Type	MH Message Function
Home Agent Address Discovery Request	This mobile node sends this message to initiate the home agent dynamic discovery mechanism, discussed in the next section. The message is sent to the home agent's anycast address for its subnet.
Home Agent Address Discovery Reply	The home agent sends this message in response to the Home Agent Address Discovery Request message and includes the home agent IP address.
Mobile Prefix Solicitation	The mobile node sends this message to the home agent when in a foreign network. This message solicits a Mobile Prefix Advertisement.
Mobile Prefix Advertisement	The home agent sends this message to the mobile node in response to a Mobile Prefix Solicitation message. The message distributes information about the home link so that the mobile node can configure and update home addresses.

Prefix	Interface Identifier	
	1111111...111111	Anycast ID = 7E

Figure 5-34   *IPv6 Home Agent's Anycast Address Structure*

Dynamic Home Agent Discovery

Mobile IPv6 provides support for multiple home agents and reconfiguration of the home network. In these cases, the mobile node might not know the IP address of its own home agent. When a mobile node needs to send a BU message but is unaware of any home agent on its home network, the mobile node can attempt to discover the address of a home agent by sending an ICMP Home Agent Address Discovery message to the IPv6 home agent's anycast address. Figure 5-35 illustrates a mobile node using the Home Agent Address Discovery message.

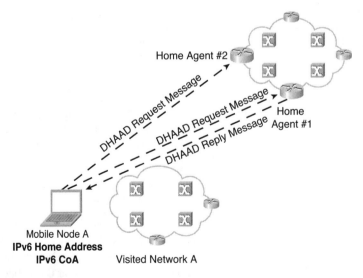

Figure 5-35   *Dynamic Home Agent Address Discovery*

Mobile IPv6 Bootstrapping

A mobile node needs a minimal amount of information to register with a home agent. The process of obtaining this information—namely, the IPv6 address, a home agent address, and a security association with the home agent—is known as *bootstrapping*. RFC 4640 provides guidelines and scenarios where bootstrapping a mobile node in a Mobile IPv6 network is preferable to statically configuring this information. Many protocols have been proposed to facilitate the bootstrapping process, including Dynamic Host Configuration Protocol version 6 (DHCPv6), IEEE 802.1x, and Protocol for carrying Authentication Network Access (PANA). It is important, independent of the bootstrap protocol, that the bootstrapping process be integrated with the AAA functions.

RADIUS Support for Mobile IPv6

Mobile IPv6 interactions with RADIUS servers have not been fully standardized in the IETF. The current working draft, defined in draft-ietf-mip6-radius, describes the set of attributes to facilitate Mobile IPv6 bootstrapping and operations.

Note   The draft-ietf-mip6-radius IETF working draft also maintains a list of RADIUS attributes and Diameter Code Values for use when communicating to the AAA infrastructure.

The network access gateway in a Mobile IPv6 network functions similarly to how a foreign agent can function from an AAA perspective in Mobile IPv4. Two scenarios might occur:

- The access network provider is the same as the mobility service provider.

- The access service provider is different from the mobility service provider.

In the first case, when network access is requested, the network access gateway interacts with the access service RADIUS server, which acts as a proxy to the mobility service RADIUS server. The network access gateway retrieves mobile node information through some already-established protocol, such as PPP, DHCPv6, or Internet Key Exchange version 2 (IKEv2). This allows the mobility service RADIUS server to provide the parameters required for the mobile node to initiate the registration request. Figure 5-36 illustrates this scenario.

In the second case, Mobile IPv6 bootstrapping is not performed as part of the network access authentication procedure. A protocol between the mobile node and the home agent is required to trigger RADIUS interactions. While there is none specifically defined, this can be Mobile IPv6 or another protocol such as IKEv2. Figure 5-37 illustrates this scenario.

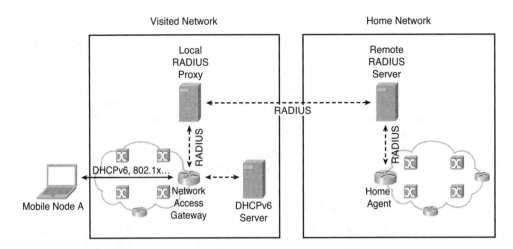

Figure 5-36 *Mobile IPv6 Bootstrapping Using Access Authentication*

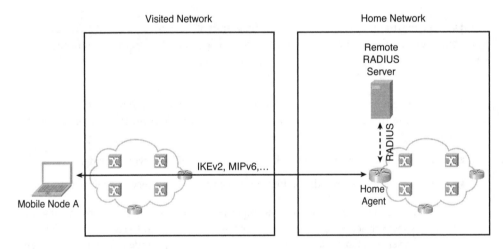

Figure 5-37 *Mobile IPv6 Bootstrapping Without Access Authentication*

Mobile Node Identifier Option for MIPv6   RFC 4283 provides a capability similar to that in Mobile IPv4 that allows the mobile node to identify itself by some other mechanism than home IP address. Identifiers such as the NAI, fully qualified domain name (FQDN), Mobile Subscriber Number (MSISDN), and International Mobile Station Identifier (IMSI) are some examples of this identification. The Mobile Node Identifier header is included after the Mobility header in an IPv6 packet to allow the AAA infrastructure to authenticate a mobile node, authorize the mobile node for service, allocate a home agent IP address, and assign a home address.

RADIUS Attributes

While the network access gateway makes use of a number of existing RADIUS attributes, including User-Name, Service-Type, NAS-Port-Type, and Calling-Station-ID, a number of new attributes are also defined for Mobile IPv6, as summarized in Table 5-6.

Table 5-6   *MIPv6 RADIUS Attributes*

Attribute	Definition
MIP6-HA	This attribute can be present in either the RADIUS Access Request or Access Accept packet to denote the home agent IP addresses that the mobile node can access.
MIP6-HA-FQDN	This attribute can be present in either the RADIUS Accept Request or Access Accept packet to denote the FQDN of the home agent.
MIP6-HL-Prefix	This attribute can be present in either the RADIUS Accept Request or Access Accept packet to denote the home link prefix of the mobile node.
MIP6-HOA	This attribute is present in the Access Accept packet to denote the home IP address assigned to the mobile node.
MIP6-DNS-MO	This attribute is sent by the network access gateway in the Access Request message to request that the RADIUS server perform a Dynamic DNS update using the mobile node's FQDN.
MIP6-Careof-Address	The home agent sends this attribute in the Access Request message to notify the RADIUS server of the CoA received in the MIPv6 Binding Update message.

Mobility Message Authentication Option   Additional RADIUS attributes have been defined in support of RFC 4285, "Authentication Protocol for Mobile IPv6." This authentication protocol defines a new signaling option, the Mobility Message Authentication Option. This authentication option provides a method of securely transporting information in Binding Update and Binding Acknowledgment messages between the mobile node and home agent.

This confidentiality capability is useful when the mobile node is authenticated for access in one operator domain and authenticated for mobility in a different operator domain.

The Authentication Protocol for Mobile IPv6 is one option for confidentiality of credentials in the transport network, in addition to an IPsec Security Association (SA) option that exists in the Mobile IPv6 RFC.

Diameter Support for Mobile IPv6

Mobile IPv6 interactions with Diameter servers are standardized in IETF RFC 5447. The same scenarios presented in the section "RADIUS Support for Mobile IPv6," earlier in this chapter, are applicable to the Diameter protocol. Similar to the RADIUS attributes defined for Mobile IPv6, Diameter Attribute-Value Pairs (AVP) have been defined, as summarized in Table 5-7.

Table 5-7   *MIPv6 Diameter AVPs*

AVP	Definition
MIP6-Agent-Info	This AVP contains the necessary information to assign a home agent to the mobile node. The AVP contains the following values: ■ MIP-Home-Agent-Address ■ MIP-Home-Agent-Host ■ MIP6-Home-Link-Prefix
MIP-Home-Agent-Address	This AVP contains the IPv6 or IPv4 address of the Mobile IPv6 home agent.
MIP-Home-Agent-Host	This AVP contains the identity of the assigned Mobile IPv6 home agent. The AVP contains the following Diameter base values: ■ Destination-Realm ■ Destination-Host The usage of this AVP is identical to the usage of the MIP-Home-Agent-Address AVP, except this attribute relies on updated information from DNS rather than a stored IP address.
MIP6-Home-Link-Prefix	This AVP contains the Mobile IPv6 home network prefix information.
MIP6-DNS-MO	This attribute is sent by the network access gateway in the Access Request message to request that the RADIUS server perform a Dynamic DNS update using the mobile node's FQDN.
MIP6-Careof-Address	The home agent sends this attribute in the Access Request message to notify the RADIUS server of the CoA received in the MIPv6 Binding Update message.

Network Mobility Basic Support Protocol

Network Mobility (NEMO), defined in RFC 3963, is an extension of Mobile IPv6 that enables session continuity for all nodes connected to a mobile network. NEMO introduces the concept of a mobile router, which is a Mobile IPv6 mobile node that can route traffic between its CoA and a subnet that moves with the router. This allows reachability to all nodes behind the mobile router, regardless of their support for any mobility protocol, as the router changes its point of attachment to the network.

NEMO works by using the bidirectional tunnel mode of Mobile IPv6 to tunnel all traffic between the mobile router and the home agent. For nodes that reside on the mobile router's network, known as the mobile network, the mobile router acts as the default gateway.

The mobile router acts as a mobile node from a home agent perspective, including the normal BU/BA sequence and Binding Update messages to the home agent. However, the mobile router can also notify the home agent of the mobile prefix assigned to its subnet so that the home agent can provide routing functions for that mobile network and ensure that traffic is sent to the mobile router.

Mobile Network Routing   While NEMO relies on the home agent to route all traffic to the mobile router and the prefixes that reside behind the mobile router, this can also be accomplished outside the scope of the NEMO protocol. Rather than notifying the home agent of network prefixes through Mobile IPv6 header options, the mobile router and home agent can also use standard routing protocols, such as Open Shortest Path First (OSPF) or Border Gateway Protocol (BGP).

Figure 5-38 illustrates NEMO.

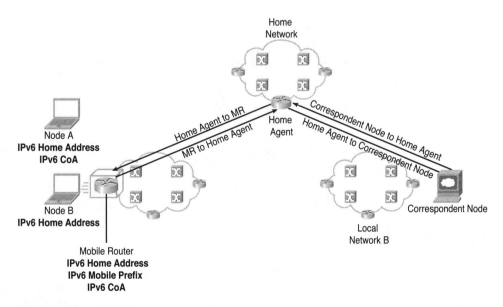

Figure 5-38   *NEMO*

Mobile IPv6 in Practice

Mobile IPv6 is well documented in the IETF, but it has yet to reach significant deployment because the majority of the Internet is still IPv4 based. Mobile IPv6 is standardized across numerous mobile standards organizations, including both 3GPP2 and WiMAX Forum NWG.

The following sections discuss specific implementations of Mobile IPv6 relative to mobile standards organizations. These sections will examine a Mobile IPv6 example from WiMAX Forum Network Working Group (NWG) standards.

WiMAX Forum NWG Implementation of Mobile IPv6

NWG R1.0 Network Architecture defines the WiMAX network architecture in support of both Client Mobile IP (CMIP) and Proxy Mobile IP (PMIP) (see Chapter 4, "Data Link Layer Mobility"). This architecture is depicted in Figure 5-39, and includes the following network nodes:

- **Access router:** The access router is the network access gateway in a WiMAX Mobile IPv6 network. This device serves as the default router for the Mobile IPv6 node.

- **Home agent (HA):** The HA provides standards-compliant Mobile IPv6 home agent functions for mobile node session continuity.

- **AAA server:** The AAA server provides authentication and authorization services for both the Access Service Network Gateway (ASNGW) and HA.

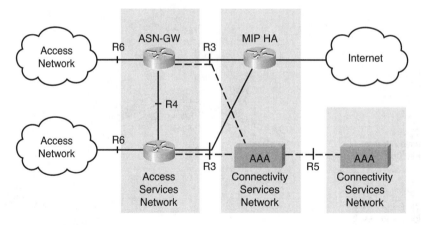

Figure 5-39   *WiMAX Network Architecture*

To facilitate mobility in a WiMAX network, each ASN is a unique foreign/visited network. The home agent, located in the Connectivity Service Node (CSN), provides Mobile IPv6 mobility services across all ASNs within an operator domain. The Mobile IPv6 protocol is carried across the R3 reference point in WiMAX standards.

On initial connection to the WiMAX network, the mobile node listens for Router Advertisement messages. Because there is no foreign agent function in a Mobile IPv6 network, the mobile node must acquire bootstrap information from the network infrastructure. This is done through either DHCPv6 or through the AAA server. The Access Router can also perform access authentication and retrieve dynamic home agent assignment, home link assignment, and home address assignment information from the AAA server.

After the bootstrap information, including the home link, the Home Address (HoA), and home agent address are received, the mobile node issues a Binding Update message to the home agent. This BU message includes the following information:

- Destination Option Header

- MN-NAI value

- MN-AAA Authentication Option

The mobile node also generates a CoA, based on the subnet it received in the Router Advertisement message.

The home agent triggers an Authentication Request message to the AAA server through either RADIUS or Diameter based on information received in the BU message.

The AAA server replies with a message indicating the status (Accept/Reject) and the MN-HA key for subsequent message processing. The HA also performs a replay check to ensure that the mobile node is not using expired data for authentication and responds with a Binding Acknowledgment message. This BA message includes the following information:

- Type 2 Routing Header

- MN-NAI Mobility Option

- MN-HA Authentication Option

Figure 5-40 illustrates a call flow for a WiMAX Mobile IPv6 session setup.

When a mobile node changes point of attachment in a WiMAX network, the access router servicing the mobile node can be changed. In this event, the mobile node must listen for, or solicit, a new Router Advertisement message. This new RA provides subnet information that the mobile node uses to determine a new CoA.

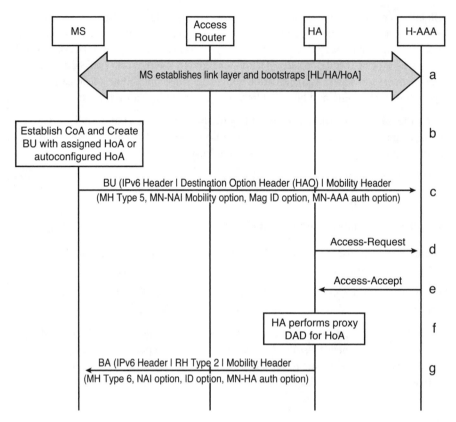

NWG R1.0.0 Stage 2 Part 2 7-81

Figure 5-40 *WiMAX Mobile IPv6 Session Setup*

After the CoA has been calculated, the mobile node sends a Binding Update message to the home agent. During the relocation of the R3 interface from the old access router to the new access router, a data path tunnel is established between the two access routers to ensure that no data traffic is lost. Figure 5-41 depicts the call flow for R3 reanchoring.

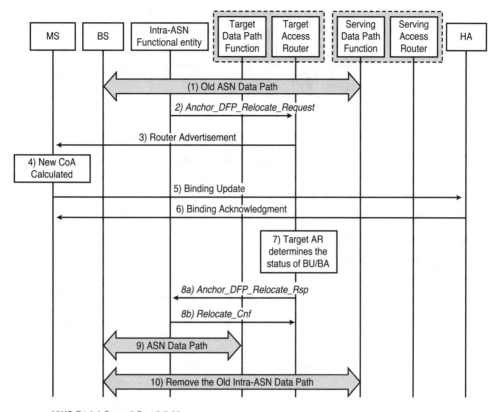

NWG R1.0.0 Stage 2 Part 2 7-83

Figure 5-41   *WiMAX Mobile IPv6 Session Handoff*

Figure 5-42 illustrates the end-to-end WiMAX IPv6 protocol stack for both bidirectional tunnel and route optimization modes.

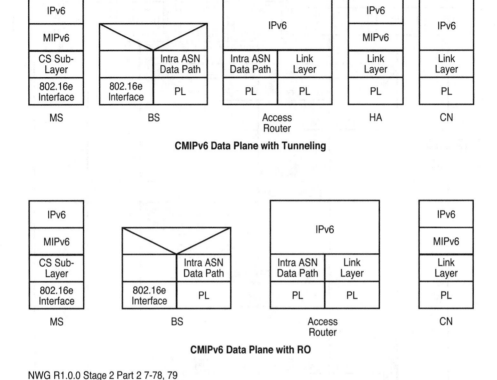

CMIPv6 Data Plane with Tunneling

CMIPv6 Data Plane with RO

NWG R1.0.0 Stage 2 Part 2 7-78, 79

Figure 5-42   *End-to-End WiMAX Mobile IPv6 Protocol Stack*

Dual-Stack Mobile IP

Mobile IPv4 and Mobile IPv6 provide technologies for mobility for mobile networks using IPv4 and IPv6 protocols, respectively. These mobility management techniques share a common name and a common function, namely, providing session continuity for a mobile node; however, the protocols themselves are indeed separate and noninteroperable.

This does not create a challenge in a network that is built on IPv4 or a network that is built on IPv6. As networks migrate from IPv4 to IPv6 for either business or technical reasons, a new challenge arises in providing session continuity as a mobile node changes point of attachment from an IPv4 domain to an IPv6 domain.

Nodes that support both IPv4 and IPv6 protocol stacks are known as *dual-stack nodes*. These nodes can establish connectivity through IPv4, through IPv6, or through both IPv4 and IPv6 simultaneously. With Mobile IPv4, the node can ensure that applications reliant on IPv4 persist as the node moves from IPv4 subnet to IPv4 subnet. With Mobile IPv6, the node can ensure that applications reliant on IPv6 persist as the node moves from IPv6 subnet to IPv6 subnet. The need to support session persistence as a mobile node moves from IPv4 subnet to IPv6 subnet, or from IPv6 subnet to IPv4 subnet, requires either:

■ A single mobility management protocol

■ Interactions and visibility between Mobile IPv4 and Mobile IPv6 protocols

Dual-stack mobility, a problem discussed in draft RFC draft-ietf-mip6-dsmip-problem, provides solution requirements for both Mobile IPv4 and Mobile IPv6 so that they can support mobility management for dual-stack devices. In addition, RFC 5454, "Dual-Stack Mobile IPv4," and RFC 5555, "Mobile IPv6 Support for Dual-Stack Hosts and Routers," provide extensions and modifications to Mobile IPv4 and Mobile IPv6, respectively, to allow these protocols to understand and manage mobility across the IPv4 and IPv6 domains.

Mobile IPv4 Extensions to Support IPv6

The extensions to Mobile IPv4 in support of IPv6 allow the mobile node to maintain connectivity using only the Mobile IPv4 protocol while moving in an IPv4 or dual-stack network. These extensions provide separation between the signaling protocol (Mobile IPv4) and the IP transport network that tunnels it. This allows Mobile IPv4 to establish both IPv4 and IPv6 tunnels over the IPv4 transport network.

Note   Because the signaling protocol is Mobile IPv4, the required mode of operation to support both IPv4 and IPv6 is reverse tunneling or bidirectional tunneling. The route optimization mode provided by Mobile IPv6 cannot be used, because correspondent nodes in a Mobile IPv4 network are unaware of the mobility signaling.

The mobile node communicates information about the IPv6 prefixes to the Mobile IPv4 home agent through RRQ/RRP extensions. Three extensions are added to the RRQ/RRP flows:

■ **IPv6 Prefix Request:** The mobile node can include one or more of the IPv6 Prefix Request extensions in an RRQ message. This extensions carries information about the IPv6 prefixes that the mobile node is using.

■ **IPv6 Prefix Reply:** The Mobile IPv4 home agent responds to the IPv6 Prefix Request in the RRQ with an IPv6 Prefix Reply in the RRP. This extension notifies the mobile node whether the request was accepted or rejected.

■ **IPv6 Tunneling Mode:** The mobile node includes a single IPv6 Tunneling Mode extension in an RRQ message. This extension notifies the home agent as to which tunneling protocol should be used for tunneling IPv6 packets.

Upon successful registration to a Mobile IPv4 home agent, a dual-stack mobile node can receive traffic for either its IPv4 home address or IPv6 home address through the mobile IPv4 tunnel to the home agent. Because the home agent encapsulates this traffic in Mobile IPv4, the traffic can even traverse a foreign agent (if foreign agent CoA is negotiated). Figure 5-43 illustrates Mobile IPv4 being used to tunnel IPv6 traffic to a mobile node.

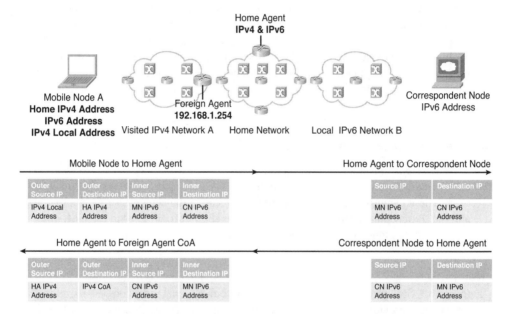

Figure 5-43   *Mobile IPv4 Tunneling IPv6 Packets*

Mobile IPv6 Extensions to Support IPv4

The options added to Mobile IPv6 in support of IPv4 allow the mobile node to maintain connectivity using only the Mobile IPv6 protocol while moving in an IPv4 or dual-stack network. Like the extensions for Mobile IPv4 RRQ/RRP, these options to the Mobile IPv6 Binding Update and Acknowledgment headers allow the mobile node to use a single mobility management protocol (Mobile IPv6) while changing point of attachment.

A dual-stack mobile node updates the home agent with its IPv6 CoA. The home agent creates a binding cache entry for each home address, IPv4 and IPv6, to this CoA. These Binding Updates can be sent to the home agent through IPv6, or encapsulated in IPv4, depending on the network protocol support within the foreign network.

Note   Because the signaling protocol is Mobile IPv6, the mobile node can use router optimization mode when communicating through an IPv6 CoA with a node that supports Mobile IPv6. If the mobile node is located in a foreign network that does not support IPv6, or is communicating with an IPv4 correspondent node, bidirectional tunneling mode is used.

The options added to the Binding Update header include the following:

- **IPv4 Home Address Option:** This option notifies the Mobile IPv6 home agent of the mobile node's IPv4 home address. The Mobile IPv6 home agent can also provide dynamic IPv4 home address assignment for the mobile node.

- **IPv4 CoA Option:** This option notifies the Mobile IPv6 home agent of the mobile node's current IPv4 CoA when the mobile node is located in a network that only supports IPv4.

The Binding Acknowledgment Header also includes the IPv4 Address Acknowledgment Option. This option notifies the mobile node that the home agent has created a binding entry for the mobile node's IPv4 home address. If the home agent assigned this address dynamically, it includes this IP address to notify the mobile node. If the mobile node had specified a home address, the home agent copies the value from the IPv4 Home Address Option in the Binding Update message.

Figure 5-44 illustrates Mobile IPv4 being used to tunnel IPv6 traffic to a mobile node.

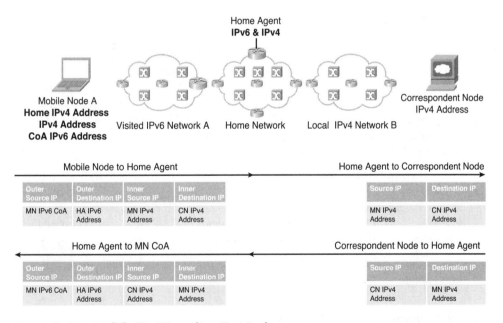

Figure 5-44 *Mobile IPv6 Tunneling IPv4 Packets*

MOBIKE Technology Overview

The Internet Key Exchange version 2 (IKEv2) Mobility and Multihoming (MOBIKE) protocol was specified in RFC 4555 as a means of providing two main functions:

- **Mobility:** MOBIKE allows a mobile node encrypting traffic through IKEv2 to change point of attachment while maintaining a Virtual Private Network (VPN) session. At a high level, the MOBIKE protocol functions similarly to the Mobile IPv4 protocol.

■ **Multihoming:** MOBIKE allows a host that has multiple simultaneous points of attachment to a network to change which interface is forwarding traffic while maintaining a VPN session. Figure 5-45 illustrates the multihoming scenario.

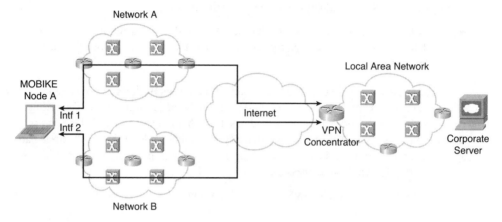

Figure 5-45   *MOBIKE Multihoming*

MOBIKE provides a secure mobility protocol that allows a remote-access worker to work uninterrupted in the mobile environments such as commuter trains. MOBIKE allows the remote worker to maintain connectivity to the enterprise intranet while changing points of attachment on the Internet, without reestablishing security associations (SAs). This is an important distinction versus traditional IP Security (IPSec) protocol, which built SAs based on IP address, and therefore suffered from a similar deficiency as standard IP. This is discussed in more detail later in this chapter.

In recent years, MOBIKE has also been proposed as a mechanism of providing secure connectivity for mobile hosts or routers that are connected to the mobile network over untrusted connections. One example, discussed later in this chapter, is the 3GPP Interworking with Wireless LAN (iWLAN) standards. MOBIKE can also be applied in a service provider environment for enabling femtocells.

Prior to understanding MOBIKE, however, it is important to understand how IKEv2 works and to see the challenges that mobility presents.

IKEv2 Terminology and Processes

Internet Protocol Security (IPsec) provides security services at the IP layer for other TCP/IP protocols and applications to use. IPsec provides a suite of protocols for securing IP communications by authenticating and encrypting each IP packet of a data stream.

Several services are offered by IPsec:

■ Encryption of user data for privacy

■ Authentication of the integrity of a message to ensure that it is not changed en route

■ Protection against certain types of security attacks, such as replay attacks

■ The ability for devices to negotiate the security algorithms and keys required to meet their security needs

Initially, endpoints must agree on a set of security protocols to use so that each one sends data in a format the other can understand. They must decide on a specific encryption algorithm to use in encoding data. They must exchange keys that are used to decrypt data that has been cryptographically encoded. IPsec uses the Internet Key Exchange (IKE) protocol for these functions.

IKE is a protocol for providing mutual authentication and security association establishment for IPsec VPNs. IKE has countless deployments and almost as many RFCs. RFC 2407, 2408, and 2409 all provide base IKE protocol definition, and numerous RFCs exist for supporting Network Address Translation (NAT) traversal, Extensible Authentication Protocol (EAP), remote address acquisition, and so on.[2]

IKEv2, standardized in RFC 4306, centralized all IKE functions into a common RFC and included enhancements to the original IKE protocol for more efficient call setup and lower latency.

IKEv2 provides a mechanism for mutual authentication between two Internet nodes andestablishment a Security Association (SA) based on shared secret information and a set of cryptographic algorithms to ensure data confidentiality. Each SA is a logical, simplex connection that provides the secure data connection between devices.

IKEv2 communications are request/response-based message flows known as exchanges. An IKE SA is established with two exchanges (four messages)—the IKE_SA_INIT and IKE_AUTH—as described in the sections that follow.

IKEv2 IKE_SA_INIT

The IKE_SA_INIT exchange is used to negotiate cryptographic algorithms; to exchange pseudorandom numbers, known as *nonces*, for replay attack prevention; and to establish a symmetric shared key. This process provides the two nodes with enough information to securely transport information required for IKE_AUTH exchange.

The node that sends the initial request message is known as the *initiator*. The initiator sends the initial request with the following information:

■ **Security Parameter Index (SPI):** The SPI is a random number used to reference the specific SA.

■ **SAi1:** The SAi1 provides the cryptographic algorithms supported by the initiator.

■ **KEi:** The KEi provides a random private value used by the SA peer to generate the shared key for traffic flowing from the initiator to the responder. All messages following the IKE_SA_INIT are encrypted and integrity-protected with this shared key.

■ **Ni:** The Ni provides the initiator's nonce value. This nonce is used as part of replay protection.

The node that responds to the initial request is known as the *responder*. The responder sends the response with the following information:

- **Security Parameter Index (SPI):** The SPI is a random number used to reference the specific SA.

- **SAr1:** The SAr1 provides the cryptographic algorithm that will be used for all communication. The responder selects this algorithm from the list presented by the initiator.

- **KEr:** The KEr provides a random private value used by the SA peer to generate the shared key for traffic flowing from the responder to the initiator. Because the SA is a simplex connection, this shared key can be different than the one generated for the initiator-to-responder direction.

- **Nr:** The Nr provides the responder's nonce value. This nonce is used as part of replay protection.

Following this exchange, both the initiator and responder have sufficient information to generate a secret shared key, known as an *SKEYSEED*. Individual keys are then generated from this shared key to determine a unique encryption key and integrity protection key. These keys are used to ensure that all subsequent communication is confidential.

IKEv2 IKE_AUTH

The IKE_AUTH exchange is used to authenticate messages between the two peers, exchange identity information, exchange certificates, and establish the SA.

The IKE_AUTH exchange when the initiator sends an encrypted message to the responder includes:

- **SPI:** The SPI is a random number used to reference the specific SA.

- **IDi:** The IDi provides the initiator's identity information.

- **Certificates:** The certificate provides validation of identity. This validation is provided by a third-party, trusted validation server.

- **IDr:** If the responder has multiple identities all hosted by the same IP address, the initiator can send the IDr value to indicate which identity it is attempting to communicate with.

- **SAi2:** The SAi2 value contains SA offers from the initiator to the responder.

- **TSi:** The TSi value contains the traffic selector of the initiator.

- **TSr:** The TSr value contains the traffic selector of the responder.

In this message, the initial payload attributes—namely, the SPI, IDi, Certificates, and IDr—are used to establish identity, while the remaining attributes (SAi2, TSi, and TSr) are used to establish the SA.

When the responder receives this request, it validates the information by verifying signatures, comparing computed MAC values, and validating the names used in the ID payload. The responder then issues a response message with the following information:

- **SPI:** The SPI is a random number used to reference the specific SA.

- **IDr:** The IDr provides the responder's identity information.

- **Certificates:** The certificate provides validation of identity. This validation is provided by a third-party, trusted validation server.

- **SAr2:** The SAr2 value contains an accepted SA offer.

- **TSi:** The TSi value contains the traffic selector of the initiator.

- **TSr:** The TSr value contains the traffic selector of the responder.

Upon conclusion of the IKE_AUTH phase, the two nodes communicate over a secure tunnel. This secure IP tunnel provides data confidentiality for the duration of communications. Figure 5-46 illustrates the IPsec setup and data call flow.

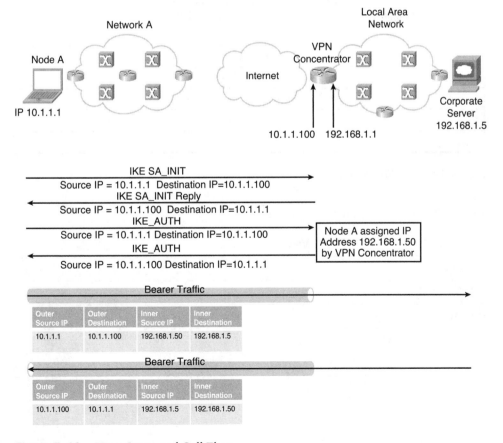

Figure 5-46 *IPsec Setup and Call Flow*

IPsec/IKEv2 Mobility Limitations   As Figure 5-46 illustrates, the IKE authentication and security association information used to build the IPsec tunnel is bound to the IP addresses of the IPsec endpoints. The IPsec tunnel is established based on the IP address in the header of the IKEv2 message requesting the IPsec SA. While the tunnel determines both source and destination endpoints, IPsec transport still relies on the hierarchical structure of the Internet for routing, and relies on the IP address to determine both the node identity and the node location. When a mobile node changes point of attachment and receives a new IP address, IPsec cannot continue normally, and rekeying of the IKE SA must occur. In some instances, rekeying is effective. However, in the majority of instances, rekeying the process is either too lengthy to ensure session continuity or requires manual intervention (such as a password).

IKEv2 Message Formats

The IKEv2 protocol uses UDP for transport. The IKEv2 packet is structured as follows:

- **IKEv2 header (HDR):** The IKEv2 header includes the initiator's and responder's SPI value, version (IKE version 2), exchange type (see Table 5-8), and a message ID (for resending lost messages). Figure 5-47 illustrates the IKEv2 HDR format.

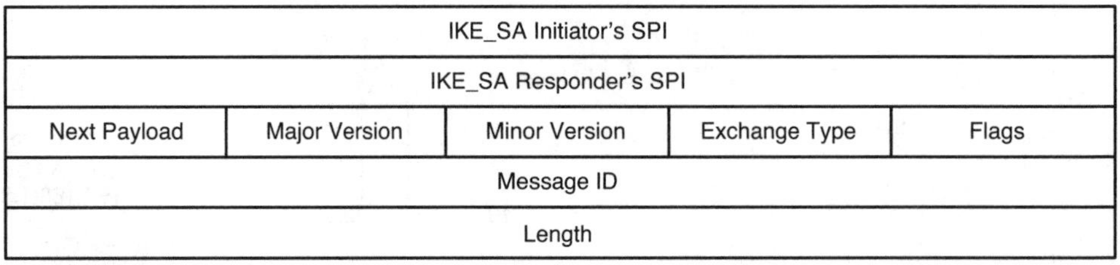

IKE_SA Initiator's SPI				
IKE_SA Responder's SPI				
Next Payload	Major Version	Minor Version	Exchange Type	Flags
Message ID				
Length				

Figure 5-47   *IKEv2 HDR Format*

Table 5-8   *IKEv2 Exchange Type Values*

Exchange Type	Value
Reserved	0–33
IKE_SA_INIT	34
IKE_AUTH	35
CREATE_CHILD_SA	36
INFORMATIONAL	37

Exchange Type	Value
Reserved to IANA	38–239
Reserved for private use	240–255

- **IKEv2 payload:** One or more payloads can be included in an IKEv2 packet. Each payload is identified by the Next Payload field in the preceding payload. Figure 5-48 illustrates a generic payload header. Table 5-9 describes the Next Payload Type field.

Next Payload	Critical	RESERVED	Payload Length

Figure 5-48 *Generic Payload Header*

Table 5-9 *Next Payload Type*

Payload Type	Value
Reserved	1–32
Security Association (SA)	33
Key Exchange (KE)	34
Identification Initiator (IDi)	35
Identification Responder (IDr)	36
Certificate (CERT)	37
Certification Request (CERTREQ)	38
Authentication (AUTH)	39
Nonce (Ni, Nr)	40
Notify (N)	41
Delete	42
Vendor ID (V)	43
Traffic Selector – Initiator (TSi)	44
Traffic Selector – Responder (TSr)	45

continues

Table 5-9 *Next Payload Type   (continued)*

Payload Type	Value
Encrypted (E)	46
Configuration (CP)	47
Extensible Authentication Protocol (EAP)	48
Reserved to IANA	49–127
Reserved for private use	128–255

MOBIKE Protocol

The MOBIKE protocol solves the mobility problem inherent in IKEv2 by decoupling the SA from the interface IP address. This allows the end node to move between two IP points of attachment, such as an office Ethernet and Wi-Fi network, and still continue the existing VPN session without rekeying. The MOBIKE protocol provides the following capability extensions to IKEv2[3]:

■ Informs the other peer about all available addresses, known as the peer address set (multihoming)

■ Determines the preferred address from the peer address set and notifies the peer to use the preferred address

■ Ensures path connectivity and detects outages

■ Notifies the other peer of address changes (mobility)

■ Notifies the other peer of changes in the available address set (multihoming)

■ Provides NAT traversal functions

To ensure that mobility is transparent to upper layers, MOBIKE only changes the outside tunnel address of the IKE SA. Figure 5-49 illustrates a mobile node moving between two points of attachment while maintaining a VPN session.

MOBIKE allows either end of the secure tunnel to have multiple IP addresses, creating M*N possible IP address to IP address combinations. The IKE initiator is responsible for determining which address pair is used for communication. In the case of mobile, especially, the initiator is in a better position to understand interface capabilities and limitations.

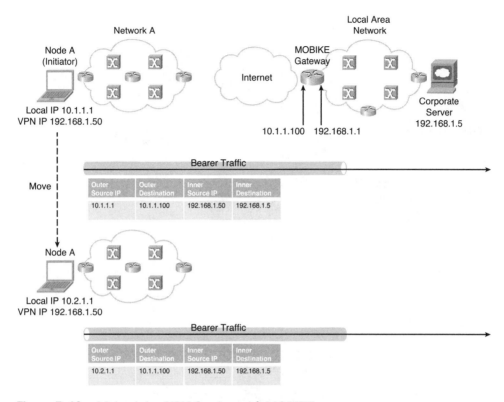

Figure 5-49   *Maintaining VPN Session with MOBIKE*

MOBIKE Call Flows

The MOBIKE call flow is similar to standard IKEv2 call flows. The IKE_INIT exchange is identical to the IKEv2 call flow; however, the IKE_AUTH exchange allows both nodes to notify the other peer that MOBIKE is supported. Either node can also include additional IP addresses with which it is associated. When the IPsec tunnel is established, the IPsec SA is based on the IP address in the IKE_SA instead of the IP header in the IKEv2 message requesting the IPsec SA. This is a key change versus the IKEv2 protocol, and it provides the separation between the SA identity and the node's location (IP address).

During data communication, MOBIKE messages notify the peer of a change in IP address. MOBIKE uses the INFORMATIONAL message to communicate the new IP address. Both the INFORMATIONAL message and all subsequent messages are sent using the new IP address. These subsequent messages are marked with an "update pending" flag until the INFORMATIONAL request is acknowledged.

Figure 5-50 illustrates this MOBIKE call flow.

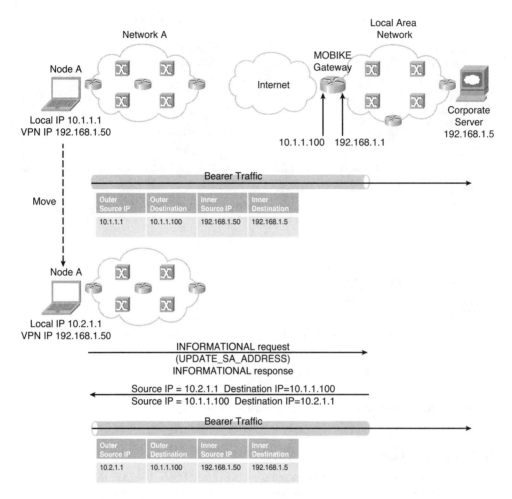

Figure 5-50   *MOBIKE Call Flow*

Connectivity Discovery

To ensure connectivity, the MOBIKE protocol relies on the IKEv2 Dead Peer Detection (DPD) mechanism. IKEv2 DPD relies on retransmit timers and windows to determine whether the IKE SA peer is no longer responding to requests. This allows the peers to determine whether the path has stopped working. MOBIKE also uses the DPD to ensure that the peer is synchronized on which address to communicate with.

While the IKEv2 DPD provides information on the existing SA between peer addresses, it does not provide insight into other available peer addresses. MOBIKE peers can use IKEv2 INFORMATIONAL message exchanges to determine whether another path works. These exchanges can be done after a failure is detected or during normal conditions.

Network Address Translation (NAT) Traversal

NAT traversal is a core function of MOBIKE. MOBIKE uses the NAT traversal functions of IKEv2; however, there are still limitations of the MOBIKE protocol when NAT devices are in the data path.

NAT detection payloads are used in MOBIKE exchanges to determine whether the address in the IP header was modified along the path. This allows both peers to learn whether there is a NAT device between the initiator and responder, and which side of the NAT device each peer is on. Figures 5-51 and 5-52 illustrate the two sides of a NAT device and the two scenarios that are possible.

Figure 5-51 illustrates a scenario where the mobile node, or the initiator, is located on the inside interface of the NAT device, and the MOBIKE gateway, or the responder, is located on the outside interface of the NAT device.

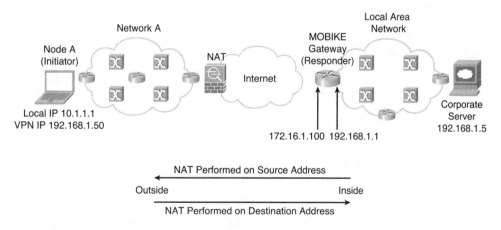

Figure 5-51   *MOBIKE NAT Scenario 1*

When a peer changes IP point of attachment, it sends an INFORMATIONAL message to the other peer, notifying it of the address change. With most NAT devices requiring that traffic is always initiated from the inside interface, these messages will get dropped by the NAT device and never reach the initiator. For this reason, MOBIKE does not support the responder changing IP point of attachment in this scenario.

Figure 5-52 illustrates an alternative scenario where the MOBIKE gateway, or the responder, is located on the inside interface of the NAT device, and the mobile node, or the initiator, is located on the outside interface of the NAT device.

Because scenarios where the mobile node, or initiator, are changing IP point of attachment are more common than cases where the MOBIKE gateway is moving, this scenario is unsupported from a MOBIKE perspective. MOBIKE peers, however, will still attempt to send INFORMATIONAL message to notify of address changes, and depending on the implementation of the NAT device, these messages can reach the SA peer.

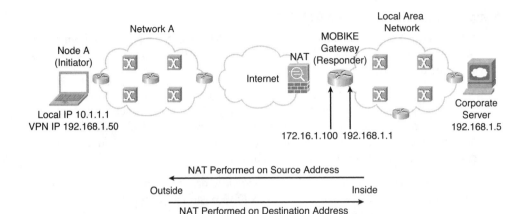

Figure 5-52   *MOBIKE NAT Scenario 2*

Authentication and Accounting

MOBIKE authentication and accounting is based on the Extensible Authentication Protocol (EAP) support inherent in IKEv2. EAP, defined in RFC 5247, provides a universal authentication framework. Rather than providing a specific authentication method, the EAP framework was designed to support both current and future authentication methods.

As discussed in Chapter 3, "Nomadicity," the three main components of the EAP framework are as follows:

- **EAP Peer:** The EAP Peer is any device that is attempting to access the network. The EAP Peer has a supplicant that allows EAP to run over a specific transport layer protocol. This transport layer protocol can be IPsec, PPP, 802.1X, or various other protocols. In MOBIKE, the initiator, or mobile node, is the EAP peer.

- **EAP Authenticator:** The EAP Authenticator is the access gateway that requires authentication prior to granting access. In MOBIKE, the EAP Authenticator is the responder, or MOBIKE gateway.

- **Authentication Server:** The Authentication Server invokes a particular EAP method for authentication, validates EAP credentials, and grants access to the network. In MOBIKE, the Authentication Server is the AAA server.

Logically, EAP authentication and connectivity are between the EAP Peer and Authentication Server. The EAP Authenticator has no specific EAP function other than to proxy EAP messages between these two points. In fact, the authentication-specific information transported in the EAP messages is encrypted, so the EAP Authenticator has a very limited role in EAP authentication. Figure 5-53 depicts the end-to-end relationship among the EAP Peer, EAP Authenticator, and Authentication Server.

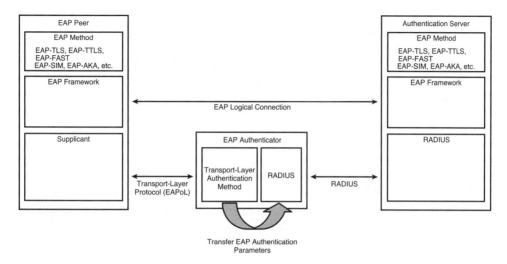

Figure 5-53   *EAP Message Communication*

During MOBIKE setup, the EAP exchange occurs as part of the IKE_AUTH exchanges, and it must be completed prior to establishing the IKE_SA. The MOBIKE gateway removes extensible authentication information from the EAP header and inserts it directly into a AAA Request (RADIUS or Diameter). The AAA server processes this information and authenticates the initiator. The MOBIKE gateway then responds to the IKE_AUTH exchange with an EAP success message. Figure 5-54 illustrates this message sequence.

After the initiator is authenticated, the IPsec SA can be established and bearer flows begin.

MOBIKE in Practice

MOBIKE is well documented in the IETF, but it has limited deployments in either an enterprise scenario or service provider scenario. Some mobile Standards Development Orgnizations (SDOs), such as 3rd Generation Partnership Project 2 (3GPP2), have chosen to implement Mobile IP (MIPv4 or MIPv6) in lieu of MOBIKE. These implementation decisions are based on a number of reasons, including the following:

- MOBIKE is more complex to implement than Mobile IP.

- Because MOBIKE uses encryption, MOBIKE headers are larger than Mobile IP headers.

- MOBIKE processing is "costly" in terms of power consumption, battery drain, and CPU utilization. Until recently, many mobile devices did not have the capabilities to encrypt/decrypt IKE.

- MOBIKE encryption has largely proved unnecessary because mobile networks implement airlink encryption and utilize dedicated backhaul circuits.

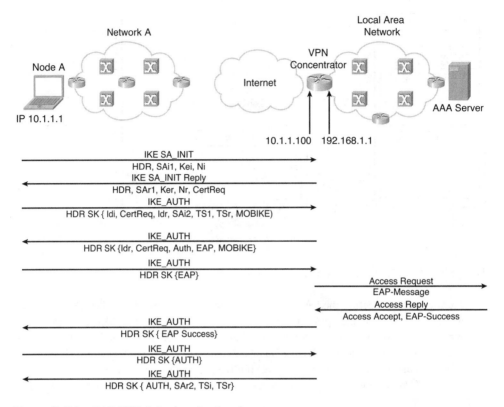

Figure 5-54   *EAP-IKEv2 Authentication Sequence*

The following section discusses specific implementations of MOBIKE relative to mobile standards organizations. This section will examine a MOBIKE example from 3rd Generation Partnership Project (3GPP) standards, in which MOBIKE is used for dual-mode voice services over Wi-Fi.

Security Architecture for Non-3GPP Access to Evolved Packet System (EPS)

Long Term Evolution (LTE) standards define 3GPP's fourth-generation (4G) high-speed packet data network. The LTE network involves the evolution of both the radio infra-structure and the mobile packet core to support scalable delivery of multiple megabits per second of service. The radio infrastructure evolution is known as the evolved UMTS Terrestrial Radio Access Network (eUTRAN), and the packet core evolution is known as the Evolved Packet Core (EPC). The total system evolution is known as the Evolved Packet System (EPS).

To facilitate access to the network and provide an offload mechanism for the eUTRAN, EPS also supports access to the network through non-3GPP radio networks, such as Wi-Fi networks. These networks are untrusted and therefore require that the mobile node's bearer traffic be delivered in a secure fashion. The security architecture for this non-3GPP access to EPS is documented in 3GPP TS 33.402. Figure 5-55 illustrates this security architecture.

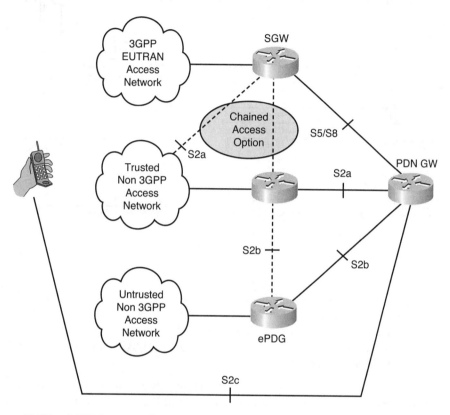

Figure 5-55   *3GPP Untrusted Access Architecture*

The architecture defines an enhanced Packet Data Gateway (ePDG) that resides between the untrusted access network and the EPC. This ePDG provides confidentiality of the mobile node identity and encryption of data flows when the mobile node is sending traffic from within the untrusted network. These functions are provided through IKEv2, with MOBIKE signaling used for mobility purposes.

Authentication of the mobile node is done through the EAP extensions to IKEv2 using Extensible Authentication Protocol–Authentication and Key Agreement (EAP-AKA). EAP-AKA, defined in RFC 4187, was developed as a secure authentication mechanism through Universal Subscriber Identity Module (USIM) for 3GPP devices connected to an IP network, such as Wi-Fi. EAP-AKA provides the same mutual-authentication capabilities as standard SIM authentication. Figure 5-56 depicts the EAP-AKA authentication mechanism with the AAA server.

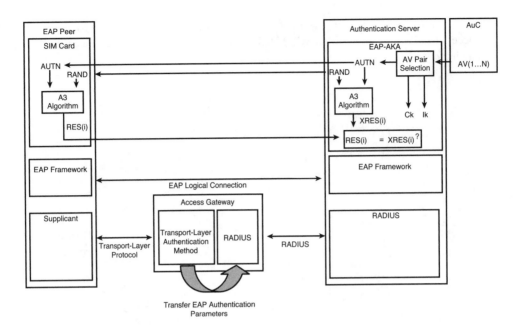

Figure 5-56   *EAP-AKA*

During mobile node authentication, the International Mobile Subscriber Identity (IMSI) is carried in the IDi payload, and the mobile Access Point Name (APN) is carried in the IDr payload. The ePDG initiates a AAA request and inserts the EAP message so that the AAA server can provide authentication and authorization services for the mobile node. Figure 5-57 illustrates the authentication flow.

When the mobile node changes point of attachment between two non-3GPP access networks, INFORMATIONAL exchanges through MOBIKE are used to notify the ePDG of the new address.

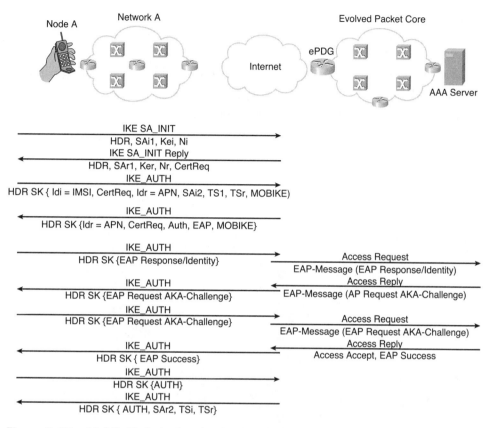

Figure 5-57 *Mobile Node Authentication in a Non-3GPP Network*

Summary

This chapter provided an overview of a number of network layer solutions for ensuring seamless mobility and session continuity. Mobile standards organizations have historically solved macro-mobility and interaccess mobility through these Layer 3 mechanisms. All these solutions are common in their approach to disassociate the IP address of the mobile node from the identity of the mobile node, and instead use the IP address only as a locator.

With capabilities to deliver network layer mobility solutions over IPv4 transport networks, IPv6 transport networks, and across domains, these technologies provide solutions for today, tomorrow, and the transition between.

Endnotes

1. RFC 3588, "The Diameter Base Protocol."

2. "Understanding IKEv2: Tutorial and Rationale for Decisions," draft-ietf-ipsec-ikev2-tutorial-01.txt.

3. RFC 4621, "Design of the MOBIKE Protocol."

Chapter 6

Transport/Session Layer Mobility

The TCP/IP transport layer sits above the network layer and is responsible for providing data transport between two end users. While the Open Systems Interconnection (OSI) model defines five classes of transport protocols depending on capabilities[1], the two most common transport protocols are Transmission Control Protocol (TCP), documented in RFC 793, and User Datagram Protocol (UDP), documented in RFC 768.

As discussed in Chapter 5, "Network Layer Mobility," when a mobile node changes point of attachment, the disassociation of the node's current IP address to that being used by a connection-oriented transport layer protocol for existing connections causes the connection to break. While this is not intended, the protocol is acting properly in tearing down the session. As a refresher, Figure 6-1 illustrates this case.

Transport layer mobility provides inherent benefits above and beyond those provided by lower-layer mobility protocols. These benefits include the following:

- **Inherent route optimization:** Lower-layer mobility protocols rely on tunnels for mobility, which, by nature, obscure the mobile node's changing point of attachment by presenting a single, persistent IP address to all corresponding nodes. A transport layer mobility approach avoids the triangular routing that occurs from handling mobility at lower layers.

- **Inherent traversal of security elements:** Lower-layer protocols, such as Mobile IP, can use topologically incorrect source IP addresses on the mobile node for transmission. This leads to many security elements, such as firewalls, impeding data transmission. A transport layer mobility approach always uses topologically correct source IP addresses and therefore does not suffer from the same problems with security mechanisms.

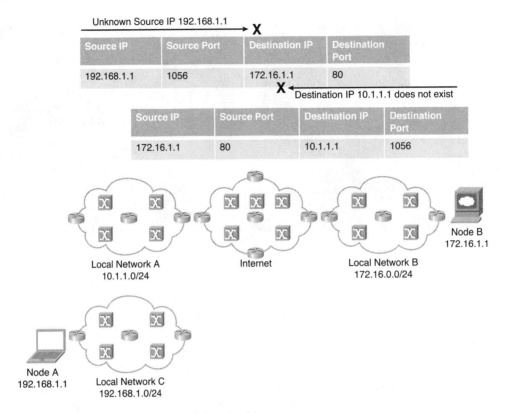

Figure 6-1   *Transport Layer Mobility Problem*

■ **Ability to pause transmissions during temporary disconnection:** When changing point of attachment, the mobile node can temporarily be unreachable while lower-layer protocols reconnect the node to the new network. Because the transport layer is aware of the mobility-induced disconnection, existing transmissions might be paused until reachability is reestablished.

■ **Ability to apply unique mobility optimization mechanisms to different flows from the same mobile node:** For a single end user, transport layer mechanisms can apply unique policies, or optimization mechanisms, based on 5-tuple information, at any point within the path from source to destination.

Lower-Layer Mobility Implications to the Transport Layer

TCP, in particular, is relevant when discussing mobility, because the protocol is connection oriented and therefore maintains flow-level information about the connection, including source and destination IP address, source and destination port number, and protocol number.

Although TCP has limited support for congestion control, TCP assumes that the end-to-end path between two end nodes remains stable. These congestion control algorithms are slow to adapt to new path characteristics, creating inefficiencies at the transport layer when the path characteristic changes are significant.

In cases where lower-layer mobility protocols mask mobility from the transport layer, nodes changing point of attachment can create abrupt changes in available bandwidth, packet loss, or path latency. Because the transport layer provides congestion control mechanisms for the Internet, transparently changing point of attachment and network connection type is problematic for proper quality controls. As mobile nodes become the standard, rather than the exception, rapidly changing path conditions will become more common. Figure 6-2 illustrates the impact to the transport layer congestion control mechanisms due to path changes.

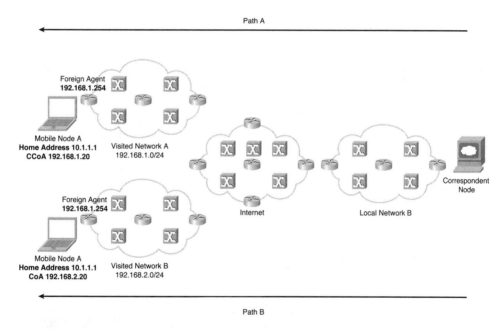

Figure 6-2   *Transport Layer Congestion Control Impact Due to Path Change*

In Figure 6-2, the mobile node is initially located on Network A with a Care-of Address (CoA) of 192.168.1.20. When a TCP connection is established between the mobile node and a correspondent node, all packets follow Path A. However, when the mobile node changes point of attachment into Network B, a forwarding disruption occurs for packets that are in transit, and Network A cannot deliver packets to the mobile node. This packet loss associated with handoff can trigger TCP backoff algorithms or other congestion control mechanisms, which, given that Network B might not be experiencing any congestion, is costly from a retransmission perspective.

Many techniques have been proposed to resolve TCP's performance over wireless networks, including the following:

■   Link layer performance improvements that allow establishment of link layer connectivity to occur rapidly, link layer retransmit techniques that hide the transmit delay from TCP, and IP multicast solutions. Figure 6-3 depicts a redirected packet stream between foreign agents during handover. This technique creates an additional layer of uncertainty because of temporary path modification.

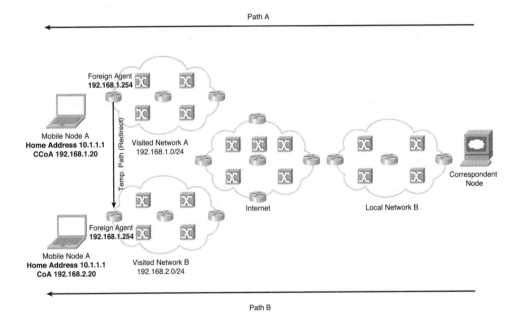

Figure 6-3   *Path Redirect During Handover*

Note   The Third Generation Partnership Project 2 (3GPP2) standards organization standardized this "horizontal tunnel" model for Evolution-Data Optimized (EV-DO) networks. The interface, called the PDSN-PDSN, or P-P, interface, provided a point-to-point (PPP) tunnel between two PDSNs involved in an intra-PDSN handoff.

■   Cross-layer enhancements that allow TCP to receive information from lower layers, such as Connectivity Change Indications (CCI)[2] or Explicit Bad State Notification (EBSN)[3], or relying on signaling from existing lower-layer messages, such as Internet Control Message Protocol (ICMP), for informing the sender about wireless failures[4].

Solving Mobility Above the Network Layer

Transport layer approaches to mobility are not entirely contained in the transport layer of the OSI stack. While the transport layer handles session persistence, location management functions are handled separately. Solving mobility above the network layer requires that the underlying layers perform their normal functions, including detecting new networks, building link layer connectivity, and obtaining network-relevant IP addresses. This might create potential problems, because Dynamic Domain Name System (DNS) and other location management approaches take significant time to update globally and converge to a mobile node's new IP address. By the time this update occurs, the mobile node might be changing point of attachment again!

The functions required to support mobility at either the transport layer or session layer are largely grouped into three key functions:

- **Reconfiguration of the host for its new network:** Protocols discussed in Chapter 1, "Introduction to "Mobility"," such as Dynamic Host Configuration Protocol (DHCP), IP auto-configuration, and router discovery mechanisms, are widely deployed techniques for accomplishing this function.

- **Ensuring reachability for new connections:** Protocols discussed in Chapter 2, "Internet "Sessions"," such as Dynamic DNS, provide sufficient capabilities for this function.

- **Updating existing connections and rebinding these connections to the new IP address:** Numerous protocols can provide this function.

This chapter will look at three techniques designed to solve the third function at the transport layer:

- **Stream Control Transmission Protocol (SCTP):** Provides a replacement for TCP, natively supports multiple addresses per host, and allows the addition or deletion of addresses from an existing association. This chapter will also discuss two proposals—cellular SCTP and mobile SCTP—designed to provide optimized handover.

- **Multipath TCP (MPTCP):** Provides extensions to the original TCP to support many of the functions defined by SCTP, without replacing TCP on the millions of end nodes already deployed.

- **MSOCKS:** Provides an architecture for transport layer mobility, a research project conducted by IBM and Carnegie Mellon University. MSOCKS relies on a proxy to provide seamless mobility of the mobile node.

In addition, this chapter also looks at two techniques to solve mobility at the session layer—the Migrate Internet Project and Session Layer Mobility (SLM). These techniques use the often-overlooked session layer to provide the same functions as transport layer mobility without modification or replacement of the transport layer protocol. This is especially interesting because most modern Internet applications do not typically use the session layer.

SCTP

The Stream Control Transmission Protocol (SCTP) was approved for standardization as IETF RFC 2960, later updated in RFC 4960. Originally designed as a specialized transport protocol in voice-signaling networks by the Signaling Transport (SIGTRAN) working group, SCTP provides a general-purpose transport layer protocol that can be used in lieu of either TCP or UDP. Any application that runs over TCP can also run on SCTP with no functionality loss.

In many ways, SCTP is similar to TCP and provides the following transport services:

■   Point-to-point connections

■   Connection-oriented services

■   Reliable delivery

■   Congestion control mechanism

■   Packet loss recovery

■   Rate adaptation

However, for all the similarities, SCTP is also significantly different than TCP[5]. Functions such as partial multistreaming and multihoming are key differentiators.

Multistreaming allows SCTP to treat each stream within a flow between two nodes independently.

Multihoming allows SCTP to provide resilience and mobility by allowing a "session" to persist across multiple IP addresses. These addresses can be communicated at session instantiation or through session updates. The IP addresses can be IPv4, IPv6, or a combination of IPv4 and IPv6. The following sections will provide detailed workings of SCTP and extensions to the native SCTP to support mobility.

Figure 6-4 illustrates the data flows between clients using SCTP.

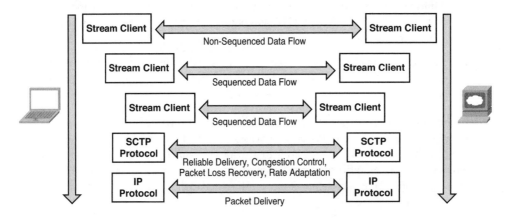

Figure 6-4   *SCTP*

SCTP Functional Overview

SCTP defines all necessary functions to establish communication, transmit data, and tear down communication. Rather than using terminology such as *session* or *connection*, which connote a communications path between two end IP addresses, SCTP creates associations that represent a logical communications path between two end nodes over multiple source or destination IP addresses. An *association* is defined as a set of IP addresses on each node (source and destination) and a port on each node. Any IP address can be used for either the source or destination IP address of data packets linked to this association. Figure 6-5 illustrates an SCTP association.

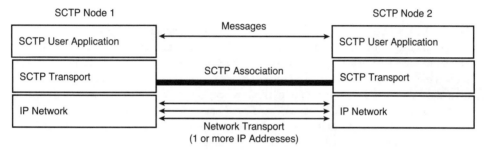

Figure 6-5   *SCTP Association*

The packets exchanged over the SCTP association are known as *chunks*. These chunks are used for both bearer and control functions. Figure 6-6 illustrates the SCTP functional architecture.

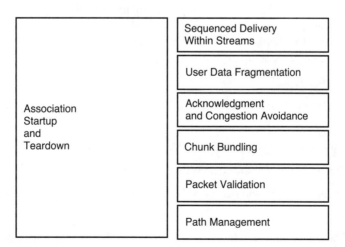

Figure 6-6   *SCTP Functional Architecture*

SCTP States

SCTP transitions through three states during the lifetime of an association. These states are initiation, data transfer, and shutdown. The sections that follow describe the SCTP states in greater detail.

Initiation

While TCP relies on a three-way handshake for session setup, SCTP uses a four-message sequence to build an association. By using a four-way handshake, SCTP avoids the common denial of service (DoS) attack known as SYN flooding.

> **Note**   A SYN flooding attack occurs when an attacker generates false TCP setup messages to a destination node. In TCP's three-way handshake mechanism, the receiver of the initial message, termed a SYN, is required to save state information and allocate resources, such as memory, for a Transmission Control Block (TCB), prior to sending a response, termed a SYN-ACK. Because the attacker has no capability to establish a session, it does not respond to this SYN-ACK message, and eventually the receiver will remove the associated TCB. However, if the attacker sends SYN messages at a rapid enough rate, the TCP server can consume all available resources responding to these false TCP setup messages. In such an overload scenario, the TCP server is unable to process legitimate TCP requests.

Figure 6-7 illustrates the four-message sequence compared to the TCP three-message sequence.

The receiver of the initial contact message, termed an *INIT chunk*, does not need to save any state information or allocate any resources. Instead it sends back its response message, an INIT-ACK chunk. Inside both the INIT and INIT-ACK chunk are a number of parameters used in the setup of the initial state:

- A list of all IP addresses that will be a part of this association

- An initial transmission sequence number (TSN) that will be used to reliably transfer data

- An initiation tag that must be included on every inbound SCTP packet

- The number of outbound streams that each side is requesting

- The number of inbound streams that each side is capable of supporting

Rather than consuming resources by building a Transmission Control Block (TCB) from the INIT sequence, the receiver builds a state cookie. The state cookie holds all the information needed by the sender of the INIT-ACK to construct its state. This state cookie is transmitted to the sender in the INIT-ACK chunk.

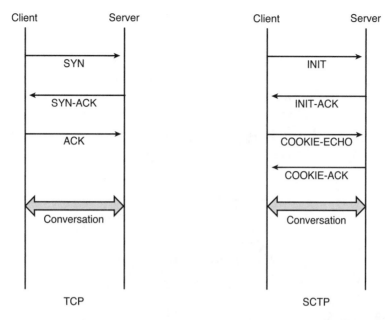

Figure 6-7   *SCTP and TCP Initiation Comparison*

In response to the INIT-ACK, the sender echoes the state cookie in a COOKIE-ECHO chunk, allowing the SCTP receiver to fully construct its state. In response to the COOK-IE-ECHO, a COOKIE-ACK message is sent that acknowledges that setup is complete.

Both chunks in the COOKIE sequence can also include data traffic, because these messages are sent after the association has been validated.

Data Transfer

TCP, unlike SCTP, relies on a single function (a sequence number) to provide perfect sequence preservation to the communicating node's transport layer. Network congestion or packet loss, however, might result in retransmission or reordering of out-of-sequence messages, either in a network node or host node. This delays the presentation of the response until proper sequencing is restored. Figure 6-8 illustrates this strict sequencing approach, denoted by the ACK value being replicated as the SYN value in a subsequent packet.

Perfect sequence preservation is not always necessary, especially for Internet sessions. While the goal is to deliver all, or virtually all, packets in a response to the requesting node, it is possible to display parts of the response while waiting for the remainder to arrive. This enables applications that rely on SCTP to achieve better perceived performance, because the end user might consume portions of information (web-page text, for example) while the remainder of the requested information arrives (web-page images, perhaps).

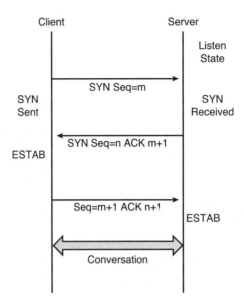

Figure 6-8   *TCP Strict Sequencing*

SCTP differentiates between ordered delivery and reliable delivery, relying on two independent functions to provide transmission and delivery functions. SCTP, instead, uses two sequence numbers:

■ Transmission sequence number (TSN) in the SCTP header ensures reliable delivery to the communicating node's transport layer. The TSN provides the transmission of packets and detection of packet loss.

■ Stream sequence number (SSN) in the SCTP packet provides per-packet sequencing to the communicating node's application layer. The SSN determines the sequence of data delivery and prioritization of buffer usage.

Data transfer in SCTP resembles TCP in many ways, including Selective Acknowledgments (SACK) and flow and congestion control algorithms. Two windows are used—the advertised receive window, which indicates the receiver's buffer occupancy, and the per-path congestion window, which is used to manage packets along the transmission path.

Multistreaming

Multistreaming enables SCTP to provide partial reordering or resequencing of a particular flow, or stream, within the SCTP "session." This allows SCTP to prioritize specific streams, such as VoIP, within a single session between two nodes, thereby eliminating latency issues that might arise because of buffer availability on either the transmitting or receiving node. Figure 6-9 illustrates how multistreaming provides more robust congestion control mechanisms.

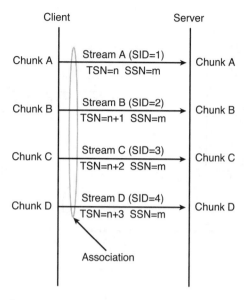

Figure 6-9 *SCTP Multistreaming*

Multihoming

Multihoming is perhaps the most recognizable feature of SCTP. Figure 6-10 illustrates SCTP multihoming from a high-level perspective.

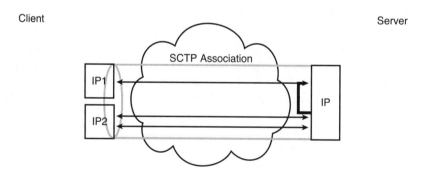

Figure 6-10 *SCTP Multihoming (High-Level)*

Multihoming enables SCTP to provide transport resiliency to failed interfaces on the host nodes, contingent upon the IP addresses in the association being reachable through mutually exclusive paths through the network. These addresses can be communicated at session instantiation or through session updates. (See the section "Dynamic Address Reconfiguration," later in this chapter.) The IP addresses can be IPv4, IPv6, or a combination of IPv4 and IPv6. Figure 6-11 illustrates a detailed view of how multihoming works.

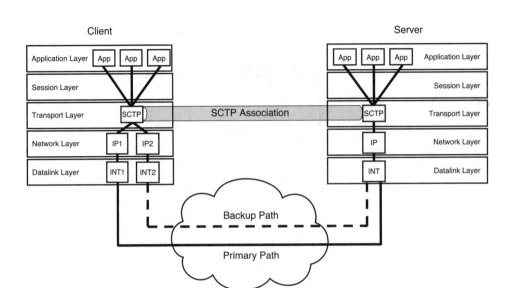

Figure 6-11   *SCTP Multihoming (Detailed View)*

Path Selection

SCTP selects a single IP address and uses this as the primary address. During normal transmission, all data chunks are sent to this primary address. If packet loss occurs, the sending node retransmits the DATA chunks using one of the alternate addresses. This improves the probability of the DATA chunk arriving at the remote node. If SCTP detects continued failures to the primary address, all DATA chunks are sent to an alternate address until reachability of the primary can be reestablished.

This reachability is established using heartbeat chunks, which are sent periodically to all idle IP addresses within an association. If no acknowledgment (ACK) is received, the particular IP address is marked inactive. Heartbeat chunks are periodically sent to inactive IP addresses to determine whether that IP address has been restored. Figure 6-12 illustrates the SCTP heartbeat mechanism.

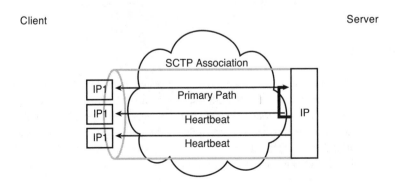

Figure 6-12   *SCTP Heartbeat Mechanism*

Shutdown

Graceful shutdown of the SCTP association is done after both nodes in an association have confirmation that the other node received all DATA chunks. TCP uses a half-open procedure, in which only one side of the TCP session acknowledges that the session has been shut down. SCTP uses a graceful shutdown procedure in which both sides of the SCTP association acknowledge that the association has been shut down. Figure 6-13 illustrates the TCP and SCTP shutdown procedures.

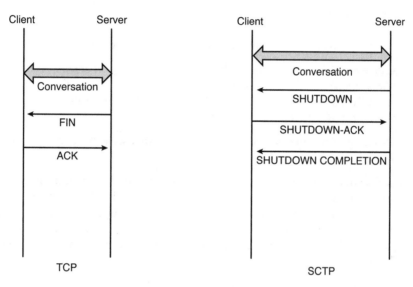

Figure 6-13   *TCP and SCTP Shutdown Procedures*

Note   In error conditions, shutdown might also be done in a nongraceful, abrupt manner. This is known as an abort procedure.

SCTP Messages

There are two types of SCTP messages—control and DATA chunks. SCTP allows bundling of these messages into a single message. This improves both transport efficiency and end-node processing of SCTP messages. Bundling is controlled by the application to ensure that retransmission of DATA chunks occurs in error cases.

Message Format

The SCTP message contains a common header followed by one or more variable-length data structures (chunks). Figure 6-14 depicts the SCTP message format.

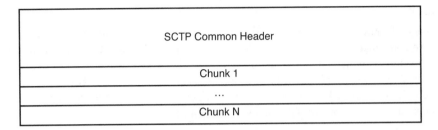

Figure 6-14   *SCTP Message Format*

The SCTP common header contains the following information:

■   **Source and destination port numbers:** These transport port addresses are used in combination with the source and destination IP addresses to identify the recipient of the SCTP packet. The port numbers allow a single IP address to support multiplexing of different SCTP associations.

■   **Checksum:** This value is used to assure data integrity while the packet transits an IP network.

■   **Verification tag:** The verification tag holds the value of the initiation tag that was first exchanged between two hosts during the four-way handshake. It must be contained in every SCTP packet that is part of an association. If a packet arrives without the correct verification tag, it is dropped. This serves as protection against old, stale packets arriving from a previous association as well as various "man-in-the-middle" attacks.

Figure 6-15 depicts the SCTP common header format.

Source Port Number	Destination Port Number
Verification Tag	
Checksum	

Figure 6-15   *SCTP Common Header Format*

Chunk Types

A chunk uses a type-length-value (TLV) format, and different chunk types are used to carry control or data information inside an SCTP packet.

Every chunk type will include TLV header information. The TLV information contains the chunk type, fragmentation and unordered delivery processing flags, and a length field. In addition, a DATA chunk will precede user payload information with the following:

■   TSN (transport sequence number)

■   Stream identifier

- SSN (stream sequence number)

- Payload protocol identifier

Figure 6-16 depicts the SCTP chunk format. Table 6-1 provides information on the type of chunks supported in SCTP.

Chunk Type	Chunk Flags	Chunk Length
Chunk Value		

Figure 6-16   *SCTP Chunk Format*

Table 6-1   *SCTP Chunk Types*

Chunk Type	Chunk Name	Chunk Function
0x00	Payload Data (DATA)	The DATA chunk is used to transmit user data between two peers in an SCTP association.
0x01	Initiation (INIT)	The INIT chunk is used to initiate an SCTP association between two endpoints.
0x02	Initiation Acknowledgment (INIT ACK)	The INIT ACK chunk is used to acknowledge the receipt of an SCTP INIT message. The endpoint sending the INIT ACK message is in the ASSOCIATE state, awaiting a COOKIE ECHO from the SCTP peer.
0x03	Selective Acknowledgment (SACK)	The SACK chunk is used to both confirm receipt of a range of chunks, denoted by the TSN, and to notify the sender of missing chunks, represented by TSN gaps.
0x04	Heartbeat Request (HEARTBEAT)	The HEARTBEAT chunk is used by an SCTP endpoint to check reachability of idle IP addresses that are part of the association. This HEARTBEAT mechanism is used to ensure that alternative paths exist in the event of a primary path failure. HEARTBEATS are exchanged between all idle IP addresses on each endpoint independently.
0x05	Heartbeat Acknowledgment (HEARTBEAT ACK)	The HEARTBEAT ACK chunk is sent in response to the HEARTBEAT message, confirming reachability.
0x06	Abort (ABORT)	The ABORT chunk is used to close an association with an SCTP peer.
0x07	Shutdown (SHUTDOWN)	The SHUTDOWN chunk is used to trigger the closing of an SCTP association.

continues

Table 6-1 *SCTP Chunk Types* *(continued)*

Chunk Type	Chunk Name	Chunk Function
0x08	Shutdown Acknowledgment (SHUTDOWN ACK)	The SHUTDOWN ACK chunk is used in response to the SHUTDOWN chunk as part of the graceful shutdown procedure.
0x09	Operation Error (ERROR)	The ERROR chunk is used to communicate some failure in the SCTP association. The ERROR chunk does not indicate a fatal failure unless it is used in conjunction with the ABORT chunk.
0x10	State Cookie (COOKIE ECHO)	The COOKIE ECHO chunk is sent in response to the INIT ACK message as part of the four-way handshake in SCTP.
0x11	Cookie Acknowledgment (COOKIE ACK)	The COOKIE ACK chunk is sent in response to the COOKIE ECHO message. This message is the fourth and final message in the SCTP initiation phase. Each SCTP endpoint has established an association with the other endpoint.
0x12	Explicit Congestion Notification Echo (ECNE)	This chunk value is reserved, but the ECNE has not been formally defined by the IETF.
0x13	Congestion Window Reduced (CWR)	This chunk value is reserved, but the CWR has not been formally defined by the IETF.
0x14	Shutdown Complete (SHUTDOWN COMPLETE)	The SHUTDOWN COMPLETE chunk is the last chunk sent and confirms that both endpoints have closed the SCTP association.

In addition to the chunk types defined in Table 6-1, SCTP also reserves chunk values for IETF-defined extensions. The following sections discuss some SCTP extensions that enable mobility.

SCTP Extensions

SCTP also allows new chunk types and parameter fields to be defined, making the protocol extensible. These extensions are maintained and managed through Internet Engineering Task Force (IETF) standards. Unlike many extensible protocols, SCTP does not permit vendor-specific extensions. One specific extension, the ADDIP extension, extends SCTP to be used as a mobility management protocol. The ADDIP extension is defined in RFC 5061, Dynamic Address Reconfiguration.

Dynamic Address Reconfiguration

As discussed earlier in this chapter, SCTP allows a multihomed device to take advantage of multiple interfaces by binding them to a single association. However, the protocol, by default, does not allow new IP addresses to be added or deleted, or for the primary address to be reset, without the Dynamic Address Reconfiguration extension defined by RFC 5061. This extension adapts SCTP from a protocol capable of providing resiliency and fault protection into one capable of providing mobility or session continuity as a node changes point of attachment.

While originally designed to provide support for hot-pluggable interfaces, the SCTP ADDIP extension maintains an SCTP association across both host and network reconfigurations. These reconfigurations can be the result of either user action, such as watching a video while a passenger in a car, or service provider action, such as IPv6 dynamic network renumbering. For these cases, the SCTP ADDIP extension allows the endpoint that has experienced a change to notify the SCTP peer of the new conditions.

The SCTP ADDIP extension consists of two new SCTP chunk types and seven new parameters. Table 6-2 provides information on the new chunk types. Figure 6-17 illustrates the ASCONF chunk format, and Figure 6-18 illustrates the ASCONF-ACK chunk format.

Table 6-2   *SCTP ADDIP Chunk Types*

Chunk Type	Chunk Name	Chunk Function
0xC1	Address Configuration Change Chunk (ASCONF)	The ASCONF chunk is used by the local endpoint to communicate an address change to an SCTP peer. This address change might be an addition or deletion of an address to a specific SCTP association, or a change of the primary address used for communication.
0x80	Address Configuration Acknowledgment (ASCONF-ACK)	The ASCONF-ACK chunk is used by a remote endpoint to acknowledge the ASCONF chunk received from a peer.

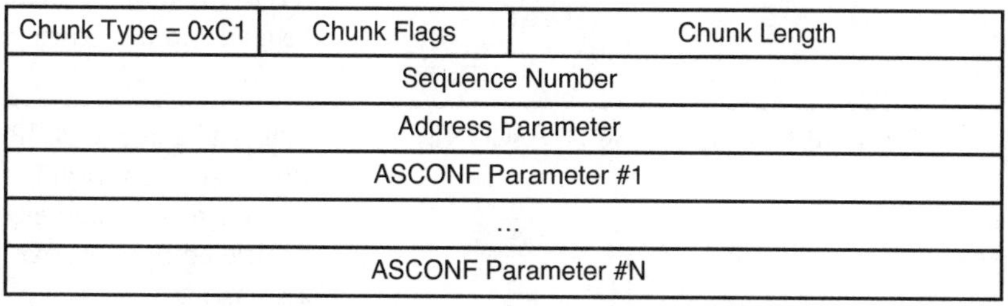

Chunk Type = 0xC1	Chunk Flags	Chunk Length
Sequence Number		
Address Parameter		
ASCONF Parameter #1		
...		
ASCONF Parameter #N		

Figure 6-17   *SCTP ASCONF Chunk Format*

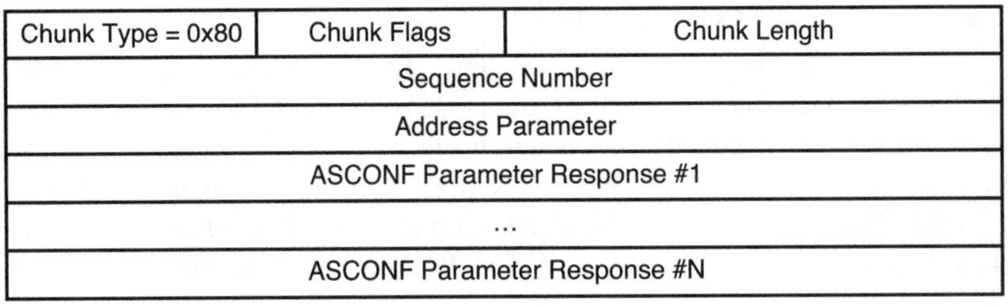

Chunk Type = 0x80	Chunk Flags	Chunk Length
Sequence Number		
Address Parameter		
ASCONF Parameter Response #1		
...		
ASCONF Parameter Response #N		

Figure 6-18 *SCTP ASCONF-ACK Chunk Format*

Table 6-3 provides information on the additional SCTP parameters defined in the ADDIP extension.

Table 6-3 *SCTP ADDIP New Parameter Types*

Parameter Type	Parameter Name	Parameter Use	Parameter Function
0xC004	Set Primary Address	SCTP INIT/INIT-ACK Chunk	This field contains an IPv4 or IPv6 address, notifying the receiver that the address is to be the primary address for sending traffic to.
0xC006	Adaptation Layer Indication	SCTP INIT/INIT-ACK Chunk	This field pertains to upper-layer protocols, such as adaptation layers that require indication to be carried in SCTP INIT/ACK.
0x8008	Supported Extensions	SCTP INIT/INIT-ACK Chunk	This field contains all the chunk types supported by the sending SCTP peer.
0xC001	Add IP Address	SCTP ASCONF	This field contains an IPv4 or IPv6 address, notifying the receiver that the address is to be added to the existing association.
0xC002	Delete IP Address	SCTP ASCONF	This field contains an IPv4 or IPv6 address, notifying the receiver that the address is to be deleted from the existing association.

Parameter Type	Parameter Name	Parameter Use	Parameter Function
0xC004	Set Primary Address	SCTP ASCONF	This field contains an IPv4 or IPv6 address, notifying the receiver that the address is to be the primary address for sending traffic to.
0xC003	Error Cause Indication	SCTP ASCONF-ACK	This field contains a cause code, identifying a standard SCTP error cause, as defined in RFC 4960.
0xC005	Success Indication	SCTP ASCONF-ACK	This field contains a success code for a specific parameter. Although, by default, if no Error Cause Indication is sent, the SCTP peer implicitly assumes success, some SCTP peers might send the Success Indication.

Mobile SCTP

Although only experimental within the IETF, the Mobile SCTP[6] variant defines a mechanism for SCTP mobility. Mobile SCTP builds on the ADDIP extension, highlighting how the SCTP protocol can be used for signaling mobility events, recommending enhancements in the mobile node, and highlighting the interaction between link layer mobility mechanisms and transport layer mobility mechanisms. While Mobile SCTP might be a promising first step, a more specified and standardized solution is required to make SCTP viable for delivering full mobility.

Multipath TCP

The Multipath TCP workgroup[7] in the IETF focuses on modifying the TCP protocol to behave in similar ways to SCTP. Most notably, multipath TCP (MPTCP) extensions allow simultaneous use of multiple paths for TCP sessions. Unlike SCTP, however, the MPTCP can provide the following benefits:

- Interworking with existing Internet infrastructure

- Stability over a wide range of existing Internet paths

- Transparency to in-path network nodes (such as Network Address Translation [NAT] devices)

Resource Pooling Principle

MPTCP operates under a resource pooling principle. The resource pooling principle allows TCP itself to use all resources, including multiple interfaces, network paths, and application servers, concurrently. As a result of this concurrent usage, the physical resources themselves appear as a single logical resource, much the same way that virtual machines and server virtualization are used today in the data center.

Numerous examples of the resource pooling principle can be seen in existing networks, including the following:

■ Link Aggregation Control Protocol (LACP), which allows multiple physical interfaces to be pooled into a single logical interface

■ Multi-Protocol Label Switching (MPLS) Traffic Engineering (MPLS-TE), which routes traffic flows across multiple physical paths in a network based on both resources required by the flow and resources available in the network

■ Virtual Local-Access Networks (VLAN), which provide virtualization and separation of broadcast domains over the same Layer 2 infrastructure

At the transport layer, however, resource pooling offers two main benefits:

■ Increased resilience by providing interface and path protection

■ Increased resource utilization by distributing TCP sessions

Figure 6-19 illustrates how resource pooling allows resilience and flexibility in traffic distribution. In the figure, source nodes send their traffic across diverse paths based on available bandwidth. The resource pooling principle demonstrates how these links are efficiently utilized.

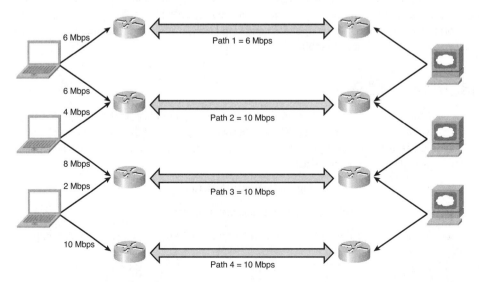

Figure 6-19   *Resource Pooling Principle Applied to Transport*

MPTCP Functional Architecture

Many of the principles on which MPTCP is based were developed as part of the Transport Next-Generation (Tng) project[8], which proposes decomposing the transport layer into application-oriented functions and network-oriented functions. Figure 6-20 illustrates this approach, creating four logical layers residing between the application and network layers.

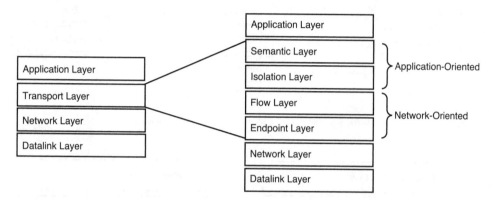

Figure 6-20   *Decomposed Transport Layer in Tng*

These logical layers are defined as follows:

- **Semantic layer:** Abstracts the communications channel from the application itself. This layer makes the communications paths, such as TCP sessions or SCTP multi-streams, available to all applications.

- **Isolation layer:** Provides end-to-end protection and reliability.

- **Flow layer:** Provides congestion control mechanisms, such as TCP windowing, and other performance management capabilities.

- **Endpoint layer:** Implements service and endpoint identification mechanisms, such as port numbers, that can be used to identify and enforce network policies.

With this model, MPTCP provides support for end-to-end, application-oriented functions while supporting in-path network nodes that intervene in segment-by-segment, network-oriented functions. Figure 6-21 illustrates this approach.

In fact, MPTCP further seeks to leverage TCP itself for the network-oriented functions, and inserts between the application and TCP layer to provide the application-oriented functions, as illustrated in Figure 6-22.

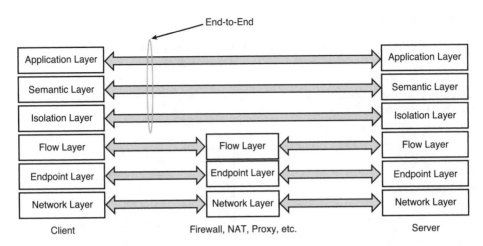

Figure 6-21   *Decomposed Transport Layer in End-to-End Model*

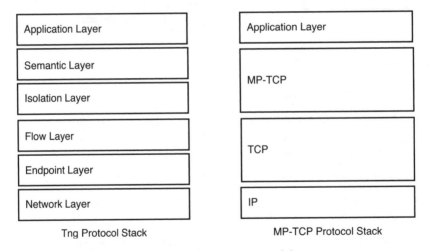

Figure 6-22   *MPTCP in the Decomposed Transport Model*

This functional decomposition of MPTCP and TCP allows MPTCP to control multiple TCP sessions independently as "subflows." MPTCP controls packet scheduling, interface selection, and path management for each individual TCP session. Figure 6-23 depicts how TCP sessions can be used as MPTCP subflows.

Similar to SCTP, MPTCP can take information from the application layer and distribute the data sequence over any number of available TCP sessions, as illustrated in Figure 6-24.

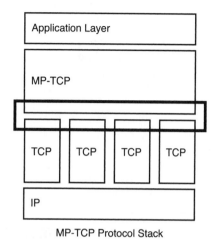

MP-TCP Protocol Stack

Figure 6-23   *MPTCP Subflows*

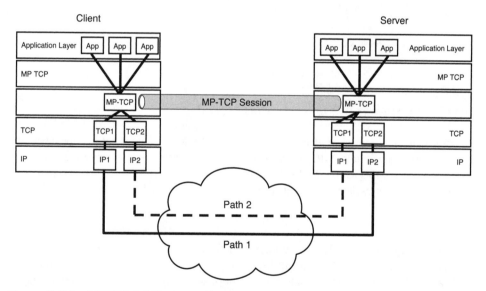

Figure 6-24   *MPTCP Subflow Distribution*

MPTCP relies on TCP options to communicate support for MPTCP in any TCP initiation sequence. MPTCP might also rely on TCP options for communicating other signaling layer information, such as availability of new addresses or reassembly information.

Path Management

Interestingly, while its name implies multiple paths, MPTCP has no way of guaranteeing disparate and unique paths through a network. While using unique interface IP addresses for each TCP session does provide some level of assurance that different paths exist, the hierarchy of the Internet might result in a single path for transport, as illustrated in Figure 6-25.

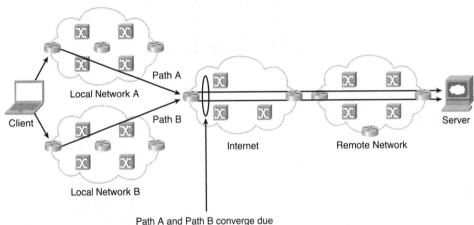

Figure 6-25   *Hierarchy of the Internet and MPTCP*

Without a mechanism of guaranteeing unique paths, MPTCP does not provide inherent path resiliency. In fact, MPTCP can only guarantee interface redundancy for ensuring reliability. For this reason, MPTCP is written as an extensible protocol that allows new methods of path selection to be incorporated and dynamic addition of new IP address pairs.

Network Layer Compatibility   While TCP is a transport layer protocol, it is closely coupled with the Internet Protocol at the network layer. This coupling allows TCP to maintain a level of awareness of the underlying network architecture itself, including the availability and utilization of either IPv4 or IPv6 for transport. MPTCP, although abstracted further from the network layer by the TCP subflows, is also capable of traversing either IPv4 or IPv6 networks. A single MPTCP session can operate over IPv4 and IPv6 networks simultaneously.

MPTCP Application Impacts

As Figures 6-21 and 6-22 illustrate, MPTCP requires support in both endpoints in a session. An MPTCP application programming interface[9] (API) is defined in the IETF to provide application developers insight into how an application can exploit the capabilities of multipath transport.

The de facto standard API for TCP is the "socket" interface. The socket interface provides transport-independent functions for setting up and tearing down sessions, data transfer, and so on. This API, in short, allows an application to use transport layer functions, including those available in both TCP and UDP.

MPTCP leverages the socket API for multihoming shim[10] to provide the application layer with access to MPTCP's path management and interface selection capabilities. Figure 6-26 illustrates how the socket API integrates into the MPTCP architecture.

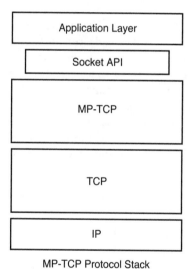

MP-TCP Protocol Stack

Figure 6-26   *Socket API in MPTCP Architecture*

MPTCP for Mobility

Given some of the inherent functions of MPTCP, including adding and deleting addresses from a session and load sharing across multiple available interfaces, MPTCP is a feasible solution for providing mobility in next-generation mobile networks. However, MPTCP suffers from many of the same concerns as other transport layer mobility mechanisms, including SCTP. To provide full mobility, MPTCP requires additional extensions and enhancements. While these enhancements do not yet exist, the Internet community and IETF working groups will undoubtedly evolve MPTCP for mobility.

MSOCKS: An Architecture for Transport Layer Mobility

MSOCKS originated as a research project at IBM's Watson Research Center. MSOCKS is largely built on the framework of SOCKS (RFC 1928), which defines a firewall traversal capability for TCP connections. The MSOCKS project creates an architecture known as Transport Layer Mobility (TLM). The TLM architecture seeks to solve a number of problems that have historically not been addressed with a common architecture. These problems are as follows:

- Providing simultaneous use of multiple interfaces on a mobile node

- Allowing the mobile node to change point of attachment

- Allowing the mobile node to determine which data flows utilize which available interface

TLM uses a proxy architecture. Proxy architectures have long been deployed in mobile networks for various functions, including delivery of Wireless Application Protocol (WAP) and video services, session-based charging, and transport optimization. An intermediate host, known as a *proxy*, is placed between the mobile node and destination server. This proxy resides directly in the communications path, mediates communication between the mobile node and server, and provides services on behalf of either. Depending on which layer the proxy functions, these services might include adaptation of HTTP traffic, transcoding/transrating of video traffic, or simply TCP session management. Figure 6-27 illustrates an architecture in which numerous proxies are deployed.

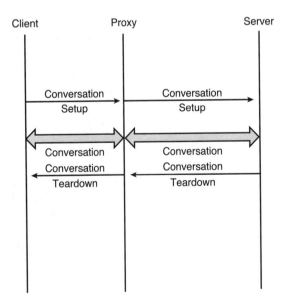

Figure 6-27   *Proxy Architecture*

Most proxies operate on a split-connection model. In this model, an end-to-end communications path between a mobile node and a server is split into two separate connections. One connection exists between the mobile node and the proxy, and another connection exists between the proxy and the server.

The TLM architecture relies on a proxy at the transport layer similar to how Mobile IP relies on a gateway at the network layer. A TLM proxy supports mobility by providing a mechanism to migrate the connection between the mobile node and the proxy to a new interface while keeping the connection between the proxy and server unchanged[11]. Figure 6-28 illustrates the TLM architecture.

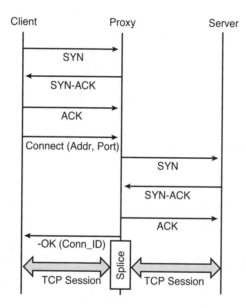

Figure 6-28   *TLM Proxy Architecture*

Like all transport layer approaches, TLM requires that the underlying layers provide IP address management functions. Upon establishing network layer connectivity, the mobile node would then request that the proxy migrate its sessions to the new interface. Figure 6-29 depicts how a TLM proxy provides mobility functions.

TLM Protocol

The TLM architecture requires an intermediate TLM proxy and modification to the mobile node TCP stack, but no modifications to either the server or the mobile node application layer. This approach allows application developers and Internet server hosts to remain unmodified. Figure 6-30 illustrates how the TLM protocol fits within the existing client and server stacks.

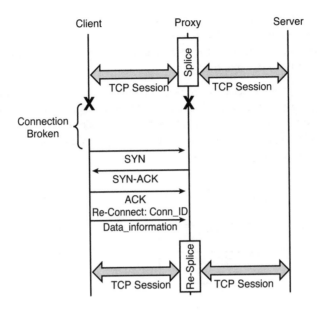

Figure 6-29   *TLM Mobility Functions*

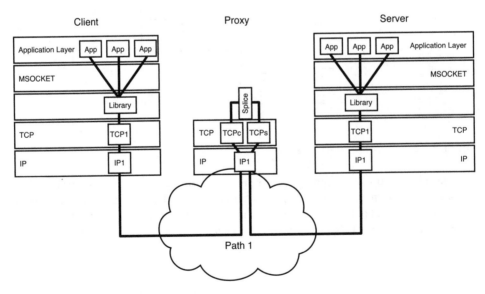

Figure 6-30   *TLM Architecture*

In addition, the TLM architecture also enables a mobile node to simultaneously use two different interfaces and control which traffic is sent over which interface. This is done by enabling multiple IP interfaces on the TLM proxy and assigning host routes, corresponding to one or more of these interfaces, on the mobile node for specific destination servers. This allows the mobile node to control not only outbound traffic but also inbound traffic. Figure 6-31 illustrates how TLM allows a mobile node to control which interface traffic uses.

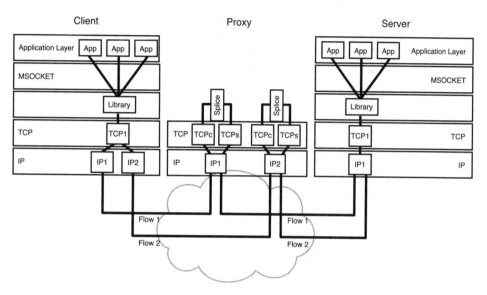

Figure 6-31   *TLM Interface Control Functions*

MSOCKS Summary

While a prototype for MSOCKS demonstrates the performance improvements and capabilities that a transport-proxy approach can deliver, TLM remains largely a research experiment, with little development in standards organizations. The most notable objection is that TLM is not well suited for interdomain, or interoperator, mobility because the proxy device is fixed, leading to triangular routing. However, the MSOCKS researchers did define a broad set of requirements for transport layer mobility that have been incorporated into both MPTCP and SCTP designs. Innovative approaches to solve mobility at the transport layer, such as MSOCKS, continue to pave the way for the viability of transport layer mobility approaches.

Other Transport Layer Mobility Approaches

Numerous other approaches to transport layer mobility have also been proposed over the last several years. Each approach has both merits and drawbacks, and certainly limited degrees of acceptance. Rather than discussing every approach to transport layer mobility, however, the following sections instead provide a few examples of transport layer mobility research projects.

Migrate Internet Project

The Migrate Internet Project[12], developed by the Massachusetts Institute of Technology (MIT) Lab for Computer Science, consists of a new session layer and TCP extensions that allow session migration. Although referred to as a session layer approach, the Migrate Internet Project is similar to TLM in that it relies on TCP options to signal and authenticate session reestablishment; however, the Migrate solution also removes the need for a proxy in the TCP flow. This, in turn, requires that both client and server are Migrate capable. Figure 6-32 illustrates the Migrate approach.

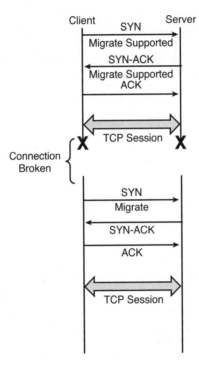

Figure 6-32   *Migrate Approach*

Migratory TCP

The Migratory TCP (M-TCP) protocol, proposed by the Discolab at Rutgers University[13], also relies on extensions to TCP to communicate and coordinate state information between clients and servers. Instead of being driven by the need to migrate an existing connection between available interfaces on a client device, M-TCP seeks to instead allow a client to move a TCP connection between two servers. Figure 6-33 illustrates M-TCP.

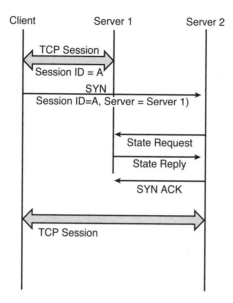

Figure 6-33   *Migratory TCP*

Session Layer Mobility Approaches

The session layer has historically been omitted from real-world implementations of data networks. Applications themselves create and use transport layer connections, rather than relying on the session layer to create them. This leads to some difficulty in using a transport layer approach to resolve mobility, because each transport layer connection that requires mobility manages itself. By placing mobility management, including the capability to monitor movement and trigger binding updates, at the session layer, these functions could be provided on a system-wide level to all overlying applications.

Providing many of the same advantages as transport layer mobility, session layer mobility has been an area of research for many years, mainly because of its simplicity. Transport layer protocols are mature and provide numerous functions. Because the session layer is mostly unutilized, adding features tends to be simpler.

SLM provides another framework for supporting end-to-end mobility on an existing Internet framework without the use of IP tunnels. SLM relies on a shim layer, called a Session Management (SM) entity, that provides connection control between the application layer and network interface. This shim layer is not significantly different from either the MPTCP architecture or the SCTP multihoming capabilities. Figure 6-34 illustrates the SM entity.

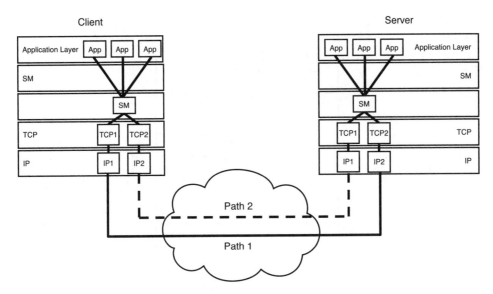

Figure 6-34   *SLM SM Entity*

Unlike the transport layer approaches discussed previously, however, the SLM session layer approach provides location management. Such a session layer might be effectively paired with a mobility-enhanced, lower-layer protocol to divide functions. A logical division of these functions would have the session layer maintaining reachability and the transport layer maintaining connections.

The SLM architecture also introduces a new network entity, called the *User Location Server (ULS)*, which is used to locate the called party and provide any address translations necessary. Any correspondent node can retrieve the mobile host's current location by querying this ULS. This functionality is similar to a home agent control plane in Mobile IP without the requirement for bearer anchoring. In addition, this functionality is similar to the Home Location Registrar (HLR) function in Global System for Mobile Communications (GSM) voice networks. Figure 6-35 illustrates the role of the ULS.

When a mobile node changes point of attachment, it sends an update to the ULS, much like the Mobile IP Binding Update message. Any protocol can be used to send this update, as long as the ULS understands the update. For example, the ULS can be an extension on existing DNS servers, and Dynamic DNS can be used to update location. Correspondent nodes learn of the ULS address for a specific mobile node either in a session setup message with the mobile node (that is, TCP options) or through a DNS query for the ULS address.

There are numerous concerns about the feasibility of this session layer approach. Most notably, this approach is not well suited for session continuity approaches because of delays in updating the ULS. In addition, the limited deployment of session layers within the current Internet architecture makes session layer approaches like SLM difficult to implement.

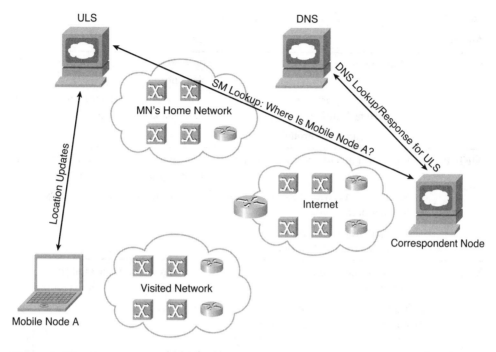

Figure 6-35   *SLM ULS*

Summary

As we continue to examine various methods of achieving mobility, the transport and session layers provide compelling advantages, including stronger alignment and integration with existing congestion control mechanisms and inherent route optimization. In fact, the majority of the mobility management capabilities provided by network layer protocols can be handled by a transport or session layer approach. These approaches, however, also have far-reaching implications. For transport layer mobility approaches, significant modifications to well-established protocols like TCP, or complete replacement of TCP with SCTP, would be required of every Internet node, mobile or fixed. At the session layer, with continued avoidance by the application development community of the session layer itself, it is highly unlikely that a session layer mobility scheme would gain significant support. Table 6-4 provides an overview of the pros and cons of each of the discussed approaches.

Table 6-4 *Transport and Session Layer Approaches to Mobility*

Approach	Pros	Cons
SCTP	Multistreaming well suited to mobile wireless networks	Poor support for in-path network elements
	Multipath support (through SCTP Concurrent Multipath Transport)	Limited known industry support for adoption and development
	Well standardized through the IETF	
MPTCP	Interworking with existing Internet infrastructure	Framework to support mobility, but no inherent mobility functions
	Stability over a wide range of existing Internet paths	Early in standardization process
	Transparency to in-path network nodes (such as NAT devices)	
MSOCKS	Interworking with existing Internet infrastructure	Proxy architecture introduces complexity
	Transparency to in-path network nodes (such as NAT devices) when not residing between source and proxy	No standardization efforts under way

Endnotes

1. H. Zimmermann. "OSI Reference Model—The ISO Model of Architecture for Open Systems Interconnection." *IEEE Transactions on Communications*, Vol. 28, No. 4, pp. 425–432: April 1980.

2. draft-schuetz-tcpm-tcp-rlci-03.

3. http://www.crhc.uiuc.edu/%7Enhv/old.papers/mobile-computing/TCP_paper.ps.

4. http://paul.rutgers.edu/%7Egsamir/research/paper.ps.

5. RFC 3286, "An Introduction to the Stream Control Transmission Protocol (SCTP)."

6. draft-riegel-tuexen-mobile-sctp-09.

7. http://tools.ietf.org/wg/mptcp/charters.

8. draft-iyengar-ford-tng-00.

9. draft-scharf-mptcp-api-00.

10. draft-ietf-shim6-multihome-shim-api-13.

11. MSOCKS: An Architecture for Transport Layer Mobility, http://ieeexplore.ieee.org/iel4/5315/14479/00662913.pdf.

12. http://nms.lcs.mit.edu/migrate.

13. http://discolab.rutgers.edu/mtcp.

Chapter 7

Application Mobility

The previous chapters have described techniques for solving the mobility problem using solutions for routing packets toward a particular device using IP identities (addresses) as endpoint identifiers. Application mobility looks to solve the mobility problem using non-IP identities as personal identifiers.

Note There might be a 1-to-1 relationship between a "personal identifier" and a particular user, an N-to-1 relationship where a particular user has multiple personal identifiers, or a 1-to-N relationship where a single personal identifier is shared among multiple users.

Solving mobility using non-IP personal identifiers allows the focus of mobility to switch from the endpoint or device toward the person. This means that we can consider a common personal identity to be associated with multiple devices, allowing application mobility use cases to include techniques for transferring contexts, including media flows, between devices. Because application mobility can solve generic cases where a common non-IP personal identifier is associated with different devices, it can also solve the trivial case where a common non-IP personal identifier is associated with different interfaces on the same devices, in effect offering a holistic approach to mobility.

This chapter will start by looking at using application mobility to solve the interdevice use case and then go on to examine any shortcomings of using the same techniques for addressing intradevice mobility.

User-Centric Mobility

Figure 7-1 shows a generic example of a user having access to three separate devices. In this example, the smartphone supports multihoming to two different access technologies: a wide-area network (for example, a cellular network) and a local-area network (for example, built using wireless LAN technology). Conversely, the cellphone and laptop can only attach to a single network, corresponding to a wide area network and a local area network, respectively. As shown, application mobility uniquely supports session mobility between different devices.

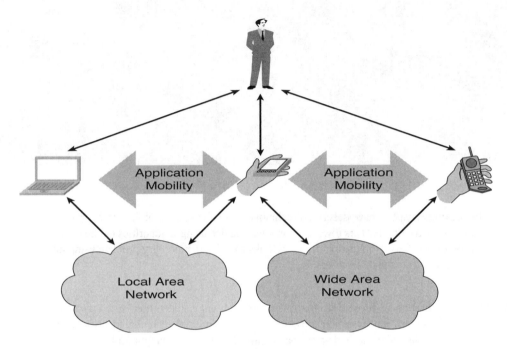

Figure 7-1   *Intradevice and Interdevice Mobility*

Schemes that support application- or user-centric mobility therefore need a common set of functions:

- **Authentication:** A user needs to be able to bind an application identity with one or more host IP addresses. Authenticating an application identity before binding to an IP address ensures that simple identity spoofing attacks are prevented.

- **Registration:** A user needs to be able to register the IP address(es) that can be used to reach a particular application identity.

- **Rendezvous service:** A correspondent node needs to be able to determine which IP address(es) is (are) bound to an application identifier.

The sections that follow describe different techniques for delivering the preceding functions as well as application mobility.

Note A consequence of solving mobility at the application layer is that unlike alternative approaches to solving mobility, the correspondent node will be fully aware of any changes to the IP address associated with a particular user. Where this IP address can be used to infer the geolocation of a user, the correspondent node might be able to track the location of a particular user, raising specific privacy issues. If the privacy of a user's location is a concern, application mobility needs to be coupled with other functionality that is able to mask a user's location.

Application Mobility Using the Domain Name System

Perhaps the most widely used application identity on the Internet is the Fully Qualified Domain Name (FQDN). RFC 1123[1] requires all Internet hosts to provide and interface to the Domain Name System (DNS), which allows all information associated with a specific FQDN to be returned to the requesting application. Because DNS implements a distributed, hierarchical database for associating FQDNs with IP addresses, the same concepts can be reused for providing application layer mobility. The DNS record includes an "A" and/or "AAAA" Resource Record (RR) type that contains the IPv4 and/or IPv6 address(es) associated with the host name (for example, cisco.com A 198.133.219.25) and a domain name pointer (PTR) RR that supports "reverse" DNS lookups, whereby a correspondent node wants to determine which FQDN is associated with an IP address (for example, 25.219.133.198.in-addr.arpa PTR www9.cisco.com).

Although the DNS was originally designed for supporting static mappings of an FQDN to a host's IP address, enhancements to the system have been defined that support dynamic updates in RFC 2136[2]. Techniques for supporting secure dynamic updates to DNS are specified in RFC 3007[3] and RFC 4034[4]. These procedures leverage DNS security, including mechanisms based on scalable Public Key Infrastructure (PKI) or secret keys, which allows DNS entities to authenticate DNS requests and responses sent between them.

When it comes to who has the authority to update the A and PTR records, a DHCP client can be given the authority to update its A Resource Record. Alternatively, the DHCP server can be responsible for updating both A and PTR RRs. Both options are specified in RFC 4702[5]. Figure 7-2 shows the signaling exchange where the DHCP client is responsible for updating its A record.

The client includes the FQDN Option 81 in its DHCP Request message, setting the S bit to 0, which indicates that the DHCP client wants to have responsibility for updating its A RR. The option also includes the client's FQDN. The exact order of the Dynamic DNS (DDNS) update is not specified, but the signaling exchange shows the update happening before the DHCP Ack is sent back to the client. The DHCP server includes the option in its DHCP Ack with the S bit set to 0, indicating that the server has agreed that the client is responsible for updating its A record. Finally, the client sends the DNS Update to complete the procedure.

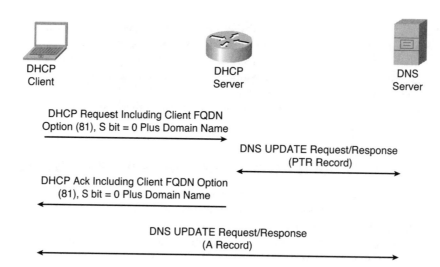

Figure 7-2   *Dynamic DNS Update Signaling by DHCP Client and Server*

Note   The DNS resource records also include a Time To Live (TTL) field. The TTL for RR updated as a result of DHCP IP address assignment should be less than the initial lease time of the IP address.

You can see how Dynamic DNS provides the three key functionalities for supporting user/application-centric mobility:

- **Authentication:** Implemented using DNS security extensions.

- **Registration:** Implemented using dynamic DNS updates to PTR and A records by hosts and/or DHCP servers.

- Rendezvous service: Implemented using the FQDN–to–IP address mapping service provided by DNS.

Applicability of DDNS to Interdevice and Intradevice Mobility

Applications will typically request information associated with a specific FQDN only once and assume this information to be static throughout the application session. Any dynamic updates to a correspondent node's resource records that are involved with an ongoing application session will cause applications to fail. Hence, DDNS-based approaches are most suited to use cases where mobility events are rare—for example, intradevice scenarios with nomadic mobility.

Interdevice mobility can also be supported if a signature that is used to authorize request updates is present in individual devices. This then ensures that dynamic update requests sent by a different host can be suitably authenticated.

Application Mobility Using the Session Initiation Protocol

Specified by IETF RFC 3261[6], the Session Initiation Protocol (SIP) is an application layer control protocol that provides signaling for the creation, termination, and modification of sessions. Perhaps the most common session type associated with SIP is the media associated with a voice call, where SIP provides the signaling for voice calls in the IP domain to enable Voice over IP (VoIP) services to be deployed.

SIP and Capabilities

SIP provides a generic session initiation framework rather than a structured method and protocol for session instantiation and control. Most frequently, the detailed session parameters are agreed between two SIP endpoints using the Session Description Protocol (SDP) that can be embedded within SIP messages, and the actual media session is transported using the Real Time Protocol (RTP).

The basic functionality established by SIP can be summarized in three broad capabilities:

- **Addressing:** SIP addressing is achieved using the SIP Uniform Resource Identifier (URI). A SIP URI has the form of sip:username@host. The username part of the URL can be a username, device name, or telephone number. The host part of the URL is either a domain name or a numeric network address, such as an IP address.

- **Registration:** SIP provides a registration service that allows one or more IP addresses to be associated with a particular SIP URI.

- **Session control:** SIP provides the ability to invite another user agent to a particular session, to modify an ongoing session, and to terminate a session.

Architecturally, SIP consists of a number of elements, as illustrated in Figure 7-3. These elements include the following:

- **SIP user agent:** SIP relies on a client-server request-response mechanism for session initiation. A User Agent Client (UAC) initiates SIP requests. A User Agent Server (UAS) responds to SIP requests.

- **SIP proxy server:** A proxy server acts as a signaling router for SIP messages. It receives a SIP message from a SIP user agent or another proxy and routes it toward its destination. The proxy server might also provide security or authentication capabilities on the local network (through a client challenge mechanism) to ensure the identity of a SIP client.

- **SIP registrar:** A registrar is a SIP component that accepts SIP user registrations. These registrations are used to establish the reachability of a SIP URI, associating it with one or more host IP addresses.

- **SIP redirect server:** A redirect server can be used to redirect a SIP client session to a new SIP URI, enabling call diversion services to be realized. Redirect servers do not proxy the message on to this new location, instead instructing the originating entity to try a new location.

- **Location server:** The location server maintains the location database for registered SIP user agents.

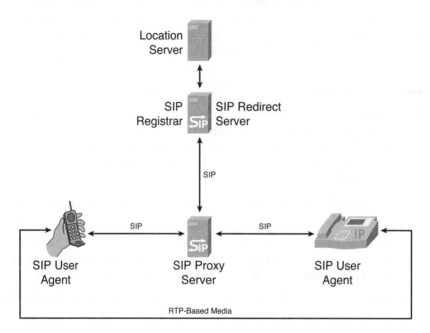

Figure 7-3   *SIP Architectural Elements*

SIP Methods

SIP defines a number of methods, which are essentially requests and responses between SIP clients (or proxy servers), termed SIP *transactions* that can be used for call control. The basic SIP RFC defines six methods:

- **REGISTER:** For registering contact information.

- **INVITE, ACK,** and **CANCEL:** For session establishment.

- **BYE:** For session termination.

- **OPTIONS:** For determining the capabilities of a SIP UA.

More methods have been defined in ancillary specifications that provide additional capabilities. The following list presents some examples of SIP extensions. A comprehensive list of SIP extensions is available in RFC 5411[7].

- **PRACK:** A method for signaling a Provisional Response ACKnowledgment (PRACK), which allows reliable information to be signaled concerning the progress of a request and is defined in RFC 3262.

- **SUBSCRIBE/NOTIFY:** Enables SIP UAs to be signaled with event notifications that can be used to convey presence information and is defined in RFC 3265.

- **UPDATE:** Allows a session to be modified and is defined in RFC 3311.

- **REFER:** Enables call transfer and is defined in RFC 3515.

- **MESSAGE:** Used for instant messaging and is defined in RFC 3428.

SIP Message Format

Having introduced SIP and its methods, the following sections provide some examples of SIP message formats and signaling flows that will be used as a foundation to understand how SIP can provide mobility services. Unlike previous voice signaling protocols, which make extensive use of Abstract Syntax Notation (ASN.1) defined Type Length Value (TLV) encoding to describe message contents, SIP is a text-based protocol similar in many respects to HTTP.

SIP Request and Status Lines

SIP request messages begin with a request line, and SIP responses begin with a status line. These lines are followed by header fields that are identical in both request and response messages.

The following is an example of a request line:

INVITE sip:charlie@example.com SIP/2.0

where:

- INVITE indicates the SIP method.

- sip:charlie@example.com is a SIP URI.

- SIP/2.0 indicates the protocol version.

The following is an example of a status line:

SIP/2.0 180 Ringing

where:

- SIP/2.0 indicates the protocol version.

- 180 provides a numerical status code of the transaction.

- Ringing provides a human-readable format of the transaction status.

Different status codes are defined and range from 100 to 699. Table 7-1 indicates how the status codes are grouped in specific numerical ranges to indicate specific meanings.

Table 7-1   *SIP Numerical Status Code Ranges and Their Meanings*

Status Code Range	Meaning
100–199	Provisional
200–299	Success
300–399	Redirection
400–499	Client error
500–599	Server error
600–699	Global failure

SIP Header Fields

RFC 3261 defines the six mandatory header fields that are included in every SIP message:

- **To:** This header field contains a destination of the transaction request in the form of a human-readable SIP URI.

- **From:** This header field contains the originator of the transaction request in the form of a human-readable SIP URI.

- **Cseq:** This header field contains a sequence number and a method name.

- **Call-ID:** This header contains a unique identifier for the SIP message exchange.

- **Max-forwards:** This header is used to avoid routing loops between SIP proxies. Every proxy that forwards the SIP message will decrement the value of this header by 1. If this value reaches 0, the message is discarded.

- **Via:** This header is used to ensure that SIP messages are routed symmetrically. In other words, a SIP proxy that handles a SIP request can use the Via header to ensure that it handles the SIP response to the transaction.

Another header field that, although not mandatory, plays a critical role in how SIP provides application mobility is the Contact header. This header field contains a SIP URI and is used to indicate how the message originator can be directly contacted—for example, avoiding subsequent SIP exchanges having to be processed by a SIP proxy.

Note   SIP also provides the capability to enforce routing of SIP messages by a SIP proxy. In such circumstances, the SIP proxy includes a Record-Route header containing the proxy's SIP URI in a request. The Record-Route header is included in the response, ensuring that both the originator and destination know that the SIP proxy is required to be included in future transactions. This is ensured by the originator including the Route header in subsequent SIP request messages containing the SIP URI of the proxy recovered from the Record-Route header field.

SIP Message Body

After the header fields in the SIP message, there is a blank line followed by the SIP message body. When SIP is used to provide VoIP services, one of the most common types of message bodies is the Session Description Protocol (SDP). SDP is specified in RFC 4566[8] and, when embedded in SIP messages, is used together with an offer/answer model[9] to allow two SIP UAs to agree on a multimedia session.

Example 7-1 shows an example of an SDP offer by Charlie and a subsequent SDP answer by Harry. The o= field gives the originator's username and IP address plus a session identifier. The c= line indicates connection data or the IP address where Charlie wants to receive the media stream(s). In this example, Charlie wants to establish two media streams and hence includes two m= lines, one describing the offered audio stream and the other the video stream. The m= lines include the port number where Charlie wants to receive the media stream (20000 for audio and 20002 for video), the audio and video codecs that Charlie's terminal supports (indicating that the terminal supports both the G.711 μ-law [corresponding to type 0] and GSM [corresponding to type 3] audio codecs and the H.261 video codec [corresponding to type 31]), and the protocol used to transport the media (in this case, RTP/UDP/IP).

Example 7-1   *SDP Session Description Offer and Answer*

```
v=0
o=Charlie 2790844767 2867892087 IN IP4 64.103.25.233
c=IN IPv4 64.103.25.233
t=0 0
m=audio 20000 RTP/AVP 0 3
a=sendrecv
m=video 20002 RTP/AVP 31

v=0
o=Harry 2345662566 236376607 IN IP4 64.103.12.167
c=IN IPv4 64.103.12.167
t=0 0
m=audio 30000 RTP/AVP 0
a=sendrecv
```

Example 7-1 also shows the SDP answer that Harry responds with. This answer indicates that Harry's terminal does not support the H.261 video codec (no m= line corresponding to video media is included in the answer) but does support the same G.711 μ-law codec included in Charlie's offer. The SDP answer then allows a common audio codec to be negotiated between Charlie and Harry, as well as the IP addresses and ports where incoming media is expected to be received by both terminals.

> **Note**   The SDP offer/answer shown in Example 7-1 includes other lines:
>
> ■   The v= line is used to indicate which version of SDP is being used.
>
> ■   The t= line is used to indicate the start and stop times for the media session. In this instance, t=0, where 0 is used to indicate that the session is supposed to be initiated immediately.
>
> ■   The a= line is termed an attribute line and is used to extend SDP. In the example shown, this line is used to indicate that the negotiated media is bidirectional.

Basic SIP Mobility

You have already seen how applications require three fundamental services to be delivered to provide mobility: registration, authentication, and rendezvous. Here we see examples of how SIP delivers all three services.

SIP Registration

Charlie powers on his mobile phone that performs a SIP registration. Figure 7-4 shows the message flow with the Registrar responding with a 200 (OK), indicating successful registration.

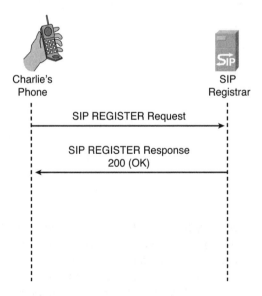

Figure 7-4   *SIP Registration Signaling*

The detailed REGISTER request message is shown in Example 7-2, with the key lines/fields explained in the list that follows.

Example 7-2   *SIP REGISTER Message*

```
REGISTER sip:example.com SIP/2.0
To: Charlie <sip:charlie@example.com>
From: Charlie <sip:charlie@example.com>; tag=a73kszlfl
Call-ID: 1j9FpLxk3uxtm8tn@example.com
Cseq: 1 REGISTER
Max-Forwards: 70
Via: SIP/2.0/UDP 64.103.25.233:5060;branch=z9hG4bKnashds7
Contact: <sip:64.103.25.233>
Content-Length: 0
```

- The request line shows the SIP method as well as the SIP URI identifying the location service for example.com.

- The To header field contains the SIP URI identifying the record whose registration status is being created.

- The From header field contains the SIP URI of the person creating the registration—in this case, Charlie.

- The Call-ID header field contains a fixed value used in all registrations.

- The CSeq (Command Sequence) header field contains an integer sequence number and the method name—in this case, REGISTER. Requests within a dialog are identified by a monotonically increasing sequence number. A SIP dialog is typically established with an INVITE/200 OK transaction and terminated with a BYE/200 OK transaction.

- The Contact header field contains the address that is requested to be bound to the registration, corresponding to a direct route by which Charlie can be contacted. It can be of the form username at a Fully Qualified Domain Name (FQDN) or, as in this case, an IP address.

The preceding description describes a single registration transaction. Of course, SIP also allows Charlie to register different contact information—for example, associating his SIP URI with the IP address of his mobile phone as well as the IP address of his softphone PC client.

SIP Authentication

You know that application mobility requires authentication services to be provided. SIP provides a challenge-response-based mechanism for authentication that is based on authentication in HTTP[10] and is known as *Digest authentication*. Authentication is typically used between a SIP UA and a SIP proxy or registrar server, whereby the server requires each SIP UA to authenticate itself prior to the server processing the method. In general, the registration procedure should always be authenticated to avoid malicious users from registering false contact information for a particular SIP URI.

Figure 7-5 shows an example signaling exchange when a SIP UA wants to register its location with a SIP registrar.

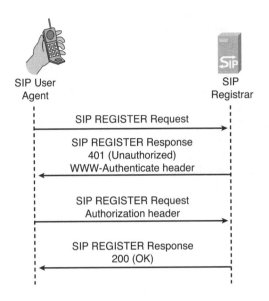

Figure 7-5 *SIP Digest Authentication*

In this example, the SIP registrar is responsible for authenticating the user and responds to the registration request with a 401 Unauthorized response. This message includes a WWW-Authenticate header, which includes realm information, at least one challenge including authentication scheme(s) supported, and an indication as to whether the server supports both authentication and integrity protection.

After the SIP UA receives the 401 response to its SIP REGISTER Request message, it reoriginates the SIP REGISTER Request, but this time includes proper credentials in an Authorization header field in the request. The Authorization header includes the user's name in the specified realm and the response to the WWW-Authenticate challenge.

Note   SIP systems can be architected to be stateless. In such scenarios, SIP authentication might be required to protect registration (SIP REGISTER method), session setup (SIP INVITE method), session modification (SIP UPDATE method), and session terminations (SIP BYE method).

Alternatively, SIP systems can be architected to be stateful. In such scenarios, SIP authentication is typically applied only to protect SIP registration. The IP Multimedia Subsystem (IMS) is one example of a stateful SIP system that has been defined by the Third Generation Partnership Project (http://www.3gpp.org) and uses SIP authentication to protect registration procedures[11,12].

SIP Rendezvous Service

The SIP proxy provides the basic rendezvous service for realizing SIP mobility. Figure 7-6 illustrates the use of the INVITE method for initiating a session, as well as the use of the SDP offer/answer exchange.

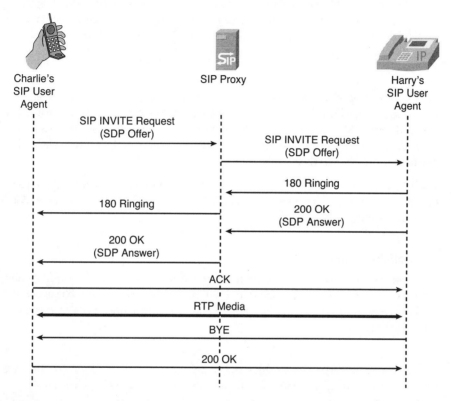

Figure 7-6   *Session Initiation and Termination*

Charlie sends an INVITE request to Harry's SIP URI (sip:harry@example.com). The INVITE also includes the SDP offer from Charlie's SIP user agent. The SIP message is routed to the proxy at example.com, which consults the location server to determine the current contact details associated with Harry's SIP URI. The proxy then relays the INVITE request to Harry at his current location.

In this example, Harry responds with the provisional response "180 Ringing" to the INVITE request. Harry can also include his IP address in the SIP URI included in the contact information of the provisional message, which allows subsequent messages to be exchanged directly between Charlie's and Harry's SIP UAs (assuming that the proxy has not requested to be included in future transactions by inserting a Record-Route header in the original INVITE request). Eventually, Harry answers his phone and the SIP UA ends the INVITE transaction by sending the 200 OK message, which in this example, includes the SDP Answer indicating that the media description has been successfully negotiated between the two endpoints.

> **Note** While Figure 7-6 shows the SDP answer being included in the 200 OK message, other options are possible, including the SDP answer being sent with the "180 Ringing" provisional response, which is used to establish "early media" between two endpoints. For example, if the terminating endpoint is a VoIP gateway, such early media can be used to send ringing tones back toward the originating endpoint.

The establishment of the SIP session is completed by Charlie's SIP UA sending an ACK request message, which does not have a response associated with it. Notice that Charlie has used Harry's SIP URI received in the contact field of the SIP response message to allow Charlie and Harry to send subsequent SIP messages directly between each other. The negotiated media is then established.

Finally, Figure 7-6 shows Harry ending the conversation by sending a SIP BYE request directly to Charlie, who responds with a 200 OK response indicating that the session has been successfully terminated.

SIP UA Mobility Example

Using the previously described functionality, you can now see how a basic SIP mobility service can be realized. If the mobility event occurs prior to session establishment, the SIP UA is responsible for registering any newly obtained IP address prior to session establishment.

> **Note** From a client perspective, there needs to be an application programming interface (API) by which the SIP application can determine that the IP address has changed (for example, by repeatedly performing a query/response exchange using a "getLocalIpAddress()" function call).

The more complicated use case is to accommodate SIP mobility during an already established session. Figure 7-7 illustrates the signaling exchanges for supporting SIP mobility when a session has already been established when Charlie's SIP UA was connected to network 1. In addition, this example highlights the case where the SIP proxy wants to enforce the routing of SIP messages by inserting a Record-Route header in the original INVITE and in particular where such a proxy requires a SIP UA to perform a SIP registration prior to the SIP server providing proxy services. Such operations might be particularly important in mobility scenarios to prevent unauthorized SIP UAs from hijacking the media stream.

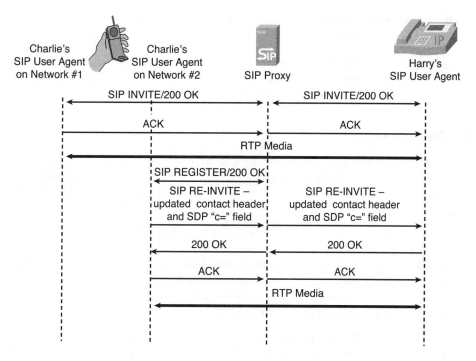

Figure 7-7   *Basic SIP Mobility*

After the media session has been established, Charlie's terminal switches IP Point of Attachment, for example, by switching from a cellular network to a wireless LAN. APIs between the OS and SIP application are assumed to be able to indicate the allocation of a new IP address, which in this case causes the SIP UA to register its new IP address with the SIP registrar prior to sending a RE-INVITE request message to Harry's SIP URI. This RE-INVITE message contains the same Call-ID used in establishing the original session, but the original Contact header and SDP c= field are replaced with values corresponding to the newly acquired IP address on network 2.

The overall performance of SIP-based mobility is impacted by several serial processes:

■ **New IP address acquisition:** The actual acquisition of a new IP address might require Layer 2 access authentication, involving multiple round trips between the host and the EAP server as well as DHCP operation.

■ **Application indication of IP address change:** The SIP application needs to detect the change of IP Point of Attachment, for example, by repeatedly polling an OS function call for any change.

■ **SIP registration delay:** Authenticated SIP registrations require multiple round trips between the SIP UA and registrar.

■ **SIP signaling delay:** The SIP RE-INVITE/200 OK signaling exchange needs to be completed between the two SIP UAs.

■   **Media updating delay:** The media needs to be updated with the newly negotiated session description.

Simulations of handover performance[13] indicate that with a wireless link delay of about 50 ms and an IP delay between SIP UAs of about 75 ms, the media interruption with a SIP-based application handover can exceed 0.8 seconds!

SIP Session Mobility

The previous analysis of mobility solutions has been very device-centric. While such approaches might be applicable when the penetration of devices is low, as technology advances, Chapter 1, "Introduction to 'Mobility'," has described a future where the number of simultaneous devices associated with a single user is set to increase.

With the Cisco Internet Business Solutions Group (IBSG) predicting that by 2010 there will be 35 billion devices connected to the Internet[14] (or nearly six devices per person on the planet), one logical consequence is that the future support of mobility must move from the device-centric view of the past (where a user is defined by a single device) toward a user-centric view of the future (where a user has a plethora of devices on which to participate in sessions and consume media).

Application mobility is unique in its capability to support interdevice mobility, allowing users to maintain service continuity even when changing the physical device on which the service is consumed. A user might initiate a session on a PC that includes video and audio components but partway through the session, might decide to leave the room in which the PC is located. Instead of terminating and reoriginating the session on a mobile device, SIP-based session mobility allows the transfer of the audio session directly from the PC to the mobile device. Two alternative approaches for realizing session transfer are as follows:

■   SIP REFER[15]

■   Third-Party Call Control (3PCC)[16]

SIP REFER-Based Session Mobility

The REFER method is a SIP extension request that causes the recipient of the request to REFER to a resource provided in the request and for the originator of the request to be subsequently informed of the outcome. The SIP REFER method can be used for realizing a call transfer service.

Figure 7-8 illustrates the signaling sequence for performing the SIP REFER-based session transfer described previously.

Charlie has an established session with Harry using his SIP UA on his PC, using the SIP URI sip:charlie@pc.example.com. Charlie decides to transfer the session to his mobile phone and so sends a SIP REFER request to Harry's SIP UA, providing the contact information for Charlie's mobile phone in a Refer-To header field:

Refer-To: sip:charlie@mobile.example.com

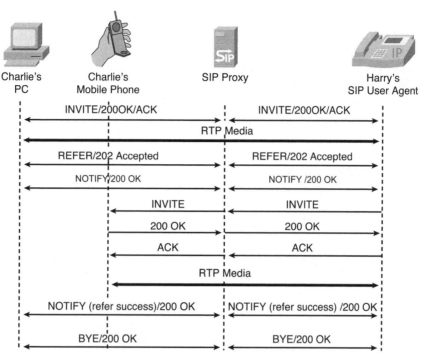

Charlie's PC	Charlie's Mobile Phone	SIP Proxy	Harry's SIP User Agent

Figure 7-8   *Successful SIP REFER-Based Session Transfer, BYE Sent by Originator*

Assuming that Harry has authorized call transfer operations, Harry's SIP UA will signal its acceptance of the call transfer request by sending a 202/Accepted response back to Charlie's PC. Accepting the REFER request implicitly establishes a subscription to the refer event packages so as to allow the recipient (in this case, Harry's SIP UA) to send notifications on updates to the status of the refer to the requesting SIP UA (in this case, Charlie's PC).

Note   Normal subscription to events is triggered by a SIP SUBSCRIBE request, allowing entities in the network to subscribe to notifications of state changes, for example, related to registration or call state[17].

The implicit creation of the subscription causes an immediate NOTIFY request to be sent from Harry's SIP UA toward Charlie's PC, indicating that the Refer Event package is active; this is acknowledged with a 200 OK. Harry's SIP UA then contacts the resource identified by the URI in the Refer-To header field, in this example, corresponding to Charlie's mobile device. The normal INVITE/200 OK/ACK exchange is used to establish the new session. Harry then signals the completion of the call transfer by sending a NOTIFY request that terminates the implicit subscription to the REFER event package. Now that the session has been established between Harry and Charlie's mobile device, Charlie's PC can then end its session and the call transfer is completed.

3PCC-Based Basic Session Mobility

In 3PCC-based session mobility, a SIP Back-to-Back User Agent (B2BUA) is included in the architecture. As its name suggest, a B2BUA divides the SIP signaling between two SIP UAs into two separate call legs and maintains complete state of the session. Dividing the signaling into different call legs allows the B2BUA to perform types of SIP signaling manipulation that are forbidden for normal SIP proxy servers.

When supporting mobility, the B2BUA is used to mask most of the details of session mobility from the correspondent node. The B2BUA remains in the signaling path between all SIP UAs involved in the session and is used to present a single multimedia session toward the remote party, even though there might be more than one SIP UA communicating with the remote party. Figure 7-9 shows an example of 3PCC-based SIP mobility.

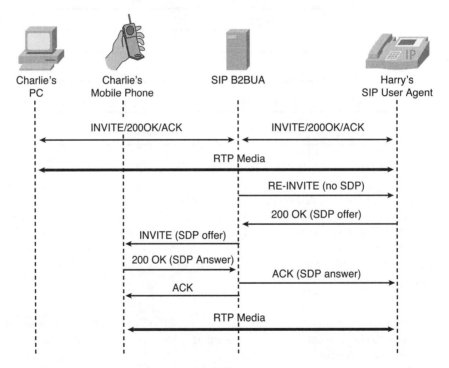

Figure 7-9   *SIP 3PCC-Based Session Mobility*

The B2BUA has established a session between Charlie's PC and Harry's IP phone using two separate SIP dialogs. The B2BUA can trigger a transfer of the session from Charlie's PC to Charlie's mobile phone by sending a re-INVITE to Harry's IP phone, with no SDP offered. Harry's SIP UA makes an SDP offer in the 200 OK message that the B2BUA then recovers and includes in an INVITE sent to Charlie's mobile device. The SDP answer from Charlie's mobile device is included in the 200 OK, and the B2BUA then takes this answer and includes it in the ACK sent back to Harry's IP phone. Finally, the B2BUA ACKs the 200 OK sent by Charlie's mobile device and the media can continue.

Note   Conceptually, the use of the SIP B2BUA for handling mobility and masking the details of session mobility from a correspondent node can be likened to the use of proxies in other alternative approaches to providing mobility.

3PCC-Based Enhanced Session Mobility

3GPP has defined an enhanced 3PCC session mobility architecture, termed *Session Continuity*[18]. This architecture defines specific roles for SIP UAs, defining a controller SIP UA role and a controllee SIP UA role. The functionality of the controller SIP UA is augmented with additional functionality for the following:

- The discovery of controllee SIP UAs

- The initiation of interdevice session transfer procedures

- 3PCC control of the media flows to/from the controllee SIP UA—for example, the ability to add, modify, and release media on the controllee SIP UA

Note   The controller SIP UA might even have no local media, in which case it acts purely as a SIP mobility management entity, remotely controlling the transfer of media sessions between one or more controllee SIP UAs.

A controller SIP UA uses the SIP SUBSCRIBE methods to discover the registration status of controllee SIP UAs by subscribing to the Registration events (reg-event) package[19]. This will trigger the SIP REGISTRAR to send a SIP NOTIFY message when the registration state of the subscribed-to SIP UA changes. After a controller UA has discovered a controllee UA, it can additionally send a SIP OPTIONS request to it to query the controllee SIP UA about its capabilities.

Note   The SIP OPTION method is a generic way for a SIP UA to discover the capabilities of another SIP UA or proxy—for example, discovering whether a UA supports a particular SIP method defined by a SIP extension, or whether a UA supports a particular codec type without having to send an INVITE to the other party.

The 3PCC session mobility architecture defined by 3GPP allows the multiple controllee UAs to be involved in a "collaborative session." In particular, a multimedia session might involve multiple devices, and the controller UA is responsible for combining the services delivered using individual devices into a collaborative session. Figure 7-10 illustrates one example of a collaborative session.

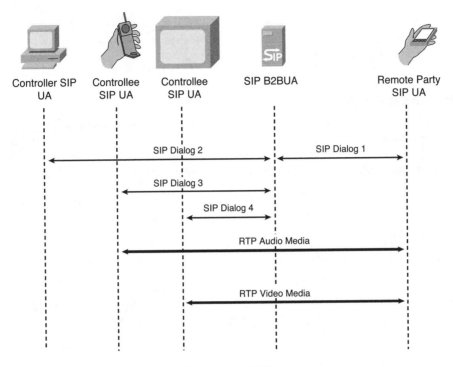

Figure 7-10   *Enhanced 3GPP-Based Session Mobility*

A B2BUA has a SIP dialog (dialog 1) with a remote party SIP UA and a SIP dialog (dialog 2) with a controller UA. This SIP UA provides the overall management of the collaborative session. In this example, the controller UA has triggered the establishment of two media sessions between two controllee UAs. The B2BUA uses SIP dialog 3 to establish audio media between the remote party UA and the handset SIP UA and uses SIP dialog 4 to establish video media between the remote party UA and the video screen–based SIP UA. The signaling to individual controllee UAs is combined by the B2BUA and presented to the remote party as a single standard SIP-based multimedia session.

Although Figure 7-10 shows a simple collaborative session, the same basic 3PCC-based mobility techniques can be used; however, these now enable mobility for individual media legs. For example, a user might decide when he changes from a SIP UA in a PC environment to a mobile phone–based SIP UA to dynamically update the media session so that the video session is terminated, but the audio session continues uninterrupted.

Other Application Aspects for Supporting Mobility

The previous examples of SIP and DDNS have described how three core functionalities required for supporting application mobility (namely, authentication, registration, and rendezvous) can be used to realize mobile functionality. While not all applications are suitable for providing such services, there are other aspects of application definition that can assist in mobilizing certain applications. In particular, how the application specification deals with asynchronous changes of IP addresses can lead to considerable improvements to the user experience when mobility events cause a host to change subnet.

One clear example of how application specification can assist in mobility is the Hypertext Transfer Protocol/HTTP 1.1, as specified in RFC 2616[20]. Importantly from a mobility perspective, HTTP 1.1 defines the client behavior when a transport connection is asynchronously closed. Whereas the HTTP 1.1 protocol designers foresaw example use cases corresponding to servers closing an "idle" connection after a client's request was in progress, the same characteristics can be attributed to the client moving subnets and receiving a new host IP address. RFC 2616 specifies that HTTP 1.1 clients and server must be able to recover from the asynchronous closing of an HTTP 1.1 connection. Client software should reopen the transport connection (reestablish the communication socket, for example using a newly allocated IP address) and retransmit the aborted sequence of requests.

Whereas such functionality does not allow sessions to be transferred between hosts, it does represent a foundation for ensuring that the impact on user experience is limited when applications are forced to operate in environments with changing IP addresses.

Note   Other applications support mobility by remaining oblivious to mobility itself. These applications ignore any changes to the protocols underneath the application layer and remain unaware of any topologically relevant attachment point. This application class grew largely because lower layers did not support such mobility capabilities. Rather than relying on a binding between an application and TCP port, or TCP port and IP address, these applications use "tokens" within the application layer header that are used to identify both the identity and the session.

While mobility protocols themselves rely on maintaining individual connections or sessions, either at the IP layer or TCP layer, these applications do not depend or rely on any level of continuity. Instead, the application itself closes and opens TCP connections as needed to ensure that user data flows continue seamlessly. In fact, these applications do not even distinguish between a loss of connection and change of IP address.

Video streamers are one example of this application class.

Summary

This chapter has introduced the key aspects of providing mobility at the application layer. Unlike other techniques described in this book, providing mobility at the application layer allows decoupling mobile operations from a particular device, allowing multi-device mobility use cases to be supported. As the number of devices that consumers have access to continues to increase, mobility functionality will increasingly have to accommodate a more subscriber-centric view rather than today's view of mobility as a device-centric function.

Starting with examining core functionality required for application mobility, key examples related to providing mobility using DDNS and SIP have been described. Examples have been provided that highlight how application mobility can provide mobility functionality for a single device, although the application quality of experience can be significantly impacted. Such single-device restrictions are not apparent when application mobility is used in a multidevice configuration, and sessions can be switched between devices to allow new mobility applications and use cases to be realized.

Endnotes

1. RFC 1123, "Requirements for Internet Hosts—Applications and Support," R. Braden, Oct. 1989.

2. RFC 2136, "Dynamic Updates in the Domain Name System (DNS UPDATE)," P. Vixie, S. Thomson, Y. Rekhter, and J. Bound, April 1997.

3. RFC 3007, "Secure Domain Name System (DNS) Dynamic Update," B. Wellington, Nov. 2000.

4. RFC 4034, "Resource Records for the DNS Security Extensions," R. Arends, et. al., March 2005.

5. RFC 4702, "The Dynamic Host Configuration Protocol (DHCP) Client Fully Qualified Domain Name (FQDN) Option," M. Stapp, B. Volz, and Y. Rekhter, Oct. 2006.

6. RFC 3261, "SIP: Session Initiation Protocol," J. Rosenberg, et. al., June 2002.

7. RFC 5411, "A Hitchhiker's Guide to the Session Initiation Protocol (SIP)," J. Rosenberg, Feb. 2009.

8. RFC 4566, "SDP: Session Description Protocol," M. Handley, V. Jacobson, and C. Perkins, July 2006.

9. RFC 3264, "An Offer/Answer Model with Session Description Protocol (SDP)," J. Rosenberg and H. Schulzrinne, June 2002.

10. RFC 2617, "HTTP Authentication: Basic and Digest Access Authentication," J. Franks, et. al., June 1999.

11. 3GPP TS 24.229, "IP multimedia call control protocol based on Session Initiation Protocol (SIP) and Session Description Protocol (SDP); Stage 3," http://www.3gpp.org/ftp/Specs/html-info/24229.htm.

12. 3GPP TS 33.203, "3G Security; Access security for IP-based services," http://www.3gpp.org/ftp/specs/html-info/33203.htm.

13. C. Politis, K.A. Chew, and R. Tafazoli, "Multiplayer Mobility Management for All-IP Networks: Pure SIP vs. Hybrid SIP/Mobile IP," IEEE Veh. Tech. Conf., 2003.

14. D. Evans, "Top 25 Technology Predictions," Cisco IBSG, 2009, https://www.cisco.com/web/about/ac79/docs/Top_25_Predictions_121409rev.pdf.

15. RFC 3515, "The Session Initiation Protocol (SIP) Refer Method," R. Sparks, April 2003.

16. RFC 3725, "Best Current Practices for Third Party Call Control (3pcc) in the Session Initiation Protocol (SIP)," J. Rosenberg, et. al., April 2004.

17. RFC 3265, "Session Initiation Protocol (SIP)—Specific Event Notification," A.B. Roach, June 2002.

18. 3GPP TS 23.237, "IP Multimedia Subsystem (IMS) Service Continuity, Stage 2," http://www.3gpp.org/ftp/specs/html-info/23237.htm.

19. RFC 3680, "A Session Initiation Protocol (SIP) Event Package for Registration," J. Rosenberg, March 2004.

20. RFC 2616, "Hypertext Transfer Protocol—HTTP 1.1," R. Fielding, et. al., June 1999.

Chapter 8

Locator-Identifier Separation

Chapter 2 discussed the Internet protocol stack and in particular the fact that the IP address functions simultaneously as a Routing Locator (which is an identifier with a topological meaning) and as an Endpoint Identifier. Figure 8-1 illustrates this dual role. In retrospect, this can be seen as a design mistake, especially in the light of mobility.

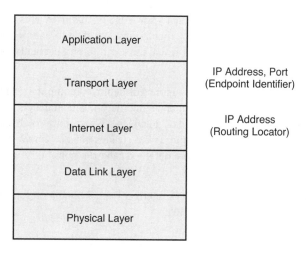

Application Layer	
Transport Layer	IP Address, Port (Endpoint Identifier)
Internet Layer	IP Address (Routing Locator)
Data Link Layer	
Physical Layer	

Figure 8-1 *Layers of the Internet Architecture*

When a host changes its point of attachment to the Internet, its IP address must change as well, and therefore all transport sessions will break. The previous chapters took the design of the Internet stack as a given and presented various ways of working around the problems that this causes for mobility.

This chapter covers a few more fundamental approaches to mobility that do not shy away from redesigning the Internet protocol stack. These proposals share a common approach to separating Routing Locators and Endpoint Identifiers to wean all identification-related functions away from topology-dependent information (such as IP addresses), whereas the solutions presented in the earlier chapters adopt a protocol stack that includes IP as the communication endpoint.

This common approach of separating the Routing Locator and Endpoint Identifier is generally called *Locator-Identifier Separation*, even though this is, strictly speaking, a misnomer. After all, the Routing Locator is also an identifier (namely, that of a location in the routing tree). Likewise, using just *identifier* as a label for an Endpoint Identifier is much too broad; after all, there are many types of identifiers that are not used to identify an endpoint. However, the remainder of this chapter sticks to this widely used terminology.

Much of the work discussed here originates from the Routing Research Group (RRG) in the Internet Research Task Force[1] (IRTF), the research-oriented sister organization of the Internet Engineering Task Force (IETF). The reason for it being discussed there is that the lack of Locator-Identifier Separation not only causes problems with mobility but also with routing scalability, multihoming, and traffic engineering. Discussion of these topics is beyond the scope of this book. One issue that is of particular importance for mobility and somewhat less for the other problems is that of user location privacy. When identifiers are long lived and a publicly available mapping exists between identifiers and locators, it is possible to gather the location of a host (a number of services exist that can map IP addresses to geographic location with reasonable accuracy), and therefore the user using it, without the permission or even knowledge of that user. This is considered an invasion of privacy and violates privacy regulations. It is therefore important that the proposed mechanisms, by default, do not reveal the location of a particular host to unknown observers.

You must realize that because of the vast amount of deployed computers, routers, and other devices that connect to the Internet, changing the fundamental architecture of the Internet is not easy; in particular, a "flag day" in which all hosts have to change is not feasible. The solutions discussed in this chapter try to strike a balance among changes needed at the hosts, changes needed in the core networks, and the possibility of adopting the solution incrementally.

This chapter discusses four solutions that have either been around a bit longer or that have recently gained momentum in the RRG:

■   The Host Identity Protocol (HIP)

■   Locator-Identifier Separation Protocol – Mobile Node (LISP-MN)

■   Network Address Translation for IPv6 to IPv6 (NAT66)

■   Identifier-Locator Network Protocol (ILNP)

Before diving into the details of these solutions, it helps to understand the basic methods for Locator-Identifier Separation, as described in the section that follows.

Approaches to Locator-Identifier Separation

Most approaches to Locator-Identifier Separation fall into two broad categories:

- Those that introduce an extra layer to hold the original Endpoint Identifiers encapsulated within packets that use Routing Locators as source and destination

- Those that split the existing IPv6 address space into a part that has topological meaning and a part that is used to identify the host

Both categories can be further divided into the following:

- Approaches that act at the host

- Approaches that act at the border between a site and the core network

The benefit of implementing Locator-Identifier Separation on the border between a site and the core network is that typically the hosts don't have to be changed, which is obviously a major obstacle in the adoption of an approach. However, this comes at the expense of end-to-end transparency of the communication, and might have implications for session persistence at the transport layer. Implementing Locator-Identifier Separation at the host does not have those downsides but requires each host to change its networking stack to benefit from Locator-Identifier Separation.

HIP, discussed in the section that follows, is an example of an approach that introduces an extra layer at the host. The encapsulation of Endpoint Identifiers at the border of a network is also called a Map-and-Encap scheme. In this approach, packets with source and destination Endpoint Identifiers are encapsulated (the Encap) into packets containing source and destination Routing Locators. To find the Routing Locator corresponding to a particular Endpoint Identifier, some sort of mapping infrastructure is used (the Map). An example of a Map-and-Encap approach is LISP-MN, described later in the chapter.

When the existing IPv6 address space is divided into separate IPv6 address spaces for a site network and for the core, this is usually called the Address Rewriting approach, because the IPv6 addresses that are used inside a side are at the border, with the rest of the Internet rewritten into addresses from the core address space. NAT66, described later in a section devoted to this topic, is an example of that.

Alternatively, the higher-order 64 bits of an IPv6 address can be designated as a Routing Locator and the lower-order 64 bits as an Endpoint Identifier. Figure 8-2 shows what the IPv6 packet header looks like in this latter case.

Hosts in a domain are not aware what their Routing Locator is. So, when a host sends a packet to another host, only the 64 bits of the Endpoint Identifier are specified for the source address. When the packet leaves the domain, the router at the border of the domain adds the Routing Locator part of the source address. When the packet arrives at the destination domain, the router at the border of that domain removes the Routing Locator bits of the destination address and forwards the packet to the destination. This way, the hosts never have knowledge about their own Routing Locator, but they have "normal" IPv6 addresses (consisting of Routing Locator and Endpoint Identifier) for the hosts they correspond with. ILNP, discussed later, is an example of this approach at the host.

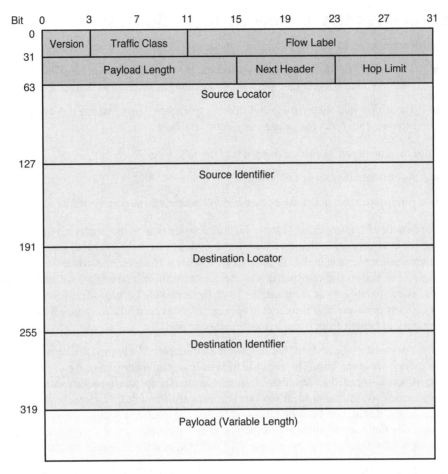

Figure 8-2   *Packet Header When Splitting an IPv6 Address into an Endpoint Identifier and a Routing Locator Part*

HIP

The Host Identity Protocol (HIP), described in RFC 4423[2] and RFC 5201[3], introduces a new layer to the Internet protocol stack that sits between the Internet layer and the transport layer (see Figure 8-3). For this new layer, the host identity layer, a new namespace is introduced with Host Identifiers (HI).

Each host will have at least one Host Identity and the corresponding identifier. Each Host Identity uniquely identifies a single host.

Sockets are no longer bound to IP addresses but rather to HIs, thereby separating the Routing Locator (IP address) and Endpoint Identifier (HI). HIs are translated to IP addresses in the kernel. The HI for a particular server can typically be found in the Domain Name System (DNS). HIs are location independent and persistent (but can be changed).

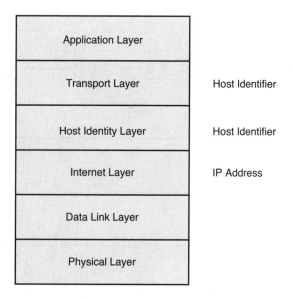

Figure 8-3   *HIP Stack*

HIs are implemented as public keys of a public/private key pair, of which the private keys are stored at the host. Each host is responsible for creating its own public/private key pair. Because having different key lengths is cumbersome for applications, a 128-bit hash value of the HI is used instead of the HI itself—the Host ID Tag (HIT).

In addition to providing mobility (change of IP address does not break the socket connection), the use of cryptographic identifiers also allows verification of the corresponding host as well as end-to-end encryption between the hosts (using IPsec Encapsulating Security Payload).

Figure 8-4 shows how two hosts that want to communicate establish a shared state using the HIP base exchange.

The system that initiates the HIP exchange is called the *Initiator*, and the peer is the *Responder*. The Initiator and Responder establish a shared secret for their communication using the Diffie-Hellman (D-H) key exchange[4], a protocol that makes it possible for two parties that have no prior knowledge of each other to establish such a shared secret:

1. The Initiator sends a packet containing its HIT to the Responder.

2. The Responder answers by sending a puzzle (a cryptographic challenge), D-H parameters, a signature of part of the message using the HI, and the HI itself.

3. The Initiator verifies the signature, computes the answer to the puzzle, and sends the latter along with the D-H parameter, a signature over part of the message using its HI, and its HI to the Responder.

4. The Responder verifies the answer to the puzzle and sends a signed message back to the Initiator. The signature is verified by the Initiator.

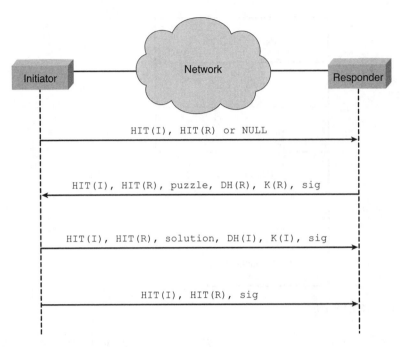

Figure 8-4 *HIP Base Exchange*

So, after this key exchange, both the Initiator and Responder have a shared key that can be used to identify each other and to encrypt traffic between them. And furthermore, they have verified that the other host indeed possesses the private key that corresponds to the HI.

The puzzle mechanism is used to defend the Responder against some denial of service attacks. In particular, the responder does not have to do cryptographic computations to establish state until the Initiator has done so first. This makes it hard for a malicious Initiator to trick the Responder into spending all its computing cycles calculating for bogus connection setup attempts.

To locate a host (that is, find the IP address that is associated with a particular HI), some kind of rendezvous system needs to be implemented. If a host moves, it needs to update its registration with the rendezvous server. If two hosts have already established a shared state, they can also inform each other directly of location changes.

Applications typically can run unmodified on top of HIP, because HITs manifest themselves as 128-bit identifiers, just like IPv6 addresses.

Benefits and Challenges

HIP has a number of benefits. Routing Locators and Endpoint Identifiers are separated, so hosts can change their point of attachment without breaking sessions. HIs can, in theory, be changed at the host, so anonymity and location privacy can be achieved; however, it is questionable how realistic that is. Confidentiality and integrity of the communication between peers are achieved by using IPsec.

At the time of introduction (around 2006), HIP didn't get much traction, however, because of the fact that HIP requires IPv6 and because of the computational overhead of using IPsec. At that time, there was no strong need for an IP mobility solution because of the fact that mobile devices were, to a large extent, mobile phones that were using the Layer 2 mobility solutions in the mobile phone networks.

Now that that situation has changed, it appears that existing and relatively widespread solutions such as Mobile IP and Proxy Mobile IP address most of the use cases for which HIP was envisioned.

Locator-Identifier Separation Protocol – Mobile Node (LISP-MN)

Locator-Identifier Separation Protocol – Mobile Node (LISP-MN) aims to make it possible for mobile devices to roam while keeping TCP sessions alive and to be simultaneously connected to two different networks (multihomed). LISP-MN achieves this goal by leveraging a LISP infrastructure, so a description of LISP is given first.

LISP

LISP[5] implements a Map-and-Encap scheme. Packets are encapsulated at the border router of the sender domain (called the Ingress Tunnel Router [ITR] in LISP) and decapsulated at the border router of the receiving domain (the Egress Tunnel Router [ETR] in LISP). This makes it possible for the core routing (the routing between the domains) to be independent of the encapsulated Endpoint Identifiers and thus be optimized for the topological characteristics of the core network.

LISP can be seen as adding an extra Internet layer below the existing one, as illustrated in Figure 8-5.

So, if a host in one LISP-capable domain wants to send a packet to a host in another LISP-enabled domain, the following happens:

1. The host looks up the name of the correspondent host in DNS, which gives an Endpoint Identifier.

2. The host puts its Endpoint Identifier as the source and the correspondent host's Endpoint Identifier as the destination.

3. The packet traverses to the ITR. The ITR encapsulates the packet in a new packet with the Routing Locator of the ITR as the source and the Routing Locator of an ETR for the domain as the target (this mapping is either previously cached or is determined by the mapping mechanism).

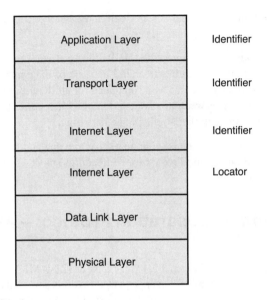

Figure 8-5   *LISP Stack*

4.   The packet traverses to the ETR.

5.   The ETR decapsulates the packet and sends it on to the destination Endpoint Identifier.

For the mapping infrastructure, a number of approaches have been proposed. The most widely used approach is called LISP-Alternative Topology (LISP-ALT). LISP-ALT uses the Border Gateway Protocol (BGP) and generic routing encapsulation (GRE) to construct an overlay network for advertising Endpoint Identifier prefixes. Because the mapping mechanism is decoupled from the forwarding mechanism, however, any mapping mechanism can be used.

Figure 8-6 shows a typical LISP scenario.

The host with Endpoint Identifier 1.0.0.1 wants to send a packet to the host with Endpoint Identifier 2.0.0.2. This is done as follows:

1.   The packet arrives at ITR2 (that has Routing Locator 11.0.0.1).

2.   ITR2 looks up the Routing Locators corresponding with Endpoint Identifier 2.0.0.2, and finds 12.0.0.2 and 13.0.0.2, of which the first has the higher priority.

3.   ITR2 encapsulates the packet with source 1.0.0.1 and destination 2.0.0.2 in a packet with source 11.0.0.1 and destination 12.0.0.2 and forwards the packet as normal over the Internet core.

4.   ETR1 receives the packet and decapsulates it.

5.   ETR1 forwards the packet to 2.0.0.2.

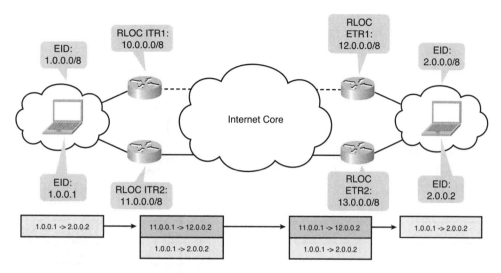

Figure 8-6   *Typical LISP Scenario*

LISP-MN

The idea behind LISP-MN[6] is now to leverage the mapping infrastructure of LISP to support mobile devices. This is achieved by turning the mobile device into a LISP ITR and ETR for itself (in fact, you could say that the mobile device turns into a mini-LISP site). This means that the mobile device sends Map Requests and furthermore that all packets originating at the mobile device are LISP encapsulated.

A mobile device can answer itself to Map Requests coming in, or it can designate its Map Server as a proxy for replying to those requests. Packets destined for non-LISP-enabled nodes are decapsulated by a proxy ETR.

Map Servers that act as proxy Map Reply behave like anchoring points for the mobile devices, similar to home agents in Mobile IP, with the big difference being that unlike in Mobile IP, the actual data never flows through these nodes; they just answer to the mapping requests. Furthermore, home agents never provide mapping info because that is left to the mobile node.

The mobile device registers with its provisioned Map Server that advertises the Endpoint Identifiers for which it is responsible (including the Endpoint Identifier of the mobile device). This way, neither the current location nor updates to it have to be exposed to the ALT infrastructure. Only the Map Server stores the Routing Locator of the mobile device.

Figure 8-7 is similar to Figure 8-6, but here the destination host is a LISP site in itself instead of being *inside* a LISP site.

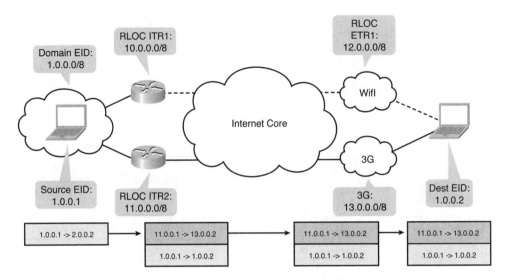

Figure 8-7   *LISP-MN Operation*

Consider a scenario in which the host with Endpoint Identifier 1.0.0.1 wants to send a packet to the host with Endpoint Identifier 1.0.0.2. That mobile host has lost its Wi-Fi connection but remains connected to the 3G network.

What happens is the following:

1.   The mobile node updates the mapping server to indicate that it is no longer reachable through 12.0.0.2 but only through 13.0.0.2.

2.   The packet arrives at ITR2 (that has Routing Locator 11.0.0.1).

3.   ITR2 looks up the Routing Locators corresponding with Endpoint Identifier 1.0.0.2 and finds 13.0.0.2.

4.   ITR2 encapsulates the packet with source 1.0.0.1 and destination 1.0.0.2 in a packet with source 11.0.0.1 and destination 13.0.0.2 and forwards the packet as normal over the Internet core.

5.   The mobile host receives the packet and decapsulates it.

Benefits and Challenges

LISP implements the separation of Routing Locators and Endpoint Identifiers without the need for changes at the hosts. The addressing in the core network is independent from that at the edge, so for example, the core network could use IPv6, whereas the edge network would use IPv4 and vice versa.

By turning a mobile node into a LISP-site-in-a-box, mobile nodes can change their point of attachment without breaking transport sessions. Unfortunately, the latter does require changes at the host, undoing one of the advantages of LISP.

In LISP, a proxy Map Reply server can be used that is like an anchoring point in Mobile IP; however, unlike with Mobile IP, the actual data flow is never through that server. Given the assumption that Endpoint Identifiers are persistent, this introduces location privacy concerns.

The largest obstacle appears to be the requirement for an operational LISP infrastructure. Until LISP is widely deployed, the benefits of LISP-MN are small.

NAT66

Network Address Translation for IPv6 to IPv6[7] (NAT66) describes a method for providing address independence. Address independence in this context means that the IPv6 addresses that are in use inside a local network do not have to change if the IPv6 prefix that is announced to the outside world changes (if the ISP changes the prefix or when the site changes ISPs).

NAT is also widely used for IPv4, both for address independence and as a way of connecting many hosts to the Internet while only using a small amount of global IP addresses. The latter argument obviously doesn't apply for IPv6; there is no address shortage in IPv6.

NAT in an IPv4 environment causes a number of problems for transport and application layer protocols. These problems are extensively documented in RFC 2993[8], but are often summarized with the phrase "NAT is evil." Most importantly, NAT for IPv4 requires the translation device to maintain per-node or per-connection state information and to rewrite transport layer headers. NAT will also break security mechanisms that provide integrity protection of the IP header (after all, the IP header changes when the address changes).

NAT66 addresses these issues, with the exception of the integrity of the IP header protection, by using no port mapping function (used in IPv4 NAT to map many internal addresses to only one external IP address) and a default mapping mechanism that does not require maintaining state.

Figure 8-8 shows the typical operation using NAT66:

1.   The host with internal IPv6 address FD01:0203:0405:0001::1234 in the site with Internal Prefix FD01:0203:0405:/48 sends a packet to the host with IPv6 address 2001:0DB8:5555:0001::1234.

2.   At the NAT66 device, the internal address is rewritten to the external address 2001:0DB8:0001:D550::1234 out of the 2001:0DB8:0001:/48 External Prefix.

3.   The receiving host sends return packets with a source 2001:0DB8:555:0001::1234 and a destination the external address 2001:0DB8:0001:D550::1234.

4.   At the NAT66 device, the external destination address 2001:0DB8:0001:D550::1234 is rewritten to FD01:0203:0405:0001::1234.

5.   The original sending host receives the return packet from 2001:0DB8:5555:0001::1234.

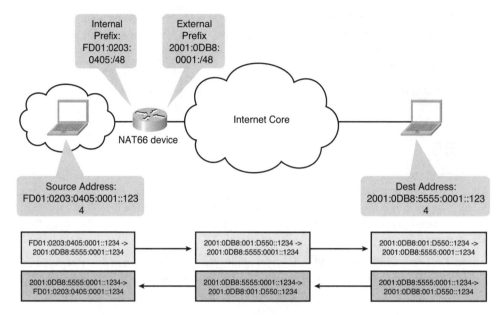

Figure 8-8   *NAT66 Operation*

Changing the source or destination IP address changes the IPv6 pseudoheader and thus the pseudoheader checksum. Changing the value of another field in the pseudoheader offsets this, resulting in unchanged checksums. This means that transport protocols that use the checksum, like TCP and UDP, can be used unmodified.

Benefits and Challenges

NAT66 achieves separation of the Routing Locator and the Endpoint Identifier by separating the core network from the site network, each using its own address space. This allows easy site mobility and multihoming. The way the addresses are rewritten allows a much higher level of transparency than could be achieved with NAT in an IPv4 environment; still, protocols that require unchanged IP headers will break. NAT66 does not require any changes in the host and can therefore be deployed incrementally.

The fact that the internal address (the Endpoint Identifier) cannot be used to look up the external address (the Routing Locator) gives a reasonable level of location privacy.

The problem with NAT66 from a mobility point of view is that NAT66 works particularly well when the external addresses change (the site moves to another ISP or is multihomed), but when a host moves, the host will still typically get a new address prefix, and thus sessions will still be interrupted.

Identifier-Locator Network Protocol (ILNP)

The Identifier-Locator Network Protocol[9] (ILNP) is an example of the approach in which the existing address space is divided into Endpoint Identifiers and Routing Locators. In ILNP, the 128-bit IPv6 addresses in the packet headers are split into 64 bits for the Routing Locator and 64 bits for the Endpoint Identifier. The Locator has significance only in the network layer, and the Identifier has significance only in the transport layer. In addition to that, whereas the use of IP addresses at the application layer is quite common, ILNP is strict about only using fully qualified domain names (FQDN) at the application layer, as illustrated in Figure 8-9.

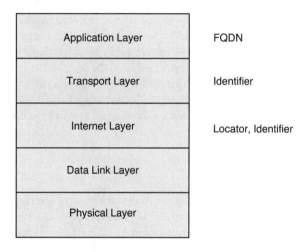

Figure 8-9   *ILNP Stack*

Identifiers are, by default, in the IEEE EUI-64 format[10], which is a method for encoding MAC addresses into 64-bit IPv6 addresses. Typically, the MAC address of one of the interfaces of the host is used to construct the Identifier so that the Identifier is likely to be globally unique (not strictly necessary for ILNP, but this reduces the burden of checking for duplicate addresses). The Locators name a subnetwork and are used only for packet forwarding, not for anything above the network layer.

Instead of using IP addresses at the transport layer, only the Identifier is used. When a host changes its point of attachment, the Locator changes but the Identifier remains the same, so the sessions at the transport layer remain intact.

To reflect the fact that IP addresses are split into Locators and Identifiers, new record types are introduced into the DNS for looking up the Identifiers and Locators for a given host and vice versa.

If a host changes its point of attachment, it will have to update its DNS to reflect the change of Locator. To minimize the risk for denial of service attacks by inserting false information in DNS, hosts should use Secure DNS Dynamic Updates[11], and the use of DNS Secure (DNSSEC)[12] is assumed.

Benefits and Challenges

ILNP achieves separation of Routing Locators and Endpoint Identifiers. Only the hosts need to change; the routers don't. This allows an incremental upgrade path. Two hosts that want to communicate can implement ILNP and benefit from the session mobility that is achieved through that without a need for other hosts to upgrade. At the same time, that is challenge, because changes in the host operating systems are not easy to deploy; it basically requires buy-in from the large OS manufacturers.

The reliance on DNS casts some doubt as to whether ILNP will work when the host changes point of attachment quickly. Subsecond update rates of DNS information generally don't work.

A more fundamental problem with the use of DNS for looking up the Routing Locator given an Endpoint Identifier is the lack of location privacy this introduces—anyone can look up the location of a particular host at any time, given the Endpoint Identifier. The Endpoint Identifier is, by default, constructed from the MAC address and is therefore persistent. Anyone that has ever learned the MAC address of a particular host can keep track of its location. This issue can be solved by not using EUI-64 addresses and/or by using proxies that mask the actual location; however, that is not the default mode of operation.

Summary

There are a number of approaches that try to deal with one of the fundamental flaws of the current Internet architecture: the use of IP addresses both as Routing Locators and as Endpoint Identifiers, resulting in sessions breaking when the host changes its point of attachment. The various approaches fall into two broad categories:

- Those that introduce an extra layer to hold the original Endpoint Identifiers encapsulated within packets that use Routing Locators as source and destination, either implemented at the border between the site network and the rest of the Internet or at the host

- Those that split the existing IPv6 address space into a part that has topological meaning and a part that is used to identify the host also implemented at either the border or at the host

This chapter discussed HIP, LISP-MN, NAT66, and ILNP as typical examples of Locator-Identifier Separation. Time will tell whether one or more of these solutions will be widely deployed.

Parting Thoughts

With the Internet becoming an infrastructure in which the majority of the devices are mobile, a number of challenges surface. They stem from the fact that the Internet has not been designed for large numbers of hosts that change their point of attachment on a regular basis. In particular, the fact that a communication session is associated with the IP address of the communicating parties causes trouble when either of them moves. This book introduced a number of solutions to partly overcome this fundamental flaw in the original design of the Internet. Depending on the use case, one or more of these solutions can be applied. And while, as this last chapter illustrates, there is currently no final, all-encompassing solution for this fundamental flaw, there is really no reason not to embrace the mobile Internet.

Endnotes

1. Internet Research Task Force, http://www.irtf.org.

2. RFC 4423, "Host Identity Protocol (HIP) Architecture," R. Moskowitz and P. Nikander, http://www.ietf.org/rfc/rfc4423.txt, May 2006.

3. RFC 5201, "Host Identity Protocol," R. Moskowitz, P. Nikander, P. Jokela, and T. Henderson, http://www.ietf.org/rfc/rfc5201.txt, April 2008.

4. RFC 2631, "Diffie-Hellman Key Agreement Method," E. Rescorla, http://www.ietf.org/rfc/rfc2631.txt, June 1999.

5. D. Meyer. "LISP." *The Internet Protocol Journal*, Vol. 11, No. 1: March 2008, http://www.cisco.com/web/about/ac123/ac147/archived_issues/ipj_11-1/111_lisp.html.

6. "LISP Mobile Node," Presentation at IETF, D. Farinacci, V. Fuller, D. Lewis, and D. Meyer, http://www.1-4-5.net/~dmm/talks/IETF76/lisp-ietf-arn-mn.final.pdf, July 2009.

7. I-D.mrw-nat66, "IPv6-to-IPv6 Network Address Translation (NAT66)," M. Wasserman and F. Baker, http://tools.ietf.org/id/draft-mrw-nat66-00.txt (work in progress), October 2010.

8. RFC 2993, "Architectural Implications of NAT," T. Hain, http://www.ietf.org/rfc/rfc2993.txt, November 2000.

9. "An Introduction to the Identifier-Locator Network Protocol (ILNP)," R. Atkinson and S. Bhatti, http://www.cs.st-andrews.ac.uk/~saleem/papers/2006/lcs/ilnp/ab2006.pdf, July 2006.

10. RFC 4291, "IPv6 Addressing Architecture," R. Hinden and S. Deering, http://www.ietf.org/rfc/rfc4291.txt, February 2006.

11. RFC 3007, "Secure Domain Name System (DNS) Dynamic Update," B. Wellington, http://www.ietf.org/rfc/rfc3007.txt, September 2000.

12. RFC 4033, "DNS Security Introduction and Requirements," R. Arends, R. Austein, M. Larson, D. Massey, and S. Rose, http://www.ietf.org/rfc/rfc4033.txt, March 2005.

Index

Numbers

A

D

H

I-J

K-L

M

O

P

S

CISCO™

ciscopress.com: Your Cisco Certification and Networking Learning Resource

Subscribe to the monthly Cisco Press newsletter to be the first to learn about new releases and special promotions.

Visit **ciscopress.com/newsletters.**

While you are visiting, check out the offerings available at your finger tips.

–Free Podcasts from experts:
  · OnNetworking
  · OnCertification
  · OnSecurity

Podcasts

View them at **ciscopress.com/podcasts.**

–Read the latest author **articles** and **sample chapters** at **ciscopress.com/articles.**

–Bookmark the Certification Reference Guide available through our partner site at **informit.com/certguide.**

Connect with Cisco Press authors and editors via Facebook and Twitter, visit **informit.com/socialconnect.**

cisco
Cisco Learning Network
Free Test Prep and Beyond.
Access review questions
Watch Quick Learning Modules (QLMS)
Search for jobs and network with others
Take self-assessments
Participate in study groups
Play online learning games
Register for a free membership
and get started now.
www.cisco.com/go/learningnetwork
Cisco Learning Network
A social learning site brought to you by Learning@Cisco

FREE Online Edition

Your purchase of Building the Mobile Internet includes access to a free online edition for 45 days through the Safari Books Online subscription service. Nearly every Cisco Press book is available online through Safari Books Online, along with more than 5,000 other technical books and videos from publishers such as Addison-Wesley Professional, Exam Cram, IBM Press, O'Reilly, Prentice Hall, Que, and Sams.

SAFARI BOOKS ONLINE allows you to search for a specific answer, cut and paste code, download chapters, and stay current with emerging technologies.

Activate your FREE Online Edition at
www.informit.com/safarifree

> **STEP 1:** Enter the coupon code: SYAEHBI.

> **STEP 2:** New Safari users, complete the brief registration form.
> Safari subscribers, just log in.

If you have difficulty registering on Safari or accessing the online edition, please e-mail customer-service@safaribooksonline.com